AN A – Z OF APPLIED LINGUISTICS RESEARCH METHODS

WITHDRAWN

An A – Z of Applied Linguistics Research Methods

Shawn Loewen and Luke Plonsky

 palgrave

First published 2016 by
PALGRAVE

Palgrave in the UK is an imprint of Macmillan Publishers Limited, registered in England, company number 785998, of 4 Crinan Street, London, N1 9XW.

Palgrave Macmillan in the US is a division of St Martin's Press LLC, 175 Fifth Avenue, New York, NY 10010.

Palgrave is the global imprint of the above companies and is represented throughout the world.

Palgrave® and Macmillan® are registered trademarks in the United States, the United Kingdom, Europe and other countries.

ISBN 978–1–137–40321–6 paperback

This book is printed on paper suitable for recycling and made from fully managed and sustained forest sources. Logging, pulping and manufacturing processes are expected to conform to the environmental regulations of the country of origin.

A catalogue record for this book is available from the British Library.

A catalog record for this book is available from the Library of Congress.

Loewen, Shawn, author.

An A – Z of applied linguistics research methods / Shawn Loewen and Luke Plonsky.

pages cm

Includes index.

Summary: "A brief and accessible introduction to the concepts and techniques used in applied linguistics research, which will be illustrated using real-life examples. The book covers both qualitative and quantitative research design, sampling procedures, instrumentation and analyses found in applied linguistics research" — Provided by publisher.

ISBN 978–1–137–40321–6 (paperback)

1. Applied linguistics—Research—Handbooks, manuals, etc.   2. Applied linguistics—Resesarch—Methodology—Handbooks, manuals, etc.   I. Plonsky, Luke, author.   II. Title.

P129.L64 2015

418.0072'1—dc23

2015033257

Shawn:

To Treva, who taught me how to write.

Luke:

To my father, Matthew Plonsky, and grandfather, Andrew Plonsky, who passed on to me a love of numbers.

Contents

Acknowledgments

We are indebted to numerous individuals who have helped us as we have written this book. First and foremost we would like to thank our editors, Paul Stevens and Aléta Bezuidenhout, for their encouragement and support throughout the entire process. This book would simply not have been possible without them. Next, enormous thanks go to Magda Tigchelaar and Dan Brown, who worked as our research assistants and helped us with all the things that professors do poorly, such as chasing up examples for entries, securing copyright permissions, and creating an index. Special mention also goes to Talip Gonulal for his helpful comments on drafts of the manuscript. We would also like to thank Cambridge University Press for their enlightened copyright policy which made it possible for us to include numerous graphics without going into debt. Figure 34: "Facets map resulting from a Rasch Analysis" is reproduced courtesy of © R Foundation: http://www.r-project.org. Figure 39: "Data view screen in SPSS" is reproduced courtesy of International Business Machines Corporation, © International Business Machines Corporation. Finally, we would like to thank our long-suffering families for their support throughout this process. To Pamela Loewen for the sacrifices she made, and to the Loewen kids—Winona, Patrick, and Austin—who dread to hear the words "Dad is working on a book deadline." I couldn't do it without the love, support, encouragement, and distraction that I get from all of you! Big thanks to Pamela Plonsky as well! And I (Luke) thank Mateo, Ruby, and Rose, precisely because they have no idea about research methods or book deadlines. You keep me "normal."

Introduction and User Guide

Conducting research is not always easy. Each study involves making numerous choices, many of which are not inherently good or bad but rather, represent a unique theoretical or methodological stance, and present several advantages and disadvantages. After we decide what phenomenon we will study (no small feat in and of itself), we have to make a host of decisions about our sample, design, data collection instruments, procedures, analyses, and interpretations. And, of course, each of these major decision points leads to additional considerations and choices, all requiring an understanding of their corresponding strengths and weaknesses relative to numerous possible alternatives.

Further complicating the researcher's life are the seemingly endless terms for the concepts and techniques that must be learned and applied. Researchers in applied linguistics must distinguish, for example, between terms such as nominal and interval data, Type I and Type II errors, reliability and validity, and case studies and ethnographies, just to name a few. We understand this challenge, and we're here to help!

Our goal in writing this book is to enable researchers, reviewers, consumers of research, and students of research methods in applied linguistics to quickly access an overview or refresher on critical terms and the methodological practices and issues associated with them. We also tried to do so in a format that can be taken advantage of quickly, almost at a glance. Traditional methodological texts necessarily describe key concepts and terminology embedded deep within larger discussions. The entries in this book—more substantial than a glossary but not as lengthy as an encyclopedia entry—give the reader "bite-sized" overviews of key terms, explaining their background, meaning, purpose, and place in the field. We also recognize, however, that many of the concepts described here are related. It's difficult to talk about parametric statistics, for example, without some understanding of a normal distribution. Likewise, it makes little sense to consider epistemology in isolation from ontology. We have therefore emboldened terms with entries found elsewhere in the book; we've done this in an effort to preserve and alert readers to the interrelatedness of terms and concepts. It's very likely, in fact, that skipping around from entry to entry will be the most useful way to use this book. We don't actually envision that anyone would use this as their stand-alone research methods textbook, nor would most people read the book cover to cover. Rather, we recommend the use of this book as an accompaniment—a sidekick, if you will—to whatever text or texts readers use as their go-to, comprehensive guide to research methods.

In addition to explaining a bit about our purpose and approach in writing this book, we also wanted to share a few tips that might make it more useful as a reference and research companion. For one, the text provides numerous examples from real applied linguistics research in order to provide context to the terms and concepts. We use these to illustrate and exemplify the sometimes abstract concepts we cover. References to such studies and to further reading are also provided, along with their relevant entries, to allow readers to track them down for additional information. Another aid we've included are visuals, lots of them. If you haven't done so yet, take a moment to flip through the book. Many of the concepts we cover here lend themselves very nicely to graphic displays, and we've tried to take advantage of this as often as possible as a kind of pedagogical tool.

Another issue that comes up in reading a text on research methods (or any kind of text, really) is the target audience. That is, who is this book written for? In short, everyone. We'll explain. First of all, we tried to keep a number of diverse audiences in mind while writing this book. We especially sought to consider the needs of students and novice researchers. But this book is not only for those new to the field or to research. This book is for anyone who has ever needed a quick reminder on the difference between construct validity and face validity. This book is for anyone looking for an example of a longitudinal study. This book is for anyone wanting a quick review of the different types of reliability. In other words, this book is for anyone who conducts, reads, or reviews research in applied linguistics. Meanwhile, we are well aware of the challenges in preparing a text for an audience that is potentially very diverse in terms of training, background, research interests, theoretical approaches, and so forth. We also admit that there may be moments in the book when we have presented what some would consider to be an oversimplification of certain concepts and/ or techniques for the sake of clarity. At the same time, despite our efforts to keep the novice researcher in mind at all times, it is also possible that certain entries may appear overly technical or complex. If you find yourself in this situation, please don't lose heart! Everyone feels this way at some point or other regarding research methods.

Despite these and many other challenges, an understanding of research methods is critical to our field. It's actually difficult to overstate the importance of methodological knowledge. If applied linguistics researchers—individually or collectively—lack conceptual or technical know-how, the studies we produce cannot accurately inform theory or practice. Furthermore, it is critical that those of us who produce research possess a keen understanding of methodological concepts, practices, and so forth, since trusted gatekeepers, journal reviewers, and editors need to be able to assess the value of the thousands of reports submitted each year to applied linguistics journals. Likewise, consumers and practitioners, such as teachers, test developers, and language program administrators, must be able to evaluate studies relevant to their work as a means to know what and how they can be applied to their own contexts. In other words, all of us within the applied linguistics community must possess some level of methodological knowledge.

We have tried to make this book as comprehensive as possible, including general research terms from α to *z- score*. In addition, we have focused on discipline-specific topics from *action research* to *VARBRUL* for applied linguists. However, without reading too many entries, it will become clear that our own specialized area of research within applied linguistics pertains to second language acquisition (SLA). Many of the studies we have chosen to illustrate specific terms are from SLA, and even from our own research. The reason for this is primarily a practical one. These are the studies that are most familiar to us. However, the terms in this book were chosen specifically for their broader appeal, and we do not regard SLA research as more valuable than other areas within applied linguistics.

Also, it is our aim to encourage good research practices, both in conducting and reporting research. That being said, not all published articles contain all of the information that we might hope for. In considering the examples to include in the entries, we sometimes found studies that were good, but did not report everything that we might recommend. In such cases, we used the example as-is, but we would ask readers to be aware that, consequently, there may be a discrepancy between what we recommend reporting compared to what we include in the real-life examples.

In the end, we hope you will find this volume useful for you, whatever your level of research experience. In addition, we wish you many happy years of research design, data collection, analysis, and reporting!

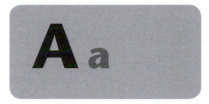

α (see Alpha)

A priori test (see Pretest)

Action research

Research generally conducted by teachers or teacher trainees in order to investigate a **research question** that is relevant to their particular pedagogical context. Action research often involves the examination of a practical problem or issue in the classroom. In many cases, action research is an iterative process in which an initial question or **hypothesis** is proposed, and an effort is made to address the question. Based on the results of the investigation, a new hypothesis might be put forward and investigated. An example of a collaborative action research project is presented by Banegas, Pavese, Velázquez, and Vélez (2013), who examined the integration of content and language learning in their own English as a foreign language classes using a three cycle process. In cycle 1, the researchers identified specific issues related to content and language integrated learning (CLIL) in their context, and subsequently designed, implemented, and evaluated teaching materials. Cycles 2 and 3 involved similar action, intervention, and evaluation activities based on information gained from previous cycles. Banegas et al. reported on the positive impact of action research for their own professional development, and the resulting benefits for their students.

In many cases, the information gained from action research is intended primarily for the teachers conducting the research and not for a wider audience. Because action research addresses questions that are of interest to specific teachers in specific contexts, there is often not a concern with generalizing the results to other settings. Action research is sometimes discounted because it is not viewed as being as rigorous or systematic as **experimental**, **quasi-experimental**, or other types of research; nevertheless, it can be quite informative, and it has become an important component of applied linguistics research.

Banegas, D., Pavese, A., Velázquez, A., & Vélez, S. (2013). Teacher professional development through collaborative action research: Impact on foreign English-language teaching and learning. *Educational Action Research, 21*, 185–201.

Burns, A. (2010). *Doing action research in English language teaching: A guide for practitioners*. Abingdon: Routledge.

McDonough, K. (2006). Action research and the professional development of graduate teaching assistants. *Modern Language Journal, 90,* 33–47.

Yuan, R., & Lee, I. (2015). Action research facilitated by university-school collaboration. *ELT Journal, 69,* 1–10.

Adjusted R^2

A statistical value, based on R^2, that indicates how well a regression model generalizes from a **sample** to an entire **population**. When conducting a regression, researchers want to determine how well certain variables (called predictor variables) predict scores on another variable (called an outcome variable). For example, Venkatagiri and Levis (2007) wanted to know how closely L2 speakers' phonological awareness was associated with their comprehensibility when speaking. Their **linear regression** analysis resulted in an R^2 value of .241, indicating that 24% of the **variance** in speaker comprehensibility could be accounted for by the **predictor variable** of phonological awareness. The R^2 value applies only to the group being investigated in the research study; consequently, in order to generalize to the larger population, an adjusted R^2 value was calculated. Venkatagiri and Levis reported an adjusted R^2 of .190, leading the authors to claim that, conservatively, phonological awareness accounts for 19% of the variance in comprehensibility scores. The adjusted R^2 value indicates the loss of predictive power that occurs if the model were applied to the larger population. The less difference there is between the R^2 and the adjusted R^2 values, the better the model.

Venkatagiri, H. S., & Levis, J. (2007). Phonological awareness and speech comprehensibility: An exploratory study. *Language Awareness, 16,* 263–277.

Alpha (level)

A numeric cutoff point for determining if a statistical test has produced a significant result. Often represented by the Greek letter α, the alpha level is typically set at .05, meaning that there is a less than 5% probability that the result of the statistical test is interpreted as significant when it should not be, and that a **Type I error** has been committed. The alpha level desired by a researcher should be determined at the beginning of statistical analysis, based on the level of statistical certainty required for the research study. In more exploratory, low-stakes research, an alpha level of .10 or .20 is considered acceptable. For instance, Ammar and Spada (2006) set their cutoff for statistical significance in comparing **pretest** results at .10. This choice was motivated by an interest in ensuring that any pretreatment differences between groups would be detected. With the more traditional but stricter alpha of .05, they might have missed group differences that ought to be taken into account in the **posttest** analyses (see Plonsky, 2015a, 2015b). Such a mistake, a **Type II error**, would pose a threat to the **validity** of the

A

findings. For the same reason, in medical research, a much stricter alpha level of .001 is often set, due to the need for precise results.

The **p-value** produced by the statistical test is compared to the alpha level to determine if a test result should be considered statistically signifi-cant. In **Null Hypothesis Significance Testing (NHST)**, the alpha level is often treated as invariant and dichotomous, with all values greater than .05 being viewed as non-significant and all values less than .05 being sig-nificant; however, there is much criticism of such a categorical use of the alpha level because according to such a strict criterion, the values of .06 and .96 are both treated equally, as non-significant, even though they express a 6% as opposed to 96% probability of obtaining the observed data or effect, assuming such an effect does not exist in the **population**. Consequently, there has been a call for caution in using NHST, with suggestions to use additional values, such as **effect sizes** and **confidence intervals**, to assess the importance and stability of a finding (e.g., Norris, 2015; Plonsky, 2015b).

Ammar, A., & Spada, N. (2006). One size fits all? Recasts, prompts, and L2 learning. *Studies in Second Language Acquisition, 28*, 543, 574.

Norris, J. M. (2015). Statistical significance testing in second language research: Basic problems and suggestions for reform. *Language Learning, 65*(Supp. 1), 97–126.

Plonsky, L. (2015a). Quantitative considerations for improving replicability in CALL and applied linguistics. *CALICO Journal, 32*, 232–244.

Plonsky, L. (2015b). Statistical power, *p* values, descriptive statistics, and effect sizes: A "back-to-basics" approach to advancing quantitative methods in L2 research. In L. Plonsky (Ed.), *Advancing quantitative methods in second language research* (pp. 23–45). New York: Routledge.

Analysis of covariance (ANCOVA)

A type of **analysis of variance** that attempts to account for the effects of a moderating variable on a **dependent variable**. The goal of ANCOVA is, therefore, to arrive at a more accurate estimate of the effect of the **inde-pendent variable**(s) on the dependent variable(s), without the influence of other intervening variables. One of the ways that ANCOVA is sometimes used in applied linguistics research is in **quasi-experimental designs** investigating the effects of an instructional treatment by including a **pre-test** and at least one **posttest**. Ideally, all groups should score similarly on the pretest in order to ensure that any gains made on the posttest are due to the treatment and not to other variables, such as initial differences in proficiency levels between the groups. However, if there are differences between the groups on the pretest, such as may occur when using **intact classes**, then the pretest scores can be treated as a **covariate** in the ANCOVA, and the analysis will examine the effects of the treatment after the moderating variable of proficiency level has been accounted for. In this way, researchers can obtain a clearer picture of the effects of the instruc-tional treatment. Ammar and Spada (2006), for example, were interested in

A

comparing the effects of two types of feedback—recasts and prompts—on the development of English third-person possessive determiners *his* and *her*. The pretests revealed, however, that there were proficiency differences between the groups at the beginning of the study. Therefore, the authors used ANCOVA, instead of ANOVA, to compare the two treatment groups and the **comparison group**. The use of ANCOVA is somewhat controversial, with some people suggesting that the effects of a covariate can never really be partialled out (Field, 2013). Nevertheless, ANCOVA is still sometimes used in applied linguistics research. Assumptions to be investigated before conducting an ANCOVA include: (a) homogeneity of regression slopes, and (b) independence of the covariate and treatment effect (Field, 2013).

Ammar, A., & Spada, N. (2006). One size fits all? Recasts, prompts, and L2 learning. *Studies in Second Language Acquisition, 28*, 543, 574.

Field, A. (2013). *Discovering statistics using SPSS* (4th ed.). Thousand Oaks, CA: Sage.

Analysis of variance (ANOVA)

A statistical procedure that compares the differences in the means of three or more groups. ANOVA is the most commonly used statistical test in applied linguistics research (Gass, 2009; Plonsky & Gass, 2011). By enabling the researcher to compare the means of more than two groups, ANOVA expands on the *t*-test, which compares the means of just two groups.

There are several different types of ANOVAs, and the naming conventions used to refer to them are sometimes confusing and inconsistent (see Table 1, which contains example studies). However, one thing that all ANOVAs have in common is that they allow only one **dependent variable** measured on a **continuous scale**, while **independent variables**, of which there may be multiple, are **categorical** in nature. Another important distinction between different types of ANOVAs involves determining whether the data being analyzed come from different groups (**between-groups**) or the same group (**within-groups**). Below are described several different types of ANOVAs, beginning with the simplest and continuing with more complex ones:

- A one-way analysis of variance has one dependent variable and one independent variable with three or more different levels or groups. This test compares the means of those groups to see if there are statistically significant differences between the groups. In order to interpret a statistically significant one-way ANOVA, a **post hoc** analysis must be conducted in order to determine the exact nature and location of the differences. Because there are three groups, it might be the case that only two groups differ significantly from each other, or it might be the case that each group differs significantly from the others. A post hoc test (e.g., LSD, Tukey's HSD, Scheffe) will reveal these differences.

A

Table 1 Examples of different types of ANOVAs in SLA

Study	Type of ANOVA (reported)	Type of ANOVA (as described here)	Dependent variable	Between-groups variable(s)	Within-groups variable(s)
Lyster (2004)	Analysis of variance	Mixed design ANOVA	Test scores	Group (FFI-prompt, FFI-recast, FFI-only, Comparison)	Time (Pretest, Posttest 1, Posttest 2)
Riazantseva (2012)	Repeated measures ANOVA	Repeated measures ANOVA	Accuracy rate	None	Outcome measure (in-class essay, in-class summary, at-home summary)
Saito (2013)	Three-factor ANOVA	Mixed design ANOVA	Test scores	Treatment group (FFI+EI, FFI only, Control)	1. Test (controlled versus spontaneous production) 2. Test Time (pretest versus posttest)
Sheen (2008)	One-way ANOVA	One-way ANOVA	Anxiety scores	Group (high anxiety-recast, low anxiety-recast, high anxiety-control, low anxiety-control)	None

Note: Tukey's pairwise comparisons were carried out as post hoc tests in each of the studies except for Riazantseva, who did not conduct post hoc tests.

A

- A factorial ANOVA includes two or more independent variables, and each variable contains different groups, meaning that it is an independent, rather than repeated measures, ANOVA. Sometimes when referring to ANOVAs, the number of independent variables is indicated in the name. For example, a two-way ANOVA has two independent variables, while a three-way ANOVA has three independent variables, and so on. Just to add to the confusion, sometimes researchers use the number of levels in each independent variable to name the ANOVA. So, a 2 × 3 ANOVA has two independent variables, one with two levels and one with three levels of measurement. A 2 × 3 × 3 ANOVA has three independent variables, with one measured with two levels and the others with three levels. A factorial ANOVA will produce **main effects** for each independent variable, as well as **interaction effects** that compare each variable against the others. With two independent variables, there will be two main effects (X, Y) and one interaction effect (X × Y), while with three independent variables there will be three main effects (X, Y, Z), three two-way interaction effects (X × Y, X × Z, Y × Z), and one three-way interaction effect (X × Y × Z). Three-way interaction effects and greater can be difficult to interpret; consequently, other types of analysis such as **multiple regression** may be preferable with three or more independent variables. As with one-way ANOVAs, post hoc tests should be conducted following statistically significant factorial ANOVAs in order to determine the exact location and direction of the differences.
- Repeated measures ANOVAs compare three or more independent variables (e.g., tests) taken from the same group. As such, it is similar to a paired-samples *t*-test. For example, a repeated measures ANOVA might compare the performance of one group on three different tasks, or at three different times (such as a **pretest**, **posttest**, and **delayed posttest**).
- Mixed design ANOVAs have at least two independent variables, one or more of which is between-groups and one or more of which is within-groups. This is a common design in SLA research when a researcher compares two or more treatment groups on a pretest and one or more posttests in order to gauge the effectiveness of some type of instructional treatment.

Each of these ANOVA types has specific **assumptions** that should be met before conducting the analysis. The two primary assumptions for the between-groups ANOVAs are a **normal distribution** of data and **homogeneity of variance**. A main assumption for repeated measures ANOVAs is **sphericity**, which is conceptually similar to homogeneity of variance.

In addition to running post hoc analyses, another good way of visualizing the relationships between the groups is through graphs, especially **line graphs**, which provide evidence of interaction effects when lines are distinctly non-parallel.

In addition to indicating statistical differences between groups, it is important to note the **eta-squared** value associated with an ANOVA. This value is an **effect size** for ANOVA and indicates the amount of variance in the dependent variable that can be accounted for by the **categorical variable**(s) under investigation. Also, because post hoc analyses for ANOVA involve comparing individual pairs of mean scores, the **Cohen's *d*** effect size is generally more appropriate at this phase of the analysis.

Gass, S. (2009). A survey of SLA research. In W. Ritchie & T. Bhatia (Eds.), *Handbook of second language acquisition* (pp. 3–28). Bingley: Emerald.

Lyster, R. (2004). Differential effects of prompts and recast in form-focused instruction. *Studies in Second Language Acquisition, 26,* 399–432.

Plonsky, L., & Gass, S. (2011). Quantitative research methods, study quality, and outcomes: The case of interaction research. *Language Learning, 61,* 325–366.

Riazantseva, A. (2012). Outcome measure of L2 writing as a mediator of the effects of corrective feedback on students' ability to write accurately. *System, 40,* 421–430.

Saito, K. (2013). Reexamining effects of form-focused instruction on L2 pronunciation development: The role of explicit phonetic information. *Studies in Second Language Acquisition, 35*(1), 1–29.

Sheen, Y. (2008). Recasts, language anxiety, modified output, and L2 learning. *Language Learning, 58,* 835–874.

ANCOVA (see Analysis of covariance)

ANOVA (see Analysis of variance)

Aptitude-treatment interaction (ATI)

Research that attempts to investigate the ways in which the effects of different types of instruction vary according to individual learner differences, such as general learning abilities, learning styles, and language learning ability. The goals of ATI research are both theoretical and practical. From a theoretical perspective, research in this domain can help inform the interaction between learner-external and learner-internal variables. More practically speaking, one of the goals of ATI research is to match specific types of instruction with learners who will maximally benefit from that type of instruction based on specific individual difference characteristics. Interest in ATI research is often traced back to educational psychology, where over half a century ago Cronbach (1957) called for greater collaboration between researchers examining causal relationships (e.g., instructional effects) and those interested in correlation relationships (e.g., individual differences). In applied linguistics, interest in ATI research has been gaining some momentum. Yilmaz (2013),

A

for example, examined working memory and language analytic ability as moderators of the effects of two types of corrective feedback, namely explicit correction and recasts. Among other results, Yilmaz found that explicit feedback was more effective than recasts only among participants with higher working memory and language analytic ability. In a comparable design, Li (2013) also found an interaction between the effects of implicit feedback and learners' language analytic ability, suggesting that higher analytic ability allowed learners to benefit from implicit feedback.

Cronbach, L. J. (1957). The two disciplines of scientific psychology. *American Psychologist, 12*, 671–684.

DeKeyser, R. (2009, October). *Variable interaction in SLA: Much more than a nuisance*. Plenary address given at the Second Language Research Forum, East Lansing, MI.

Li, S. (2013). The interactions between the effects of implicit and explicit feedback and individual differences in language analytic ability and working memory. *Modern Language Journal, 97*, 634–654.

Yilmaz, Y. (2013). Relative effects of explicit and implicit feedback: The role of working memory capacity and language analytic ability. *Applied Linguistics, 34*, 344–368.

Assumption

Conditions that must be met before conducting specific statistical analyses. All statistical tests require that the data being analyzed meet certain criteria. Some assumptions are related to the types of variables involved, whether **categorical**, **ordinal**, or **continuous**. For example, *t*-tests require a continuous **dependent variable**, such as a test score, and a categorical **independent variable**, such as treatment condition. In contrast, **chi-square tests** allow only **categorical variables**. Another type of assumption is related to the nature of the distribution of the data. For instance, **parametric statistics**, such as **ANOVAs**, require a **normal distribution** of data, while correlations and regression analyses assume both normal distributions within variables and linear relationships between them. Other assumptions about relationships among variables include: (a) **homogeneity of variance**, which assumes that the distribution of data scores is similar for groups being compared in *t*-tests or ANOVAs; (b) **sphericity**, which is similar to homogeneity of variance for repeated measures data; and (c) lack of **multicollinearity** in correlations and regressions, meaning that pairs of variables are not highly correlated. Additionally, many statistical tests assume that the data are independent, meaning that one participant's behavior does not affect the data from other participants. Finally, more advanced statistics such as **multiple regression** and **factor analysis** have additional, unique assumptions, such as homoscedasticity (residuals with equal variance) or large sample sizes.

Testing assumptions before conducting statistical analyses is an important, although often overlooked, process. If the assumptions of a specific statistical test are not met, then the results from the analysis may be unreliable or invalid, thereby causing misleading interpretations of the data. Several assumptions, such as the type of variable (e.g., categorical or continuous) and **independence** of data, can be addressed in the design of the study by choosing appropriate **instruments** and participants. Other assumptions must be assessed after the data have been collected. For example, the assumption of normal distribution of data can be checked both through visual inspection of graphic representations of the data such as **histograms** and **boxplots**, as well as through statistical tests such as the **Kolmogorov–Smirnov** or **Shapiro–Wilk** tests. Similarly, homogeneity of variance can be assessed by inspecting boxplots or conducting **Levene's test** of homogeneity of variance.

When one or more assumption is violated, there are often adjustments that can be made to the data or alternative statistical procedures that can be performed. One potential modification when comparing group means that violate the assumption of normal distribution is to apply transformational procedures, such as log or square root transformations, in which a mathematical formula is applied equally to the data. Alternatively, researchers can substitute parametric tests such as t-tests or ANOVAs with non-parametric tests such as the **Mann–Whitney U test** or a **Kruskal–Wallis test**, respectively, which do not assume a normal distribution. Additionally, in some cases, statistical corrections are available when assumptions have been violated. For example, **SPSS** provides two sets of scores for independent samples t-tests, one assuming equal variances and the other not assuming equal variances. Likewise, when the assumption of sphericity is violated in repeated measures ANOVAs, researchers can use one of several corrections, with the Greenhouse–Geisser correction being the most common.

Finally, despite the importance of checking statistical assumptions, L2 researchers often fail to do so, or to at least report having done so (Plonsky, 2013). Nevertheless, an increase in assumption testing prior to performing statistical analyses will increase **study quality** and consequently the **reliability** and **validity** of the inferences made from **quantitative research**.

Plonsky, L. (2013). Study quality in SLA: An assessment of designs, analyses, and reporting practices in quantitative L2 research. *Studies in Second Language Acquisition, 35*, 655–687.

A

ATI (see Aptitude-treatment interaction)

Attrition

The decrease in the number of participants over the course of a research study, due primarily to circumstances beyond the researcher's control. Although attrition may occur in **qualitative research**, it is often more critical in **quantitative research** in which researchers need specific sample sizes to perform certain statistical tests. In particular, classroom research can be susceptible to attrition due to variation in student attendance. In addition, longitudinal quasi-experimental studies involving a **pretest**, multiple treatment sessions, and several **posttests** are especially affected by the loss of research participants, because it is generally necessary for participants to take part in all components of the study. Consequently, participants may have to be excluded from the entire study, even if they miss only one or two elements, because such loss of data can make it difficult to make comparisons across all of the datapoints. This type of exclusion is sometimes referred to as listwise or casewise deletion. However, some statistical analyses can be conducted even if participants have missed part of the study, in which case researchers may wish to use pairwise deletion, which makes use of the participant's partial data. For example, if several participants missed a **delayed posttest**, but were present for the other components of the study, it is possible to conduct separate analyses with the full and partial samples. In other cases, the attrition can be quite prohibitive. The attrition rate by the time of the delayed posttest in Sanz and Morgan-Short (2004), for example, was so high that the authors chose not to include the data from the delayed posttests in their analyses. Another example of participant attrition is from Morgan-Short, Heil, Botero-Moriarty, and Ebert's (2012) study of attention allocation and think-aloud research methods. The researchers started with 410 university Spanish students; however, 45 did not reach a minimum threshold of attention allocation, and 4 participants did not follow the instructions properly. Consequently, only 361 were included in the final analysis, resulting in a 12% attrition rate.

See also **Missing data**.

Morgan-Short, K., Heil, J., Botero-Moriarty, A., & Ebert, S. (2012). Allocation of attention to second language form and meaning: Issues of think-alouds and depth of processing. *Studies in Second Language Acquisition, 34*, 659–685.

Sanz, C., & Morgan-Short, K. (2004). Positive evidence versus explicit rule presentation and explicit negative feedback: A computer-assisted study. *Language Learning, 54*, 35–78.

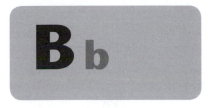

β (see Beta)

Bar graph

A technique displaying quantitative data in which the scores of one or more variables are represented with columns. Generally, the y axis represents a variable expressed in counts (**frequency**) or as a **mean** score, and the x axis represents groups. Such displays of data are useful for providing a quick overall picture of the data. It is easy to see in the bar graph in Figure 1, for example, the relationship between participants' proficiency level and their scores on the two measures: the higher the proficiency, the higher the score, on average, for both the grammaticality judgment test (GJT) and for the error correction (EC) task, where learners are asked to identify grammatical errors in a written text. This bar graph also allows us to examine the relationship between participant scores and the choice of dependent measure. Regardless of proficiency level, the participants scored higher on the GJT than on the error correction task.

Despite their ease of use, bar graphs are not always an ideal way to present quantitative data. For example, bar graphs can be somewhat

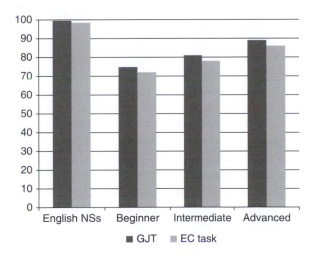

Figure 1 Bar graph

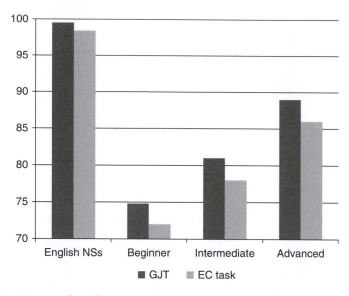

Figure 2 Bar graph with truncated scale

misleading if they do not include the entire measurement scale on the y axis. The abbreviated scale in Figure 2, where the scale begins at 70 rather than 0, presents an exaggerated view of the differences between mean scores compared with Figure 1, which presents the entire scale of 0–100. Another problem in most bar graphs, including the sample graphs here, is a lack of information about the dispersion in the data. By omitting such information, which can be included quite easily in the form of error bars, the reader is often led to overestimate group homogeneity (Weissgerber, Milic, Winham, & Garovic, 2015).

Weissgerber, T. L., Milic, N. M., Winham, S. K., & Garovic, V. D. (2015). Beyond bar and line graphs: Time for a new data presentation paradigm. *PLoS One Biology, 13*, e1002128.

Bell curve

A term used in statistical analysis to refer to the shape of a **normal distribution** of scores when they are plotted using a **histogram**, **bar graph**, or **line graph**. A bell curve has its apex at the mean, which should be in the center of the graph, as shown in Figure 3. In addition, a bell curve has equal slopes descending from both sides of the apex, with the tails extending out on both ends. Visual inspection of data can provide information about their distribution, and if a bell curve is not present, then it is possible that the data are not normally distributed but positively or negatively **skewed.**

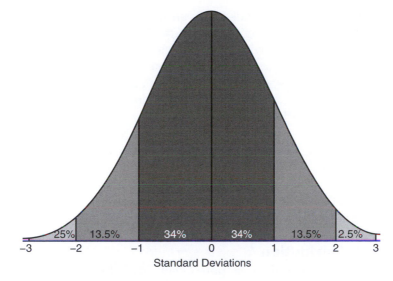

Figure 3 Bell curve

Beta (level)

The beta level, symbolized by the Greek letter β, is used in statistical analysis to refer to the probability of making a **Type II error** in which no statistical difference is found between scores, even though the difference exists within the population as a whole. The beta level contrasts with the **alpha** level, which indicates the likelihood of committing a **Type I error** in which a false positive result is found. Unlike the alpha level, which is reported quite frequently in applied linguistics research, the beta level is seldom provided.

See also **Alpha (level); Statistical power**

Between-groups design

Research that examines independent groups of individuals. By contrast, in **within-groups designs**, the same individuals appear in multiple groups or sets of scores being compared. In many cases, between-groups research studies will consist of one or more treatment groups, plus a comparison and/or control group, with different individuals in each group. For example, Loewen and Nabei (2007) employed a between-groups design in their study of corrective feedback. They had five separate groups of students, three of which received some type of corrective feedback, recast, prompt, or meta-linguistic feedback, while conducting communicative tasks. A **comparison group** performed the tasks without receiving feedback. In addition, a

B

control group was also included. This group did not receive feedback nor did they engage in the interactive tasks; rather, they continued to engage in their normal classroom activities. One benefit of a between-groups design is that the data are independent. However, sometimes the groups may not be equal in size, which may create difficulties for statistical analysis. Furthermore, it may be logistically difficult to recruit enough different individuals to achieve sufficiently large groups.

Loewen, S., & Nabei, T. (2007). Measuring the effects of oral corrective feedback on L2 knowledge. In A. Mackey (Ed.), *Conversational interaction in second language acquisition* (pp. 361–378). Oxford: Oxford University Press.

Between-subjects design
Another term for **between-groups design**.

Bimodal distribution
A type of quantitative data distribution in which two groups of scores cluster separately, forming two distinct peaks. For example, the graph in Figure 4 illustrates a bimodal distribution with a large number of scores grouping towards the left side of the graph and a smaller set of scores clustering towards the right side. A bimodal distribution contrasts with a **normal distribution** in which scores cluster around a central mean and spread out equally on both sides. Data with a bimodal distribution are not appropriate for **parametric statistical** analysis because they do not the meet the **assumption** of a normal distribution. Furthermore, when a bimodal distribution is observed, it is critical to investigate possible causes, for example, by looking at the background information of the participants

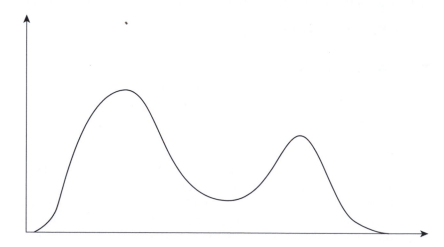

Figure 4   Bimodal distribution

who make up the two clusters. By doing so, the researcher may be able to uncover an additional grouping variable to take into account in present or future analyses.

Binary variable
Another term for **dichotomous variable**.

Bivariate correlation (see Correlation)

Bonferroni correction
A method of reducing the negative effects of conducting multiple statistical analyses on the same dataset. There is an increase in the possibility of committing a **Type I error**, in which a statistical relationship is found even though none exists in the larger **population**, when conducting multiple statistical tests (Brown, 1990). The Bonferroni correction reduces the Type I error rate in such instances. If the **alpha level** for a test is set at $p < .05$, there is a less than 5% chance that any differences found are due to chance. However, if two tests, with individual alpha levels of .05, are conducted on the same data, the overall alpha level rises to .10 (.05 * 2). The Bonferroni correction produces a more conservative alpha level by dividing the desired alpha level (usually .05) by the number of tests being performed (α/n). The resulting value is the new alpha level which is used to determine the significance of the **p-value** produced by the statistical test. For example, Isaacs and Trofimovich (2011) used a Bonferroni correction when investigating the effects of individual differences on rater judgments of L2 speech. In one instance, an alpha level of .05 was decreased to .016 due to the calculation of three different statistical tests (.05/3 = .016). As a result, one of the analyses was deemed not to be statistically significant because the p-value of .021 failed to meet the new criterion. While the Bonferroni correction reduces the potential for Type I errors, it conversely increases the possibility of a **Type II** error in which an existing difference in the larger population remains undetected in the sample, especially as the number of tests increases.

The Bonferroni correction is different from the Bonferroni **post hoc test**, which can be used after an ANOVA to investigate differences between groups. For example, after finding an initial statistically significant analysis of covariance for accuracy scores, Van Beuningen, De Jong, and Kuiken (2012) conducted Bonferroni post hoc tests in their study on the effectiveness of written corrective feedback. The pairwise comparisons revealed that the two groups that received corrective feedback significantly outperformed the two groups that did not.

Brown, J. D. (1990). The use of multiple t-tests in language research. *TESOL Quarterly, 24*, 770–773.

B

Isaacs, T., & Trofimovich, P. (2011). Phonological memory, attention control, and musical ability: Effects of individual differences on rater judgments of second language speech. *Applied Psycholinguistics, 32,* 113–140.

Van Beuningen, C. G., De Jong, N. H., & Kuiken, F. (2012). Evidence on the effectiveness of comprehensive error correction in second language writing. *Language Learning, 62,* 1–41.

Bootstrapping

A type of non-parametric, **robust statistic** that draws multiple samples from the same data set in order to simulate the effect of selecting numerous samples from the larger **population** (Beasley & Rogers, 2009; Efron, 1979). **Quantitative research** in applied linguistics often relies on samples that are necessarily small, non-normally distributed, and/or that include **outliers**. By redrawing samples from an observed data set, bootstrapping enables the researcher to obtain potentially thousands of bootstrapped samples, the aggregated results of which can then be used to calculate results that are less sensitive to any irregularities, such as non-normality, in the data. Such bootstrapped results are argued to be more accurate and stable. This technique, introduced only recently in applied linguistics (Larson-Hall & Herrington, 2010), can be applied to **descriptive statistics** (**mean**, **standard deviation**, **confidence intervals**) as well as most **inferential statistics** commonly employed in the field (i.e., **t-test**, **analysis of variance**, **correlation**). Plonsky, Egbert, and LaFlair (in press) tested the applicability of bootstrapping using raw data from 26 published applied linguistics studies. Their results showed that 25% of the statistically significant findings in the original reports were not replicated by the bootstrapped analyses (i.e., a potential **Type I error** rate five times greater than what would be expected based on an **alpha** of .05). For example, the original results of one of the re-analyzed studies found a statistically significant one-way ANOVA ($p < .05$). When the same data were bootstrapped, however, the difference across groups was no longer statistically significant. Plonsky et al. (in press) attributed this and other discrepancies to a combination of factors, including: relatively small **effect sizes** (a d value, converted from eta-squared, of just .47 in the case of this sample study); non-normal distributions; outliers; and relatively large samples, which are more likely to reach **statistical significance** even when effects are small. Based on their findings, Plonsky et al. (in press) argue in favor of bootstrapping in conjunction with—not as a replacement for—**parametric statistics**, particularly when: (a) sample sizes are especially large or small, and (b) the data display irregularities such as outliers or a non-normal distribution. For a practical tutorial on bootstrapping using both **SPSS** and **R**, see LaFlair, Egbert, and Plonsky (2015).

Beasley, W. H., & Rogers, J. L. (2009). Resampling methods. In R. E. Millsap & A. Maydeu-Olivares (Eds.), *The Sage handbook of quantitative methods in psychology* (pp. 362–386). London: Sage.

Efron, B. (1979). Bootstrap methods: Another look at the jackknife. *Annals of Statistics, 7*, 26.

LaFlair, G. T., Egbert, J., & Plonsky, L. (2015). A practical guide to bootstrapping descriptive statistics, correlations, *t* tests, and ANOVAs. In L. Plonsky (Ed.), *Advancing quantitative methods in second language research* (pp. 46–77). New York: Routledge.

Larson-Hall, J., & Herrington, R. (2010). Improving data analysis in second language acquisition by utilizing modern developments in applied statistics. *Applied Linguistics, 31*, 368–390.

Plonsky, L., Egbert J., & LaFlair, G. (in press). Bootstrapping in applied linguistics: Assessing its potential using shared data. *Applied Linguistics*.

Box-and-whisker plot (**Boxplot**)

A graphical representation of a **continuous variable** with a box and a pair of "whiskers" extending above and below it. The elements of a boxplot, illustrated in Figure 5, include: (a) a box representing the middle 50% of the data (i.e., scores falling between the 25th and 75th **percentiles**); (b) a solid line inside the box indicating the **median** score (i.e., the 50th percentile), with 25% of the data on either side of the median; whiskers at the bottom and top of the graph representing the (c) lowest and (d) highest 25% of the data,

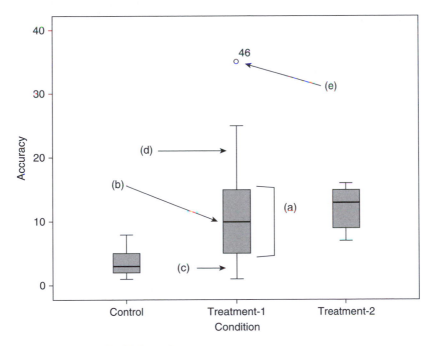

Figure 5 Box-and-whisker plot

respectively; (e) circles and/or asterisks beyond the whiskers that represent any statistical **outliers**, usually accompanied by a number that represents the number of the case or participant that the value belongs to. The plot in Figure 5 presents fabricated gain scores in writing accuracy under three conditions: a control group that received no feedback, a treatment group that received direct feedback, and another treatment group that received indirect feedback. As might be expected the accuracy of both treatment groups improved substantially more than the comparison group. Additionally, although the gains for the two treatment groups overlap, the median gain for treatment group 2 (13) was somewhat higher than that of treatment group 1 (10). In addition to enabling comparisons between group scores, box-and-whisker plots can also provide valuable information regarding normality, outliers, and the equality of variance among the groups. Of the three groups, only treatment group 1 appears to have a relatively normal distribution; the control group appears somewhat positively skewed, and the data from treatment group 2 seem to possess a slightly negative skew. In terms of equality (or homogeneity) of variance, the larger the box, and the longer the whiskers, the more variation there is in the group's scores. Thus, in this plot, not only did treatment group 2 show a higher overall (median) gain, but the participants responded more uniformly to the treatment as well in accuracy, compared to those in treatment group 1, which had more variance as indicated by the longer box and whiskers as well as the outlier (case #46).

Boxplot (see Box-and-whisker plot)

B

Case study

A type of **qualitative research** study that investigates a small number of subjects, often only one or two. The research involves in-depth description, for example, focusing on a holistic explication of the subject's context or a detailed assessment of the development of specific linguistic features. Case studies are also often longitudinal in nature. The unit of analysis in a case study can be an individual learner or a broader context, such as a classroom or school. A case study can involve multiple methods of data collection, including observations and **interviews**. Case studies may also be ethnographic in nature (e.g., Harklau, 2000). One strength of case studies is that they provide a very rich and detailed account of the participant and context in question; however, the results and conclusions may not be generalizable to other contexts and individuals. A recent case study by Polat and Kim (2014) involved tracking the development of linguistic accuracy, syntactic complexity, and lexical diversity of one Turkish immigrant in the USA over a one-year period. The participant was interviewed every two weeks, and his oral production was analyzed for the previously mentioned linguistic features. Other, seminal, case studies in applied linguistics include Schmidt's (1983) investigation of Wes and Schumann's (1978) study of Alberto. Schmidt investigated Wes's development of requests over a three-year period and concluded that the participant's communicative competence improved considerably during this time; however, there was no corresponding increase in linguistic accuracy. Similarly, Schumann conducted a 10-month research study on the linguistic development of Alberto, a naturalistic learner of English in the USA. Schumann did not find evidence of any significant linguistic growth, which he attributed to Alberto's social and psychological distance from the host society.

Duff, P. (2014). Case study research on language learning and use. *Annual Review of Applied Linguistics, 34*, 233–255.

Harklau, L. (2000). From the "Good Kids" to the "Worst": Representations of English language learners across educational settings. *TESOL Quarterly, 34*, 35–67.

Polat, B., & Kim, Y. (2014). Dynamics of complexity and accuracy: A longitudinal case study of advanced untutored development. *Applied Linguistics, 35*, 184–207.

Schmidt, R. (1983). Interaction, acculturation and the acquisition of communicative competence. In N. Wolfson & E. Judd (Eds.), *Sociolinguistics and language acquisition* (pp. 137–174). Rowley, MA: Newbury House.

Schumann, J. (1978). *The pidginization process: A model for second language acquisition.* Rowley, MA: Newbury House.

Categorical variable

A type of **variable** in **quantitative research** consisting of discrete, non-numeric categories. Categorical variables, also called **nominal variables**, contrast with ordinal and **continuous variables**. Examples of common categorical variables in applied linguistics are L1 background and L2 target language, each containing potential categories such as English, Chinese, Spanish, and so forth. Figure 6, based on data from Loewen et al. (2014), shows the responses to a categorical variable where participants had to select which academic field of study they most identified with. Thus, the category with the most frequent responses was SLA, with Applied Linguistics being the next closest category.

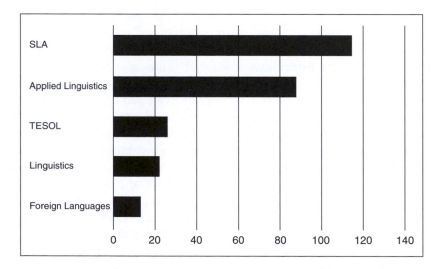

Figure 6 Categorical data [Participants' academic field of study]

It is not possible to perform many types of statistical procedures on categorical variables because they do not have mathematical properties such as a **mean** or **standard deviation**. Rather, categorical variables can only be tallied, leading to **frequency** counts and **percentages**. One **inferential statistic** that can be conducted with categorical variables is **chi-square,** which investigates whether the observed distribution of categories within one or more variables differs statistically from what would be expected if there was no association between them. Finally, when designing a data collection **instrument**, it is sometimes possible to choose whether to make a variable categorical or continuous. An example of this situation is the variable *age*. Although age is generally conceptualized as a continuous variable, it is possible to create a categorical variable by grouping participants based on a **range** of ages, such as under 18, 18–25, 26–35, over 36. In general, however, it is preferable to preserve the precision in continuous variables, because categorical variables in such cases are limited in their precision and in the types of statistical procedures that can be applied to them. In the case of a categorical age variable, a researcher can only tally the number of respondents in each age category and subject the data to a chi-square analysis. However, if age is measured as a continuous variable, with a specified number for each participant, then the data can be used for means-based analyses and **correlations**.

Agresti, A. (2013). *Categorical data analysis* (3rd ed.). Hoboken, NJ: Wiley.

Loewen, S., Lavolette, B., Spino, L., Papi, M., Schmidtke, J., Sterling, S., & Wolff, D. (2014). Statistical literacy among applied linguists and second language acquisition researchers. *TESOL Quarterly, 48*, 360–388.

Causation

When a change in one variable can be attributed to the presence or amount of another variable. In applied linguistics, as in other educational sciences, causation is principally demonstrated by means of **quasi-experimental** and **experimental** studies. The inclusion of design features such as **random assignment** to experimental conditions, **pretesting** and **posttesting**, and comparison or control groups enable the researcher to confirm whether and to what extent a change can be attributed to—that is, caused by—a treatment. By isolating the variables in question through these methods, researchers attempt to measure the effects of an **independent variable** on a **dependent variable**, without the presence of moderating or confounding variables. For example, studies of L2 corrective feedback (e.g., Ellis, Loewen, & Erlam, 2006; Lyster & Izquierdo, 2009) have used pretesting and posttesting, with treatment and **comparison groups,** to determine if one type of corrective feedback is better at causing improvement in learners' linguistic proficiency. Causation is often discussed in contrast with **correlation**, which occurs when two measured variables increase or decrease in tandem; however, correlation does not imply causation.

Ellis, R., Loewen, S., & Erlam, R. (2006). Implicit and explicit corrective feedback and the acquisition of L2 grammar. *Studies in Second Language Acquisition, 28*, 339–368.

Lyster, R., & Izquierdo, J. (2009). Prompts versus recasts in dyadic interaction. *Language Learning, 59*, 453–498.

Shadish, W. R., Cook, T. D., & Campbell, D. T. (2002). *Experimental and quasi-experimental designs for generalized causal inference.* Boston, MA: Houghton Mifflin.

Central tendency

A general function of **descriptive statistics** is to summarize a set of data. Measures of central tendency provide information about the most typical and representative scores in the data by specifying the midpoint in the data set. The most common measure of central tendency is the **mean**, which indicates the mathematical average score in the data. However, when data are heavily **skewed** or contain **outliers**, the **median,** which is the middle score in the data, can be a better indicator of central tendency. Another measure of central tendency is the **mode**, which indicates the most frequently observed value in the data. In the following hypothetical data set (1, 3, 3, 7, 10), the mean is 4.8, the median is 3, and the mode is 3.

While central tendency provides information about the center of the data, it does not provide information about the extent of the data distribution. Consequently, measures of **dispersion**, such as **range** or **standard deviation**, must also be provided in order to better understand the nature of the data set in question.

Chi-square test

A type of inferential statistic that examines whether or not the distribution of frequencies is what would be expected by chance. The chi-square value is represented by χ^2, using the Greek letter, although sometimes the Latin script X is used instead. Chi-square examines **frequency** counts rather than mean scores, and is thus suited for **categorical data** rather than **ordinal** or **interval data**. In addition, chi-square should be calculated on raw frequencies, not percentages or ratios. It is possible to compare the distribution of frequencies on one variable by comparing the observed number of counts with the number of counts to be expected by chance; such an analysis is sometimes called a **goodness of fit** analysis. However, more commonly, chi-square is used for comparing the distribution of scores across two variables to see if there is a relationship between them. For example, a study might want to compare the number of males and females from different first language backgrounds. In such cases, a **contingency table** is created, as seen in Table 2, and the observed counts are compared against the counts that would be expected if there was no relationship between the variables. Many times, a contingency table is used when each variable has only two categories. Thus, if the chi-square value is significant, it is easy to know where the differences occur because if counts are significantly higher in one cell, then they are lower in another.

However, it is also possible to create larger contingency tables in which variables have three or more levels, In such cases, it is not possible to know specifically which cells have higher or lower than expected frequency counts. Thus, in larger contingency tables, it is necessary to calculate residuals (similar to **z-scores**) for each cell which then indicate how much each observation differs from what is expected. There are several different ways of

Table 2   2 × 2 contingency table

	English	Spanish
Males	10	5
Females	11	12

calculating residuals; however, one common way is to use the adjusted standardized residual in which case, values of greater than 2.0 or less than −2.0 are considered significantly different. The closer the residuals are to zero, the less significant the differences are.

One of the **assumptions** of chi-square is that all of the observations are independent: each participant is contributing only once to a cell, because if a person or text, in the case of **corpora**, contributes more than once, they may bias the data because of their propensity for a specific category. For example, in the gender by L1 table each participant appears only once because they are either male or female, with either English or Spanish L1. Thus, each count represents one individual. However, this assumption is sometimes violated in applied linguistics research, with participants contributing multiple counts. For example, a study might want to investigate if there is a difference in the L2s that males and females study. If some participants have studied multiple L2s, then they would be contributing to more than one cell. Such data would not be independent. Another assumption is that the expected frequency count for each cell should be at least five. Finally, **Phi** and **Cramer's V** are effect sizes that can be calculated for chi-square analyses.

Classroom-based research

A type of research, fairly common in applied linguistics, that takes place inside the L2 classroom. There are several different approaches to classroom research. It may involve an investigation of the classroom as a holistic system, for instance by conducting **ethnography** or a **case study**. In these cases, the classroom environment is not manipulated by the researcher. Nevertheless, the researcher's presence affects, however slightly, what would naturally occur: a phenomenon referred to as the observer's paradox. Another type of classroom research consists of **quasi-experimental research** in which researchers instigate some type of **treatment**, often in an attempt to ascertain whether and to what extent one type of instruction, or aspect of instruction, is more effective. In these instances, the researcher may administer the treatment, or the teacher may be asked to do so.

There are several benefits to doing classroom-based research. First and foremost, compared to the artificiality of laboratory-based studies, research that takes place in a classroom is more likely to reflect the realities of the classroom, thereby possessing greater **ecological validity**. Related to this advantage, a benefit of having the regular classroom teacher administer the treatment is that the learners are familiar and more comfortable with their own teacher, and thus the treatment may be very much like a regular classroom activity. However, there are also disadvantages to conducting classroom research. First and foremost, classrooms are messy places to collect data, due to the many variables

C

that are beyond the researcher's control. While this may not be such an issue for more observational and qualitative types of research in which the primary purpose is to describe and understand the classroom context, the messiness of the classroom is a potential problem for quasi-experimental, quantitative type studies. In a classroom context, it is often difficult to control extraneous variables, which means that it can be difficult to claim that the effect of a treatment is due to the **independent variable** that the research intended to investigate. Furthermore, in studies with a **pretest**/treatment/**posttest** design, there can be participant **attrition**, whereby students miss a part of the treatment because they missed a class for whatever reason. Another difficulty is the lack of random group assignment. If **intact classes** are used, then there may be unknown factors which caused the specific group of learners to be in that class. For example, a morning class might be full of enthusiastic learners who want to start off their day with a big dose of the L2, while a late afternoon class might be filled with students who want to put off taking the class for as long as possible, or who are tired after a long day at school and/or work. Such factors can have a confounding effect on the research.

There is also an issue as to the comparability of classroom-based and **laboratory-based research**, with various researchers claiming that the findings of lab-based studies lack **generalizability** to the classroom context, and that research investigating instructed L2 acquisition should be primarily classroom-based research (see Nunan, 1991).

Foster, P. (1998). A classroom perspective on the negotiation of meaning. *Applied Linguistics, 19*, 1–23.

Gass, S., Mackey, A., & Ross-Feldman, L. (2005). Task-based interactions in classroom and laboratory settings. *Language Learning, 55*, 575–611.

Nunan, D. (1991). Methods in second language classroom-oriented research: A critical review. *Studies in Second Language Acquisition, 13*, 249–274.

Cluster analysis

A procedure for identifying groups or clusters of cases based on a set of measured variables. Applied linguists often group participants based on one or more **categorical**, **independent variables**. There are times, however, when the researcher is interested in discovering underlying or yet-undetermined groupings and, perhaps, in creating or uncovering a new independent variable. Such a situation might arise, for example, when theory in a particular area is less developed. Cluster analysis is similar to **factor analysis**, as both can be used as data reduction techniques.

Compared to other quantitative and **multivariate statistics**, cluster analysis is more descriptive and open to the interpretation of the researcher, who must decide, among other things, the number of clusters to include in the final solution. In other words, there is no statistical test to determine significance, nor does the output, which is both numeric and visual, indicate the meaning of the clusters. It is up to the researcher to decide upon a number and set of clusters that maximizes within-cluster similarity while minimizing similarities between clusters. For example, one critical step in a cluster analysis involves examining a dendrogram, which forms successive clusters or groups of participants ranging from the total sample, in which case no clusters are formed, to a single cluster comprised of all cases contributing data. In the dendrogram shown in Figure 7 (from Goslin & Floccia, 2007), the left-most initials represent each case in the data set. The lines link the cases that are most similar, in successive levels. For example, the five uppermost cases are most closely related to each other, with the sixth case being added to the cluster at the next level. At the other extreme, the entire data set can be divided into two clusters, marked by 1 and 2 on the dendrogram. These two sets of cases form the most distinct clusters. The numbers 1.1 and 1.2 go on to divide cluster 1 into two smaller clusters. In order to determine the primary characteristics of each cluster, the researcher must examine the composition of the cases within each cluster for common characteristics. In this sense, cluster analysis is comparable to factor analysis, where researchers are likewise forced to interpret groupings of data vis-à-vis their understanding of the substantive domain in question. See Staples and Biber (2015) for a guide to conducting cluster analysis in applied linguistics.

Cluster analysis has not traditionally been used very often in applied linguistics. Nevertheless, it has appeared in a variety of subdomains within the field. A number of researchers interested in individual differences, for example, have used cluster analysis to better understand different learner profiles (e.g., Papi & Teimouri, 2014; Tsuda & Nakata, 2013). For example, Papi and Teimouri examined the motivational profile of 1,278 secondary school English learners in Iran. The researchers entered 10 motivation-related variables from a survey into the cluster analysis, and they identified five motivational clusters, based on learners' high or low scores on questions related to their ideal L2 self, the ought-to L2 self, and L2 learning experiences.

In the area of **corpus** linguistics, cluster analysis has been used with texts rather than participants as the level of analysis (e.g., Biber, 2008) as a means to understand features common within and across text types. Other subdomains that have used this procedure include language assessment and language policy.

Biber, D. (2008). Corpus-based analyses of discourse: Dimensions of variation in conversation. In V. K. Bhatia, J. Flowerdew, & R. H. Jones. *Advances in discourse studies* (pp. 100–114). New York: Routledge.

Goslin, J., & Floccia, C. (2007). Comparing French syllabification in preliterate children and adults. *Applied Psycholinguistics, 28*, 341–367.

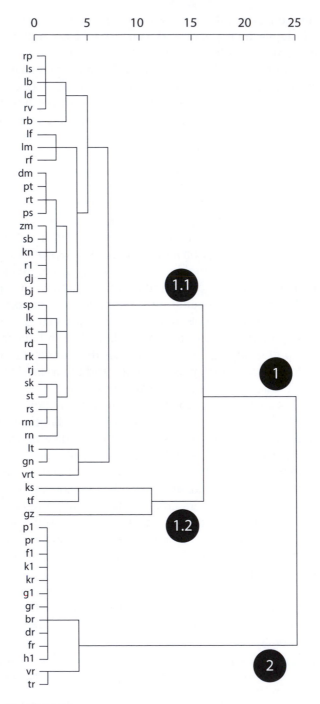

Figure 7   Dendrogram

Papi, M., & Teimouri, Y. (2014). Language learner motivational types: A cluster analysis study. *Language Learning, 64*, 493–525.

Staples, S., & Biber, D. (2015). Cluster analysis. In L. Plonsky (Ed.), *Advancing quantitative methods in second language research* (pp. 243–278). New York: Routledge.

Tsuda, A., & Nakata, Y. (2013). Exploring self-regulation in language learning: A study of Japanese high school EFL students. *Innovation in Language Learning and Teaching, 7*(1), 72–88.

Cohen's *d*

An **effect size** used to express the magnitude of difference between two mean scores. Because of the frequency of means-based comparisons in applied linguistics such as ***t*-tests** and ANOVAs, this effect size is appropriate in a wide variety of contexts of **quantitative research**. As shown in the formula below, Cohen's *d* is calculated by dividing the difference between two mean scores by their (pooled) **standard deviation** (*SD*). (Inexplicably, **SPSS** does not compute this effect size, but there are numerous online calculators that do so, or the calculation can be done by hand.) The *SD* in the denominator of this formula acts as a kind of standardizer. That is, it enables researchers to interpret the result in *standardized* units, which can be compared across studies and/or combined via **meta-analysis**, regardless of the number of items in the scale or measure being used.

$$d = \frac{M_1 - M_2}{SD_{pooled}}$$

In (**quasi-**)**experimental design**s, Cohen's *d* can be used to indicate the strength of a treatment, either as an absolute value (in a pre–post contrast) or in contrast with an alternative treatment (i.e., treatment vs. **comparison group**). By doing so, the *d* value provides a measure of the treatment's **practical significance**. For example, as shown in Table 3, we can compare the effect sizes found by different studies investigating the effectiveness of vocabulary learning. Two meta-analyses found similar *d* values at .69 and .75, but the *d* value from Wa-Mbaleka's meta-analysis was twice as large.

Table 3   Effect sizes from meta-analyses of vocabulary teaching and learning

Meta-analysis	*k*	*d*
Won (2008)	30	0.69
Chiu (2013)	16	0.75
Wa-Mbaleka (2006)	34	1.43

For a thorough discussion on the use and interpretation of these and other effect sizes, see Plonsky and Oswald (2014).

Chiu, Y. H., (2013). Computer-assisted second language vocabulary instruction. A meta-analysis. *British Journal of Educational Technology, 44,* E52–E56.

Cohen, J. (1988). *Statistical power analysis for the behavioral sciences* (2nd ed.). Hillsdale, NJ: Erlbaum.

Plonsky, L., & Oswald, F. L. (2014). How big is "big"? Interpreting effect sizes in L2 research. *Language Learning, 64,* 878–912.

Wa-Mbaleka, S. (2006). *A meta-analysis investigating the effects of reading on second language vocabulary learning.* Unpublished doctoral dissertation. Northern Arizona University.

Won, M. (2008). *The effects of vocabulary instruction on English language learners: A meta-analysis.* Unpublished doctoral dissertation. Texas Tech University.

Cohen's kappa

A method of calculating **inter-rater agreement** when conducting a **reliability** analysis. In order to ensure the consistency with which a categorical coding scheme has been used in data analysis, researchers may have two or more individuals code the same data. In some instances, a simple **percentage** agreement score is calculated: the number of items the raters agreed on divided by the total number of items. Cohen's kappa, used when two raters apply a categorical coding scheme, is similar to percentage agreement; however, it makes statistical adjustments to correct for the fact that some rater agreement might happen by chance. For example, Loewen (2005) coded focus on form episodes according to linguistic focus, whether grammar, vocabulary, or pronunciation. A second rater coded 20% of the data, with a subsequent percentage agreement of 89% and κ = .83. As can be seen, Cohen's kappa is generally a more conservative measure of reliability than percentage agreement (Plonsky & Derrick, under review). As with many measures of reliability, there is no agreed standard for a kappa score to be considered acceptable; however, scores as low as .70 have been considered fair to good (Fleiss, Levin, & Paik, 2003).

Fleiss, J., Levin, B., & Paik, M. (2003). *Statistical methods for rates and proportions* (3rd ed.). New York: John Wiley & Sons.

Loewen, S. (2005). Incidental focus on form and second language learning. *Studies in Second Language Acquisition, 27,* 361–386.

Plonsky, L., & Derrick, D. J. (under review). A meta-analysis of reliability coefficients in second language research. [Manuscript under review.]

Communalities (see Factor analysis)

Comparison group

A feature of quasi-experimental research that enables the researcher to isolate and measure the effect of a treatment, such as a type of instruction, on the **dependent variable**, such as L2 development. In **classroom-based**

research, for instance, a comparison group would take the **pretest** and any **posttests**. Furthermore, the comparison group would engage in the same instructional activities as the treatment group(s); however, they would not receive the treatment itself. In this way, the researcher can assess the effects of the treatment by comparing the two groups, one which received the treatment and one which did not. For example, in corrective feedback research, a comparison group would engage in the same communicative activities as the treatment groups; however, the comparison group would not receive the feedback. A comparison group differs from a control group in that the latter does not participate in any of the research activities, except for the pretest and posttests. Sometimes in applied linguistics and particularly in SLA, a group is called a control group when it is actually a comparison group.

Shadish, W. R., Cook, T. D., & Campbell, D. T. (2002). *Experimental and quasi-experimental designs for generalized causal inference.* Boston, MA: Houghton Mifflin.

Confidence interval (CI)

A descriptive statistic that indicates a **range** of values within which the true **population** value is likely to be found. Each CI also has a probability associated with it—typically 95%—which indicates the likelihood that the true population value can be found within the interval. CIs can be applied and interpreted in various ways (see Cumming, 2012), but they are especially useful in helping situate observed scores from a specific sample among the many other values that might be observed if different samples were investigated, and which best represent the population. In the words of Carl Sagan (1996), "[CIs are] a quiet but insistent reminder that no knowledge is complete or perfect" (pp. 27–28).

CIs can also be particularly useful in the context of means-based comparisons. In such cases, a 95% CI can provide the same information as a *t*-test. If the mean of group B falls outside the CI of group A, the difference between them is statistically significant at the .05 level, and vice versa. Similarly, the mean difference between two groups can also be expressed as a CI. This approach is actually more informative than simply reporting means, **standard deviations**, and the results of *t*-tests. Consider the results provided by Larson-Hall's (2006) comparison of the pronunciation of /l/ and /ɹ/ by three groups: inexperienced Japanese learners of English (IJs), experienced Japanese learners of English (EJs), and native speakers of English (NSs). Comparisons between each group's mean score were presented as 95% CIs. By doing so, both the **statistical significance** and the size of the difference between mean scores were evident. In one of the conditions, for example, the CI for the comparison between EJ and IJ scores was reported as [–.67, .79], indicating that the true difference between the two groups was somewhere between negative .67 and positive .79. In this case, the CI for the mean difference crosses zero, indicating no statistically significant difference, because there is the possibility of either group having a higher mean than the other. Furthermore, the interval falls roughly equally on both sides of and not far from zero, which indicates that the true population difference here, if any, is likely very small. In a different condition, however, the mean difference between groups is expressed as [−3.46, −.39], indicating that the actual difference between the two groups is between .39 and 3.46. Here, because the interval does not cross zero, the difference between the groups is statistically significant. Additionally, one end of the interval is also relatively large, indicating that the true population difference between these two groups may be somewhat large as well.

Though CIs are most often utilized to portray error around mean scores and mean differences, they can also be constructed around many other types of statistics, such as **correlation** coefficients (r), t values, F values, and d values. For example, Lyster and Saito (2010) reported confidence intervals in their meta-analysis of corrective feedback. In Figure 8, the black dot indicates the mean d value, and the whiskers indicate the CIs. Thus, the figure illustrates that the CI for the between-group d value is the widest, while the CIs for the control group is the narrowest. Furthermore, because the CIs

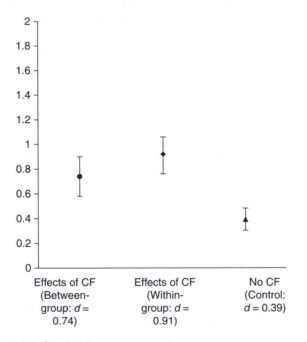

Source: Lyster & Saito (2010)

Figure 8 95% confidence intervals around meta-analytic effect sizes of CF in L2 classrooms

for those two *d* values do not overlap, Lyster and Saito concluded that their meta-analysis found a statistically significant effect for corrective feedback.

For additional details on the reporting and interpretation of CIs, see Cumming (2012) and, in the context of L2 research, Larson-Hall and Plonsky (2015).

Cumming, G. (2012). *Understanding the new statistics: Effect sizes, confidence intervals, and meta-analysis*. New York: Routledge.

Larson-Hall, J. (2006). What does more time buy you? Another look at the effects of long-term residence on production accuracy of English /ɹ/ and / l / by Japanese speakers. *Language and Speech, 49*, 521–548.

Larson-Hall, J., & Plonsky, L. (2015). Reporting and interpreting quantitative research findings: What gets reported and recommendations for the field. *Language Learning, 65*(Supp. 1), 125–157.

Lyster, R. & Saito, K. (2010). Oral feedback in classroom SLA: A meta-analysis. *Studies in Second Language Acquisition, 32*, 265–302.

Plonsky, L. (2015). Statistical power, *p* values, descriptive statistics, and effect sizes: A "back-to-basics" approach to advancing quantitative methods in L2 research. In L. Plonsky (Ed.), *Advancing quantitative methods in second language research* (pp. 23–45). New York: Routledge.

Sagan, C. (1996). *The demon-haunted world*. New York: Random House.

Confirmatory factor analysis (see Factor analysis)

Construct

An underlying concept that researchers attempt to measure and include as a variable in a study. It is a bit of an abstraction that needs to be operationalized in order to measure. Commonly examined constructs in applied linguistics include, for example, L2 proficiency, motivation, identity, and anxiety. These notions are not directly observable, but can be manifested in numerous ways. As an example, anxiety is a concept that is theorized to affect L2 learning in a variety of ways. However, anxiety cannot be measured directly. In order to do research on this construct, there must be something that is taken as evidence of anxiety. Thus, researchers have developed **surveys**, for example, that attempt to measure anxiety by asking learners to agree or disagree with questions such as: *I never feel quite sure of myself when I am speaking in my foreign language class* and *I start to panic when I have to speak without preparation in language class* (Horwitz, Horwitz, & Cope, 1986). It is also possible to measure behavioral or physiological manifestations of anxiety, such as increased heart rate.

Horwitz, E. K., Horwitz, M. B., & Cope, J. (1986). Foreign language classroom anxiety. *Modern Language Journal, 70*, 125–132.

Constructivism

A research paradigm characterized by a recognition of the existence of multiple, socially built (or constructed) realities, which researchers explore and describe. **Epistemologically**, and compared to more traditional paradigms such as (**post)positivism**, constructivism is quite aware of and open to the potential of researcher subjectivity and its interaction with participants' perspectives during data collection and particularly data analysis and inter- pretation. Researchers working in a constructivist framework often employ **qualitative methods** such as **ethnographies** and **interviews**, which take advantage of contextual information (e.g., **thick description**) as well as participants' perceptions, among other sources, to arrive at a maximally informative interpretation of the phenomenon under investigation.

Lincoln, Y. S., & Guba, E. G. (2000). Paradigmatic controversies, contradictions, and emerg- ing confluences. In N. K. Denzin & Y. S. Lincoln (Eds.), *Handbook of qualitative research* (2nd ed., pp. 163–188). Thousand Oaks, CA: Sage.

Richards, K. (2003). *Qualitative inquiry in TESOL*. New York: Palgrave Macmillan.

Construct validity

How well a specific **instrument** measures the object (or **construct**) that it is intended to measure. For example, a test in which learners have to write a story is not a good measure of oral proficiency; an oral storytell- ing task would be more appropriate and therefore have greater construct validity. The issue of construct validity has often surfaced in the context of instructed SLA research, where researchers have examined the effects of implicit and explicit instruction on implicit and explicit L2 knowledge. In order to make claims about the influence of instruction on these two types of knowledge, it is vital to know that the instruments claiming to measure each type of knowledge are actually doing so. For example, in Norris and Ortega's (2000) **meta-analysis**, it was found that explicit instruction was more effective for L2 development; however, it was claimed (Doughty, 2003) that the tests used were better measures of explicit knowledge, which would favor explicit instruction. Thus, the tests lacked construct validity in measuring implicit knowledge.

Doughty, C. (2003). Instructed SLA: Constraints, compensation, and enhancement. In C. Doughty & M. Long (Eds.), *The handbook of second language acquisition* (pp. 256–310). Malden, MA: Blackwell Publishing.

Norris, J. M., & Ortega, L. (2000). Effectiveness of L2 instruction: A research synthesis and quantitative meta-analysis. *Language Learning, 50*, 417–528.

Contingency table

A type of data display in which two **categorical variables** are compared. As such, a contingency table is a way of displaying descriptive data for **frequency** counts. The categories of each variable are displayed in the rows and columns, respectively, thereby forming cells for each combina- tion of categories. The raw frequency of occurrence of the data within each category combination is then displayed in its corresponding cell.

Table 4 2 × 4 Contingency table: Language aptitude and target language

	Arabic	French	Spanish	Japanese
High	14	10	8	12
Low	5	10	19	5

Percentages of occurrence are also sometimes presented. A contingency table is often described in terms of the number of levels of each variable. For example, a classic contingency table is 2 × 2, with each variable having only two levels. However, it is possible to have a table that is 2 × 3, 3 × 3, or any other possible combination of levels. Table 4, for instance, shows a 2 x 4 contingency table, with two categories of language aptitude and four different target languages, providing information about the relationship between individual learners' language aptitude and their choice of target language. Almost three times as many high aptitude learners chose to study Arabic, while almost twice as many low aptitude learners chose Spanish.

Finally, contingency tables provide the descriptive information about the data that goes into a **chi-square** analysis.

Continuous variable

A variable that is measured on a numeric scale. Also called interval variables, continuous variables are the most common types of variables in quantitative applied linguistics research, and they contrast with **categorical** and **ordinal** variables. L2 proficiency test scores are examples of common continuous variables. In continuous variables, participants receive scores on the variable's measurement scale, and there is equal distance between each point on the scale. For example, the difference between scoring 95 or 96 points on a 100-point test is the same as the difference between scoring 50 and 51 points, namely one point. If the 100-point test were assessing overall proficiency, we could also assume in this case that the difference in proficiency between a score of 50 and 51 was equal to the difference between 95 and 96. It is possible to calculate means and **standard deviations** for continuous variables; consequently, they can be used in means-based **inferential statistics**, such as *t*-tests and **ANOVAs**, as well as correlational statistics. Technically, continuous variables do not contain an absolute zero point on their measurement scales, where zero indicates a complete absence of the characteristic being measured. Instead, absolute zero is a property of **ratio variables**; however, in practical terms, this distinction has little impact in applied linguistics research.

Control group

A group that is compared to one or more treatment groups in order to determine the effects of the treatment (i.e., **causation**). Control groups are an important feature of **experimental** and **quasi-experimental** research. They do not receive or participate in the intervention that is provided to the treatment group(s). If there is no control group, and the treatment group improves after treatment, it is not possible to state whether those changes were due to the treatment or to some other unforeseen and uncontrolled variable. If there is a **control group** or a **comparison group** that is equal to the treatment group in every way except for the treatment, however, then the researcher can have more confidence in stating that any **posttest** differences between the two groups are due to the treatment. In many cases in applied linguistics research, there is no control group, in part because of the challenges associated with recruiting participants. In addition, sometimes a comparison group is incorrectly called a control group. However, generally a comparison group receives some type of manipulated, if only minimal, treatment as well, whereas a control group only participates in **pretesting** and posttesting activities. In Loewen and Nabei's (2007) study of the effects of oral corrective feedback during task-based interaction, they investigated: (a) three treatment groups, which received either recasts, prompts, or meta-linguistic feedback; (b) one comparison group, which participated in the tasks but did not receive feedback; and (c) a control group, which took the pretest and posttest but continued with their regular classroom activities while the other groups performed the interactive tasks.

Loewen, S., & Nabei, T. (2007). Measuring the effects of oral corrective feedback on L2 knowledge. In A. Mackey (Ed.) *Conversational interaction in second language acquisition* (pp. 361–378). Oxford: Oxford University Press.

Shadish, W. R., Cook, T. D., & Campbell, D. T. (2002). *Experimental and quasi-experimental designs for generalized causal inference.* Boston, MA: Houghton Mifflin.

Conversation analysis

A method of analyzing interaction data that is guided by a number of principles. One of the most important is that researchers are not supposed to bring external categories and perspectives to the data. Instead, the researcher is supposed to interpret how the participants themselves made sense of the interaction. In other words, the goal of conversation analysis, also known as CA, is to take an **emic** perspective, which contrasts with other approaches to the analysis of interaction (see Gass, 2004, for an illustration). As a method of analysis, CA did not start out looking at second language interaction, but instead came from the discipline of first language interaction; however, it has become widely used with second language data. An important unit of analysis in CA is the turn, with researchers looking at how turn-taking occurs, and what this might mean to the participants. Also crucial to CA are the very detailed **transcriptions** of data, representing everything from pauses to voice quality to gestures and beyond. As seen in the examples from Barraja-Rohan (2011), CA researchers use numerous transcription markers to indicate various aspects of the discourse. Barraja-Rohan used CA to raise L2 learners' awareness regarding the characteristics of conversational interaction. In particular, she had learners focus on response tokens (e.g., *yeah* or *okay*), assessments (e.g., *good* or *how terrible*), and adjacency pairs in greetings (such as the first two lines of Conversation 3 from Barraja-Rohan, 2011).

CA is also not typically concerned with making generalizations about data, in part because categories are not to be imposed on the data; consequently, researchers generally engage in detailed qualitative analyses of short segments of interaction. However, some CA researchers do attempt to quantify some of the features that they identify in discourse, in order to provide an indication of how common a specific feature is during interaction.

Conversation 3 (native speakers) (from Barraja-Rohan, 2011, p. 491)

1. *Paul*: hi Jan how are you ↓
2. *Jan*: g'day Paul↓ I'm good↑
3. *Jan*: gee it was cold this morning though, wasn't it↓
4. *Jan*: it was really hard getting out of bed↓
5. *Paul*: it certainly was↓ I really didn't want to get out of bed and to
6. *Paul*: work↓
7. *Jan*: no: still it is Friday↓
8. *Paul*: I know isn't it great↓
9. *Jan*: [yeah↓
10. *Paul*: [and it's supposed to be good on the weekend↑ the weather↑
11. *Jan*: yeah↑ barbeque weather↑ thirty degrees
12. *Paul*: fantastic
13. *Jan*: yeah, great↓

The conventions used in the transcriptions by Barraja-Rohan (2011, p. 506) include the following (based on Atkinson & Heritage, 1984; Sachs, Schegloff, & Jefferson, 1974):

=	indicates continuous stretch of talk
[ ]	indicates simultaneous talk
yea:h	the colon indicates the elongating of sound
<u>nine</u> oclock	the underline indicates sentence stress
-	the hyphen indicates abrupt cutoff or glottal stop
°it's okay°	the degree sign indicates talk that is softer than the surrounding talk
°°species°°	the double degree sign indicates unvoiced talk

↓	indicates shift in pitch going down
↑	indicates shift in pitch going up
(.)	indicates very short pause or micropause
(0.5)	indicates the length of the silence in relation to the surrounding talk
>anyway<	the signs > < indicate talk that is faster than the surrounding talk
<anyway	the sign < at the beginning indicates talk that starts quickly
<may be>	the signs < > indicate talk that is slower than its surrounding talk
huh	indicates laughter
(h)uh (h)	indicates plosive quality
$that's a pity$	the $ sign indicates laughing while talking
((clears throat))	the double brackets indicate co-activity relevant to the interaction
(.........)	indicates talk that is not clearly audible

Atkinson, J. M., & Heritage, J. (1984). *Structure of social action*. Cambridge: Cambridge University Press.

Barraja-Rohan, A. (2011). Using conversation analysis in the second language classroom to teach interactional competence. *Language Teaching Research, 15,* 479–507.

Gass, S. (2004). Conversation analysis and input-interaction. *Modern Language Journal, 88,* 597–616.

Kasper, G., & Wagner, J. (2014). Conversation analysis in applied linguistics. *Annual Review of Applied Linguistics, 34,* 171–212.

Liddicoat, A. J. (2007). *An introduction to conversation analysis*. New York: Continuum.

Markee, N. (2008). Toward a learning behavior tracking methodology for CA-for-SLA. *Applied Linguistics, 29,* 404–427.

Sachs, H., Schegloff, A. E., & Jefferson, G. (1974). A simplest systematics for the organization of turn-taking in conversation. *Language, 50,* 696–735.

Sidnell, J. (2010). *Conversation analysis: An introduction*. Malden, MA: Wiley Blackwell.

Corpora

The plural form of **corpus**.

Corpus

A large body of linguistic data used for research purposes. Corpus linguistics has developed into a substantial subfield within applied linguistics. Corpus data, generally analyzed in written form and using computer programs such as AntConc (Anthony, 2014), may be collected from any type, or combination of different types, of text such as newspapers, books, and academic articles. Corpora, the plural form of corpus, are often made up of millions of words, and the collection of large numbers of such texts has been greatly facilitated by the digital age. However, gathering corpus data in a representative and appropriate fashion (parallel to a sample of human participants) can be both deceptively difficult and time-consuming (Egbert, Biber, & Gray, forthcoming).

There are also corpora of oral language, though these are less common due to the logistical constraints involved in transcribing spoken discourse. In addition, although many corpora consist of native language speaker data, a number of corpora of second language learner production have also been compiled and analyzed for different purposes. The International Corpus of Learner English (ICLE; Granger, Dagneaux, Meunier, & Paquot, 2009), for example, contains close to 4 million words written by advanced learners of English from 16 unique first language backgrounds.

Corpus techniques have been applied in addressing a wide range of subdomains in applied linguistics, including **discourse analysis**, socio-linguistics, second language acquisition, psycholinguistics, and lexis (e.g., collocation of multiword units). Common to the interests in many of the areas, however, is the use of computer software, such as the Biber Tagger (Biber, 1988), which tags (labels) and counts lexical and/or grammatical features such as parts of speech (e.g., see **Multidimensional analysis**). One online resource for conducting corpus analyses is Lextutor (http://www.lextutor.ca/); another particularly robust set of corpora and freely accessibly analytical tools are hosted by Mark Davies (http://corpus.byu.edu/). Finally, because of the quantitative nature of many corpus analyses, the use of statistics in corpus research has advanced substantially in recent years, a trend likely to continue (e.g., Gries & Deshors, 2015).

Anthony, L. (2014). AntConc (Version 3.4.3) [Computer Software]. Tokyo: Waseda University. Available from http://www.laurenceanthony.net/

Asención-Delaney, Y., & Collentine, J. (2011). A multidimensional analysis of a written L2 Spanish corpus. *Applied Linguistics, 32*, 299–322.

Biber, D. (1988). *Variation across speech and writing.* Cambridge: Cambridge University Press.

Biber, D., Conrad, S., & Reppen, R. (1998). *Corpus linguistics: Investigating language structure and use.* Cambridge: Cambridge University Press.

Egbert, J., Biber, D., & Gray, B. (forthcoming). *Designing and evaluating language corpora.* Cambridge: Cambridge University Press.

Granger, S., Dagneaux, E., Meunier, F., & Paquot, M. (2009). *International corpus of learner English (Version 2).* Louvain-la-Neuve: Presses universitaires de Louvain.

Gries, S., & Deshors, S. (2014). Using regressions to explore deviations between corpus data and a standard/target: Two suggestions. *Corpora, 9*, 109–136.

Gries, S. Th., & Deshors, S. C. (2015). EFL and/vs. ESL? A multi-level regression modeling perspective on bridging the paradigm gap. *International Journal of Learner Corpus Research, 1*, 130–159.

Correlation

A common and more basic statistic that specifies the relationship between two **continuous variables**. Correlations assume that there is a linear relationship between the variables. As such, a positive correlation indicates that as one variable increases, the other variable increases as well. For example, in L2 learning there is hopefully a positive correlation between the amount of time an individual spends studying an L2 and his/her L2 knowledge. As one increases, the other does as well. In contrast, with a negative correlation, as one variable increases, the other decreases. A negative correlation might be observed, for example, between learners' test anxiety and test performance. In other words, the more anxious they are the worse their performance or score. It should be made clear that correlation does not equal **causation**. Thus, from a statistical point of view, it is not possible to say that because there is a strong correlation between amount of study and level of knowledge, that one causes the other, even though there may be a logical basis for such assertions. A controlled experiment, ideally with **random assignment** of participants to experimental conditions, must be conducted in order to make any claims of causation.

Correlations, like many other statistical tests, can be run with or without the assumptions of a parametric (normal) distribution. When a normal distribution is assumed, a Pearson's correlation can be used; the most commonly used non-parametric counterpart to this test is the Spearman's correlation. In either case, correlations are represented statistically by r and are expressed on a scale of -1.0 to 1.0, with the two extremes representing perfect correlations, and a score of 0 representing no relationship whatsoever. Researchers in applied linguistics often report the level of **statistical significance** associated with a correlation. It is also imperative—and certainly more interesting—to consider the strength of correlations as well. According to Plonsky and Oswald (2014), the typical correlation in L2 research is close to .40, though much weaker and much stronger correlations are also frequently observed. As the authors caution, each correlation needs to be considered in the substantive and methodological context from which it is derived. One additional and more statistical approach to interpreting a correlation is to square it. Doing so provides us with an R^2 value, which is a type of **effect size** that expresses the percent of shared variance between the two variables being correlated. Correlations are foundational in many other statistical techniques such as **factor analysis** and **multiple regression**.

Plonsky, L., & Oswald, F. L. (2014). How big is "big"? Interpreting effect sizes in L2 research. *Language Learning, 64*, 878–912.

Covariate

A variable that influences the **dependent variable** being investigated, and yet it is not an **independent variable** of primary interest. Covariates are also referred to as moderator variables and, if not handled appropriately, may act as confounding variables. In a quasi-experimental study investigating the effects of different types of L2 instruction (i.e., the independent variable), for example, learner proficiency might act as a covariate, unintentionally affecting the results of the study if the researcher does not control for level of proficiency. If pretreatment differences in group proficiency levels are observed, they need to be addressed in some way. In other words, because researchers want to have as pure a measure as possible of the effect of the independent variable, it is important to take covariates such as proficiency into account. One way to control for covariates (and prevent potential confounds) is to try to hold them constant in selecting participants. For example, if L2 learners in a study are all at the same proficiency level, then proficiency should have a minimal, if any, effect on the results. Researchers interested in comparing L2 learners who started studying the L2 either early or late may, likewise, consider years of exposure as a covariate and, therefore, attempt to recruit participants who have lived the same number of years in the target language country (see, e.g., Larson-Hall, 2008). As can be imagined, recruiting participants in a way that controls for covariates is not always possible. Fortunately, there are statistical means by which researchers can account for the influence of covariates. Both **analysis of covariance (ANCOVA)** and **multiple regression** enable the researcher to isolate the effect of the independent variable on the dependent variable after removing the influence of one or more covariates.

Larson-Hall, J. (2008). Weighing the benefits of studying a foreign language at a younger starting age in a minimal input situation. *Second Language Research, 24*, 35–63.

Cramer's V

An **effect size** that measures the strength of an association between two categorical variables, in which one variable contains more than two levels. Cramer's V is expressed on a scale from 0, indicating no relationship between the two variables, to +1, indicating a perfect association. Cramer's V can be reported with **chi-square** results, and because it uses a standardized scale, it can be used to compare the magnitude of effects between different chi-square results. Laufer and Waldman (2011) reported Cramer's V along with the chi-square results from their analysis of L2 proficiency and noun collocations, "χ^2 (df 3) = 287.77, p < .0001, Cramer's V = 0.082" (p. 661). L2 proficiency consisted of three groups (basic, intermediate, and advanced), while there were two categories of noun collocations (verb–noun collocations and non-collocating occurrences); therefore, the Cramer's V effect size was appropriate for the 3 × 2 analysis. If conducting a chi-square with variables containing only two categories, researchers should use **phi** as an effect size.

Laufer, B., & Waldman, T. (2011). Verb-noun collocations in second language writing: A corpus analysis of learners' English. *Language Learning, 61*, 647–672.

Critical discourse analysis (see Discourse analysis)

Critical value

The numeric score that is used to determine whether the result of a statistical analysis is considered statistically significant. As such, it serves as a cutoff point and corresponds with the **alpha level** and **p-value**. A critical value is determined in advance by the researcher and is dependent on the level of concern for making a **Type I error**, in which a statistically significant result is found, even though such a difference does not actually exist in the population.

Cronbach's alpha

A measure of **reliability** that is used to investigate the internal consistency across individual items on a data collection **instrument**. Statistically speaking, Cronbach's alpha is essentially an analysis of the **correlations** between each pair of items included in an instrument (or subscale of an instrument) such as a test, **survey**, or **questionnaire**. The resulting coefficient indicates the extent to which participants responded to items in a similar and consistent manner. For example, if the items on a questionnaire designed to measure learners' motivation are going to be combined (averaged or summed together) to assign each participant a motivation score, those items seeking to measure the same **construct** should be contributing relatively similar (i.e., reliable) scores. Alternatively, participants responding to a survey regarding opinions about grammar instruction should respond to items in a manner consistent with their beliefs, whether positive or negative. Using such a survey, Loewen et al. (2009) had a Cronbach's alpha coefficient of $\alpha = .84$.

Although Cronbach's alpha is the most frequently employed index of instrument reliability (i.e., internal consistency), interpretations of this index in published applied linguistics research are scarce (Plonsky & Derrick, under review). And as with other reliability coefficients, it is often difficult to know what level of reliability should be considered acceptable. With this challenge in mind, Plonsky and Derrick, examining over 2,000 reliability estimates reported in L2 research, found the **median** alpha coefficient to be .81 (**interquartile range** = .16). This finding suggests that observed reliability estimates in the neighborhood of .70–.80 may be considered normal, though higher is certainly preferable. Whether or not such values are acceptable, however, is another matter, depending on a number of other factors related to the instrument design, the construct being measured, the sample, and so forth (Brown, 2014).

Finally, it should be noted that Cronbach's alpha will not calculate properly for items with reverse phrasing, and any such items need to be recoded so that all items share the same directionality and positive responses uniformly align with higher (or lower) values. The two items seen here exemplify positive and negative phrasing, and the Likert-scale score from one of them would need to be recoded before being analyzed by Cronbach's alpha.

1. When I make errors in speaking a second language, I like my teacher to correct them.
   Strongly Disagree   1   2   3   4   5   Strongly Agree

2. I dislike it when I am corrected in class.
   Strongly Disagree   1   2   3   4   5   Strongly Agree

Brown, J. D. (2014). Classical theory reliability. In A. J. Kunnan (Ed.), *The companion to language assessment.* Oxford: Wiley Blackwell.

Douglas, D. (2001). Performance consistency in second language acquisition and language testing: A conceptual gap. *Second Language Research, 17*, 442–456.

Loewen, S., Li, S., Fei, F., Thompson, A., Nakatsukasa, K., Ahn, S., & Chen, X. (2009). Second language learners' beliefs about grammar instruction and error correction. *Modern Language Journal, 93*, 91–104.

Plonsky, L., & Derrick, D. J. (under review). A meta-analysis of reliability coefficients in second language research. [Manuscript under review.]

Cross-sectional design

A type of research design usually used to investigate differences between different levels of L2 proficiency. Often researchers want to know how L2 development occurs as learners gain proficiency. However, **longitudinal studies** that track individual learner development are time-consuming and difficult to conduct. It can also be difficult to have longitudinal data from enough participants in order to conduct statistical analyses. Because of these difficulties, researchers sometimes rely on cross-sectional research to provide information about L2 development. Rather than following specific learners over a period of time, cross-sectional research looks at different levels of learners at the same time. The assumption underlying this approach is that by looking at beginner, intermediate, and advanced learner performance simultaneously, researchers will be able to glean information about L2 development. Furthermore, because data is usually collected from numerous students in order to conduct statistical analyses, there is also the assumption that individual variation in the data will be minimized, thereby providing a relatively accurate picture of language proficiency at specific stages. A criticism of cross-sectional research is that it does not actually provide evidence of how individuals develop, and it is not always appropriate to assume that groups of different learners will accurately represent development. Nevertheless, cross-sectional designs are relatively common in L2 research. For example, in a cross-sectional study, Al-Gahtani and Roever (2012) collected role play data from four different proficiency levels in order to investigate the effects of proficiency on interaction.

C

Al-Gahtani, S., & Roever, C. (2012). Proficiency and sequential organization of L2 requests. *Applied Linguistics, 33*, 42–65.

Curvilinear relationship

A non-linear relationship between two variables, such that when it is plotted on a graph, the result is not a straight line. One such example in applied linguistics research is the relationship between strategy use and proficiency. Hong-Nam and Leavell (2006), for example, found greater use of strategies by intermediate learners, with fewer strategies used by beginner and advanced learners. Stevens (1999), likewise, identified a number of curvilinear relationships between age-related effects and self-reported L2 proficiency (see Figure 9). Because linearity is an **assumption** of correlational designs, curvilinear relationships present difficulties for such analyses. **Scatterplots** can be particularly helpful in identifying curvilinear relationships in a data set.

Hong-Nam, K., & Leavell, A. G. (2006). Language learning strategy use of ESL students in an intensive English learning context. *System, 34*, 399–415.

Stevens, G. (1999). Age at immigration and second language proficiency among foreign-born adults. *Language in Society, 28*, 555–578.

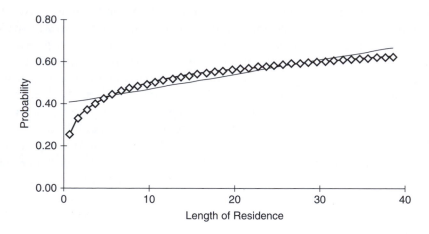

Source: Stevens (1999).

Figure 9   Example of a curvilinear relationship. Relationship between the probability of respondents reporting their level of English proficiency as "very well" and length of residence in the U.S.

Data

The material that researchers analyze. At its most basic, data is at the heart of the scientific endeavor because it is what provides researchers with evidence to answer their **research questions**. Those answers, in turn, allow researchers to confirm, disconfirm, or modify their theories. In applied linguistics, data come in multiple forms:

- Test scores—L2 learners are often given tests to assess their knowledge of the target language. These data then consist of the number of accurate responses that the learner provides. **Grammaticality judgment tests**, cloze tests, and vocabulary levels tests are all examples of tests that provide numeric data about learners' L2 knowledge for researchers to analyze.
- Language use/production—The language that users produce is another important source of data. Such production may be in the form of monologic utterances, in which a learner is producing language by him or herself, for example, when describing a set of pictures to a researcher. Language production may also involve interaction between two or more interlocutors, such as in the many communicative tasks that learners engage in. In addition, language production can be oral or written. With both types of data, there are several ways in which the data can be analyzed. One is to look at the linguistic features that are present in the data. For example, researchers may wish to look at how accurately learners use the past tense when describing their weekend activities. Alternatively, researchers may wish to examine how conversational partners structure their turn-taking during a classroom discussion. Language production can also be analyzed for the semantic content that it contains. For example, **interview** data are often analyzed for the themes that individuals express, rather than for the specific language forms used. And of course, as with other types of linguistic data, **corpus** analytic techniques can also be applied to the language used.
- **Questionnaire/Survey** data—These types of data have been frequently examined in applied linguistics research to explore numerous topics, such as anxiety, beliefs, and motivation. Questionnaires are often structured so that individuals can indicate

their agreement or disagreement with a statement by choosing a number on a specified scale. For example, several well-known surveys have been developed to measure foreign language anxiety (Foreign Language Classroom Anxiety Scale (FLCAS); Horwitz, Horwitz, & Cope, 1986) and language learning strategy use (Strategy Inventory for Language Learning (SILL); Oxford, 1990). For the FLCAS, learners must decide how strongly they agree or disagree with statements related to anxiety-producing situations in the classroom. For the SILL, students indicate on a scale from 1 to 5 how frequently they employ specific language learning strategies. Often, responses to individual survey items are collated in some way to provide a more concise picture of participants' responses. On the SILL, for example, learners tabulate their responses to items relating to different categories of learning strategies in order to identify their learning strategy preferences.

- Observational data—Researchers may also gather data by watching individuals and/or classes. Often, these types of data are analyzed from a qualitative approach in which the researcher attempts to provide a holistic picture of the context under observation. Researchers may have fewer preconceived hypotheses regarding the nature of the research study and instead, rely upon analysis of the data to provide an **emic**, insider perspective of the context under observation. There are also more focused types of observations that hone in on specific **constructs** or behaviors of interest to the researcher. For example, the Communicative Orientation of Language Teaching (COLT) (Spada & Frölich, 1995) is an observational and coding scheme that has researchers record the different types of communicative activities that teachers and students engage in during a class. This type of data has a more **etic**, researcher-imposed perspective.

- Physiological data—With recent advances in technology, data can also be collected—and used to address questions in applied linguistics—by measuring physical activity related to language processing, learning, and use. Examples include neuroimaging (fMRI), **eye tracking**, and **reaction times**. Neuroimaging studies involve measuring brain activity. For instance, Buchweitz, Shinkareva, Mason, Mitchell, and Just (2012) used fMRI imaging to record Portuguese–English bilingual participants' neural representations of concrete nouns. Their data revealed three-dimensional (multi-voxel) brain activation patterns that were the same regardless of whether participants were thinking of a noun in Portuguese or in English.

In **eye tracking** research, participants' eye movements and fixations are recorded as they read or watch something on a screen. For example, Godfroid Loewen, Jung, Park, Gass, & Ellis (2015) recorded

ESL learners' eye movements as they read **grammaticality judgment tests**. They found that learners looked at previous portions of the sentence (i.e., regressed) more frequently when the sentences were grammatical and learners had unlimited time in which to make their judgments. Godfroid et al. interpreted these data as suggesting that such conditions prompted greater cognitive processing by learners.

Finally, reaction-time data measure the amount of time it takes for participants to respond to specific stimuli. For example, Jiang (2004) studied the performance of Korean–English bilinguals in a semantic judgment task where they were asked to determine whether two English words were related. He found that participants had faster reaction times judging pairs of words that shared the same translation in Korean than pairs that had two distinct Korean translations, which Jiang interpreted as evidence for the existence of L1 semantic structures in L2 lexical representation.

Buchweitz, A., Shinkareva, S. V., Mason, R. A., Mitchell, T. M., & Just, M. A. (2012). Identifying bilingual semantic neural representations across languages. *Brain and Language, 120*, 282–289.

Godfroid, A., Loewen, S., Jung, S., Park, J., Gass, S., & Ellis, R. (2015). Timed and untimed grammaticality judgments measure distinct types of knowledge: Evidence from eye-movement patterns. *Studies in Second Language Acquisition, 37*, 269–297.

Horwitz, E. K., Horwitz, M. B., & Cope, J. (1986). Foreign language classroom anxiety. *Modern Language Journal, 70*, 125–132.

Jiang, N. (2004). Semantic transfer and its implications for vocabulary teaching in a second language. *The Modern Language Journal, 88*, 416–432.

Oxford, R. L. (1990). *Language learning strategies: What every teacher should know*. New York: Newbury House/Harper & Row.

Smith, B. (2012). Eye tracking as a measure of noticing: A study of explicit recasts in SCMS. *Language Learning & Technology, 16*, 53–81.

Spada, N., & Frölich, M. (1995). *The communicative orientation of language teaching observation scheme: Coding conventions and applications*. Sydney: National Centre for English Language Teaching and Research, Macquarie University.

Data sharing

D

The use of a researcher's data by other researchers. An important issue in scientific research is the **validity** and **generalizability** of the findings of specific studies. One way to address validity and generalizability is to allow other researchers access to one's data in order for them to attempt to replicate the research findings with the same data set. Furthermore, if data are shared, researchers may conduct additional analyses from the original study. Another way to ensure the validity and generalizability of a study is by replicating the research using similar methodologies, but varying only the participants or small details of the research design. Data sharing, like **replication**, is often applauded in applied linguistics research, but is not common. However, one example of data sharing is found in Plonsky's (2015) and Larson-Hall's (2015) textbooks on statistics in second language research, in which several authors made data available from previously published studies. Students using these textbooks are able to replicate the results found in those studies, as well as perform additional analyses. With the advent of online resources accompanying journal articles, it has become easier to make data available to others. There is also somewhat of a movement across the social sciences toward data sharing and transparency, evidenced most notably by Article 8.14 of the APA's (2010) *Ethical Principles of Psychologists and Code of Conduct*, which states that "After research results are published, psychologists do not withhold the data on which their conclusions are based from other competent professionals who seek to verify the substantive claims through reanalysis ...." However, as noted by Plonsky, Egbert, and LaFlair (in press), as their study received a disappointing response rate to requests for raw data, it is also necessary that researchers in applied linguistics begin to view their work as a more collaborative and cumulative—rather than individual—effort.

American Psychological Association. (2010). *Ethical principles of psychologists and code of conduct*. Washington, DC. Retrieved 18 April 2013 from http://www.apa.org/ethics/code/index.aspx

Larson-Hall, J. (2015). *A guide to doing statistics in second language research using SPSS and R* (2nd ed.). New York: Routledge.

Plonsky, L. (2015). *Advancing quantitative methods in second language research*. New York: Routeldge.

Plonsky, L., Egbert J., & LaFlair, G. (in press). Bootstrapping in applied linguistics: Assessing its potential using shared data. *Applied Linguistics*.

Trofimovich, P., & Ellis, N. C. (2015). Editorial. *Language Learning*, 65, v–vi.

Wicherts, J. M., Bakker, M., & Molenaar, D. (2011). Willingness to share research data is related to the strength of the evidence and the quality of reporting of statistical results. *PLoS One, 6*, 1–7.

Data transformation

A type of statistical manipulation applied to quantitative data, often when **assumptions** such as a **normal distribution** or **homogeneity of variance** are not met. Data transformation attempts to rectify the violation by applying a mathematical formula equally to all the data. Because the transformation is being applied to all the data, it alters the data in statistical, rather than substantive ways, meaning that the data can still be used for statistical analyses. For example, a square root transformation can reduce positive skew because taking the square root value has a greater effect on larger numbers. Sometimes data transformation resolves the problematic data issue; however, this is not always the case, and researchers may need to rely on other methods, such as **non-parametric statistics** or **robust statistics**, to analyze the data (Jaeger, 2008).

Jaeger, T. F. (2008). Categorical data analysis: Away from ANOVAs (transformation or not) and towards logit mixed models. *Journal of Memory and Language, 59*, 434–446.

DCT (see Discourse completion task)

Degrees of freedom

A statistical concept that is calculated by subtracting 1 from the sample size. In addition, if there is more than one group in a statistical analysis, the number of groups in the analysis is subtracted from the number of participants to arrive at the degrees of freedom. Thus, in an independent samples *t*-test, the degrees of freedom is 2 less than the sample size, because two groups are being compared. In a one-way ANOVA that compares three groups, the between-groups degrees of freedom is 2, while the within-groups degrees of freedom is 3 subtracted from the sample size. Degrees of freedom is abbreviated *df*, and is generally included in statistical output, such as this ANOVA table (Table 5). From the degrees of freedom listed in the table, it is possible to determine that three groups were compared because the between-groups *df* is 2 (i.e., 3 − 1). Additionally, the total number of participants is 60, which can be determined from the **within-groups'** degrees of freedom (60 − 3 = 57) and the total degrees of freedom (60 − 1 = 59). The significance of degrees of freedom comes from the amount of choice that a test has as it is being conducted. A concrete example of degrees of freedom is as follows. Imagine there are 10 pieces of pie and each of 10 people are allowed to choose a slice in turn. The first person has 10 pieces to choose from, the second person has

Table 5   ANOVA table

ANOVA					
	Sum of Squares	**df**	**Mean Square**	**F**	**Sig.**
Between-Groups	24,251.033	2	12,125.517	.270	.764
Within-Groups	2,560,427.950	57	44,919.789		
Total	2,584,678.983	59			

nine pieces to choose from (their respective *df*s), and so on. When it finally gets down to the last person, there is no choice to be made because there is only one piece left. Thus, the final person has zero degrees of freedom.

Delayed posttest

A test that is given some time after a **treatment** has been administered to research participants. Delayed posttests are a design feature of

experimental and **quasi-experimental** research. Usually such tests are given to gauge the long-term effectiveness of a treatment. By comparing delayed posttest results to those of a **pretest** and immediate **posttest**, it is possible to see the extent to which any post-treatment gains were made and maintained over time. The optimal timing of a delayed posttest is debated. On the one hand, there needs to be some passage of time in order to determine if the effects are durable for any meaningful length of time. On the other hand, the more time between the treatment and the delayed posttest, the less confident one can be in claiming that any effect seen on the delayed posttest is due to the treatment and not some intervening variable. This concern is a particular possibility if some aspect of L2 proficiency is being investigated and learners continue to have considerable L2 exposure after the treatment. Some studies have sought to address this issue by including multiple delayed posttests in their designs (e.g., Ellis & He, 1999). The downside to this approach is the threat of practice effects, whereby participants' performance is maintained or even improved as a result of the testing itself. In general, a common time frame for delayed posttests in applied linguistics is between one and two weeks. There are some studies that have even waited a month or two, but longer delays are not very common. It is important to note that some studies have found that treatment effects are not always seen on immediate posttests because the treatment takes time to have an effect. This may be especially true if the treatment is more implicit in nature. Along these lines, Mackey and Goo's (2007) **meta-analysis** found the effects of interaction on grammar to be larger than that of vocabulary on immediate posttests; this pattern, however, was reversed on delayed posttests. One explanation for this finding is that during the time between the immediate and delayed posttest, participants were more likely to have continued exposure and opportunities to practice targeted grammatical features than targeted lexical items.

One other consideration in delayed posttesting is the composition of the test itself. In many cases, one version of the test, with the same test items, is used for the pretest, immediate posttest, and delayed posttest. However, in such cases there is the risk of a test effect in which learners improve simply through exposure to the same test items. Another option is to use different versions, with different test items, on each occasion; however, in such cases it is important to ensure that all tests are of equal difficulty and that learners are not scoring differently on one test merely because it is easier than the others. Finally, it is possible to use a counterbalanced design in which three versions of the test are developed. A subset of learners each take one version of the test at one testing time, and the versions are rotated so that each participant does not take the same test twice.

Ellis, R., & He, X. (1999). The roles of modified input and output in the incidental acquisition of word meanings. *Studies in Second Language Acquisition, 21,* 285–301.

Ellis, R., Loewen, S., & Erlam, R. (2006). Implicit and explicit corrective feedback and the acquisition of L2 grammar. *Studies in Second Language Acquisition, 28*, 339–368.

Li, S. (2010). The effectiveness of corrective feedback in SLA: A meta-analysis. *Language Learning, 60*, 309–365.

Mackey, A. (1999). Input, interaction and second language development: An empirical study of question formation in ESL. *Studies in Second Language Acquisition, 21*, 557–587.

Mackey, A., & Goo, J. (2007). Interaction research in SLA: A meta-analysis and research synthesis. In A. Mackey (Ed.), *Conversational interaction in second language acquisition: A collection of empirical studies* (pp. 407–451). New York: Oxford University Press.

Dependent variable

The object of interest in research that gets acted upon. The dependent variable is examined for change due to the influence of the **independent variable**(s). In applied linguistics research, dependent variables often consist of scores representing some measure of L2 learners' linguistic skills, while the independent variables are hypothesized to affect those scores. Sometimes, dependent variables are test scores of global proficiency, such as IELTS or TOEFL. At other times, dependent variables might consist of test scores from more specific areas of language, such as grammar (**grammaticality judgment tests**) or vocabulary (vocabulary levels test). A dependent variable can also consist of learners' performances concerning a specific linguistic feature, such as is often seen in corrective feedback research in which learners are tested on their knowledge of individual linguistic structures, such as English past tense or French gender agreement.

There are also other types of dependent variables, such as scores on **questionnaire**s and/or tests of individual differences such as working memory, motivation, beliefs, attitudes, or anxiety. Data from these measures may be used primarily to describe learners' profiles on such **constructs** (e.g., higher or lower anxiety), or researchers may test the effects of different independent variables on the dependent ones (e.g., the influence of classroom activities on learner anxiety).

Dependent variables are often **continuous** or interval in nature, because such mathematical properties are necessary in order to conduct many statistical analyses that allow interpretation of the effects of the independent variables.

D

Descriptive statistics

Descriptive statistics are those that summarize, organize, and categorize quantitative data in some way. As such, descriptive statistics are crucial as a starting point for understanding a particular data set. In general, there are two types of descriptive statistics: those that measure **central tendency** and those that measure **dispersion**. The primary measures of central tendency for interval/continuous data include the **mean**, **median,** and **mode**, which provide information about either the

Table 6 Descriptive statistics

Groups	Pretest		Immediate posttest		Delayed posttest	
	M	*SD*	*M*	*SD*	*M*	*SD*
Treatment 1	.23	.16	.36	.22	.44	.22
Treatment 2	.39	.16	.49	.21	.69	.19
Control	.25	.15	.31	.18	.33	.15

average, middle, or most common scores in the data set. Measures of dispersion include **standard deviation, variance,** and **range**, which provide information about how diverse or spread out the scores in the data are. Thus, one could say that descriptive statistics provide information about the similarities and differences that exist within each measured variable. Descriptive statistics are often displayed in tables, such as in Table 6, which provides the means (M) and standard deviations (SD) for multiple groups on multiple tests. In addition, descriptive statistics can be displayed in graphs, such as **histograms**, **boxplots**, **bar graphs**, and **pie charts**.

The importance of descriptive statistics cannot be stressed enough. Often researchers tend to calculate **inferential statistics**, such as a **p–value**, or examine other indicators of **statistical significance** without bothering to look at the descriptive statistics, but such practices can lead to shallow, partial, or inappropriate interpretations of the data. In fact, some researchers (e.g., Larson-Hall, 2015; Plonsky, 2015) advocate for researchers to use descriptive statistics as a primary way of interpreting the data and addressing **research questions**.

Larson-Hall, J. (2015). *A guide to doing statistics in second language research using SPSS and R* (2nd ed.). New York: Routledge.

Plonsky, L. (2015). Statistical power, *p* values, descriptive statistics, and effect sizes: A "back-to-basics" approach to advancing quantitative methods in L2 research. In L. Plonsky (Ed.), *Advancing quantitative methods in second language research* (pp. 23–45). New York: Routledge.

D

Dichotomous variable

A type of **categorical variable** with only two levels or categories. Biological gender is commonly coded as a dichotomous variable; alternatively, a dichotomous variable can be used to indicate the presence or absence of a characteristic, such as pass/fail or L1/L2 speaker. Because dichotomous variables are categorical, they are limited in terms of what statistical procedures can be performed on them. For instance, the categories can be tallied to determine the **frequency** of the categories, but it is not possible to calculate a **mean** or **standard deviation**. However, dichotomous variables allow for slightly more statistical manipulation than do categorical variables with more than two levels, because the former can be meaningfully represented numerically. For example, male and female may be coded as 0 and 1, respectively. In this way, dichotomous variables can be used as one variable in a point-biserial **correlation,** or serve as a dependent or independent variable in a **logistic regression** (without the need for **dummy coding**).

Discourse analysis

A somewhat general term applied to any type of language analysis primarily focusing on linguistic or structural properties rather than semantic content. Thus, discourse analysis is concerned with the interrelation between the linguistic forms that are used and the social functions that these forms achieve. Within discourse analysis, there are several distinct theoretical and methodological perspectives, including **conversation analysis**, critical discourse analysis, and ethnography of communication. Despite these different approaches, the methods of data collection are largely similar. Researchers conducting a discourse analysis will elicit either written or oral data. In the case of oral data, **transcription** is often an initial component of the analysis. Next, a researcher will identify the linguistic structures that are the object of investigation. Often, discourse analysis is interested in turn-taking and the interaction between interlocutors. Subsequently, a description of patterns or other notable features in the data is provided. Discourse analysis has been applied in a wide variety of subfields within, and tied to, applied linguistics, including interaction, sociolinguistics, intercultural communication, and register variation. A closer look at discourse patterns in or across texts can also serve to provide a complementary and closer view of language use, as shown using more traditional **corpus** techniques (see Biber, 2012). Finally, critical discourse analysis examines the influence that social issues and power relationships have on interaction.

Biber, D. (2012). Register and discourse analysis. In J. P. Gee & M. Handford (Eds.), *The Routledge handbook of discourse analysis* (pp. 191–208). London: Routledge.

Foucault, M. (1981). The order of discourse. In R. Young (Ed.), *Untying the text: A post-structural anthology* (pp. 48–78). Boston, MA: Routledge.

Silberstein, S. (2011). Constrained but not determined: Approaches to discourse analysis. In E. Hinkel (Ed.), *Handbook of research in second language teaching and learning, Volume II* (pp. 274–289). New York: Routledge.

Discourse completion task (DCT)

A data collection **instrument** that elicits responses to previous segments of discourse. Often DCTs are used to collect data concerning pragmatic knowledge. Participants are provided with a scenario describing a specific context, and they are asked to indicate what they would say in this context,

D

often in response to a previous utterance. The following two scenarios provide examples of DCTs:

1. *You need to borrow a pen from your classmate. What would you say?*
2. *You need to ask your publisher for an extension on your book draft. What would you say?*

DCTs are often administered in writing; however, it is possible to design oral DCTs. One of the benefits of DCTs is that they allow a researcher to target specific linguistic structures or social contexts that would otherwise be difficult to access. However, a disadvantage is that participants may not supply an utterance or response that accurately reflects what they would say in the actual situation. For example, Economidou-Kogetsidis (2013) compared naturally occurring requests made during service encounter telephone situations with those elicited from a written DCT. While the discourse in the two contexts displayed similar general trends, there were considerable differences as well, suggesting the need for caution in using and interpreting DCTs.

Byon, A. (2006). Developing KFL students' pragmatic awareness of Korean speech acts: The use of discourse completion tasks. *Language Awareness, 15*, 244–263.

Economidou-Kogetsidis, M. (2013). Strategies, modification and perspective in native speakers' requests: A comparison of WDCT and naturally occurring requests. *Journal of Pragmatics, 53*, 21–38.

Discriminant function analysis

A **multivariate statistic** that attempts to differentiate groups based on specific characteristics. This procedure is most commonly employed in situations when the researcher is interested in determining which measures are best able to assign participants into one of a set of groups. Discriminant function analysis (DFA) might be used, for example, to ascertain the best constellation of linguistic features in predicting a given learner's proficiency on the ACTFL scale. One way to understand the logic of DFA is to consider its similarities and difference with and relationship to other multivariate procedures. For example, DFA is both conceptually and mathematically very closely related to **multivariate analysis of variance** (MANOVA). However, the direction, so to speak, of the two procedures run counter to each other. Whereas a MANOVA compares multiple groups' scores on a number of outcome or dependent measures, DFA seeks to assign groups of participants on the basis of multiple measures. Conceptual and statistical parallels can also be found between **logistic regression**, **cluster analysis**, and **factor analysis** (see Norris, 2015). A DFA is also often conducted in conjunction with other statistical tests such as factor analysis or MANOVA as a type of post hoc test. For example, Loewen et al. (2009) used a DFA after conducting a factor analysis on L2 learners' responses to a 37-item questionnaire concerning their beliefs about grammar instruction and error correction. After finding six factors, the researchers used a DFA to determine which groups of learners best fit which factors. Results indicated that L2 learners of English were the least enthusiastic about error correction and grammatical accuracy, while L2 learners of Japanese were the least likely to prioritize communication over grammar.

Discriminant function analysis is seldom found in applied linguistics, though it has been applied in several different areas of the field, including SLA (e.g., Collentine & Collentine, 2013), corpus linguistics (Biber, 2003), and language assessment (Fulcher, 1996), among others. See Norris (2015) for an annotated list of studies in applied linguistics that have used DFA, and for a practical guide to the use of this procedure.

Biber, D. (2003). Variation among university spoken and written registers: A new multidimensional analysis. In C. Meyer & P. Leistyna (Eds.), *Corpus analysis: Language structure and language use* (pp. 47–70). Amsterdam: Rodopi.

Collentine, J., & Collentine, K. (2013). A corpus approach to studying structural convergence in task-based Spanish L2 interactions. In K. McDonough & A. Mackey (Eds.), *Second language interaction in diverse educational contexts* (pp. 167–188). Amsterdam: John Benjamins.

Fulcher, G. (1996). Does thick description lead to smart tests? A data-based approach to rating scale construction. *Language Testing, 13*, 208–238.

Loewen, S., Li, S., Fei, F., Thompson, A., Nakatsukasa, K., Ahn, S., & Chen, X. (2009). Second language learners' beliefs about grammar instruction and error correction. *Modern Language Journal, 93*, 91–104.

Norris, J. M. (2015). Discriminant analysis. In L. Plonsky (Ed.), *Advancing quantitative methods in second language research* (pp. 309–332). New York: Routledge.

Dispersion

A **descriptive statistic** indicating the spread of data scores. Measures of dispersion typically accompany measures of **central tendency** to provide information about the distribution of the data. For example, the **standard deviation** is generally presented along with its corresponding mean to indicate how closely the scores cluster to the mean. The larger the standard deviation, the more spread out the scores. Other statistics that express dispersion are the **range**, which notes the highest and lowest scores in a sample, and the **interquartile range**, which indicates the distance from the 25th to the 75th **percentile**. In addition, **variance** provides an indication of the spread of data. Plotting data on **histograms**, **box-and-whisker plots**, or other types of graphs can be useful in understanding the dispersion of scores in a set or sample.

D

Dummy coding

A method of recoding categorical variables that have more than two levels or categories into dichotomous variables. The newly created variables, the "dummy" variables, are dichotomous with values of 0 or 1. The main purpose for dummy coding is to prepare a categorical variable for inclusion in certain types of correlation and regression analyses that require such data to be dichotomous. In order to create dummy variables, a researcher first creates as many new variables as there are groups in the original categorical variable minus one. Imagine, for example, that one of the predictor variables in a multiple regression analysis was participant L1. If there were four different L1s in the sample (Korean, Polish, Spanish, Thai), as shown in Table 7, the researcher would recode this four-level variable into three new categorical predictor variables. As shown in Table 8, each L1 becomes a new dichotomous variable and participants are coded for whether or not they belong to that group. For the Korean L1 variable, for example, the Korean L1 participants are given a value of 1, and all other participants are given a value of 0. Based on this process, the researcher has a slightly expanded data set in which each variable represents only one of the groups in the data. It is not necessary to recode the original four-level variable into four new dichotomous variables, however. Doing so would actually be redundant, because the participants in group four, Thai, are identified by means of a value of zero in the three other newly created variables.

Table 7 Non-dummy-coded predictor variable

Participant ID	L1*
1	1
2	1
3	1
4	2
5	2
6	2
7	3
8	3
9	3
10	4
11	4
12	4

*1 = Korean, 2 = Polish, 3 = Spanish, 4 = Thai.

Table 8 Dummy-coded predictor variable

Participant ID	Korean	Polish	Spanish
1	1	0	0
2	1	0	0
3	1	0	0
4	0	1	0
5	0	1	0
6	0	1	0
7	0	0	1
8	0	0	1
9	0	0	1
10	0	0	0
11	0	0	0
12	0	0	0

Dyad

Pairs of participants in a research study. Dyads, rather than individuals, sometimes constitute the unit of analysis, especially in interaction research. For example, Bowles, Adams, and Toth (2014) investigated the task-based interaction of two different pairings of Spanish learners: matched L2 learner dyads (L2–L2) and mixed L2 learner–heritage learner dyads (L2–HL). The L2–L2 pairings consisted of two learners with no familial exposure to Spanish, while the L2–HL dyads contained one learner with a Spanish-speaking family background. *Dyad* is perhaps viewed as a more scholarly term than *pair*; however, the meaning is the same.

Bowles, M., Adams, R., & Toth, P. (2014). A comparison of L2–L2 and L2-heritage learner interactions in Spanish language classrooms. *Modern Language Journal, 98*, 497–517.

D

E e

Ecological validity

The degree of similarity between a research study and the authentic context that the study is purportedly investigating. For example, a current debate in instructed SLA research pertains to the ecological validity of laboratory studies on instruction because the conditions that learners experience in a laboratory may be considerably different from the classroom, thereby reducing the confidence with which researchers can generalize the results of laboratory-based studies to the classroom. Indeed, Li's (2010) **meta-analysis** of 33 corrective feedback studies found that feedback was more effective in laboratory contexts than in classrooms, suggesting that laboratory-based studies may overestimate the effects likely to be found in the L2 classroom. In contrast, Gass, Mackey, and Ross-Feldman (2005) found that interaction between L2 learners of Spanish was similar in both classroom and laboratory settings.

In instructed SLA contexts, researchers may have difficulty isolating specific variables and controlling for moderator variables because of the often unpredictable and unsystematic nature of classroom events. Therefore, a study may have lower **internal validity** or **construct validity** because the researcher has not been able to control extraneous variables. Nevertheless, the researcher may claim high ecological validity because the study authentically captures the inconsistent nature of the research context. In this sense, there is often a trade-off between the degree to which research studies reflect the realities of a research context versus the degree of control over the **constructs** under investigation.

Gass, S., Mackey, A., & Ross-Feldman, L. (2005). Task-based interactions in classroom and laboratory setting. *Language Learning, 55*, 575–611.

Li, S. (2010). The effectiveness of corrective feedback in SLA: A meta-analysis. *Language Learning, 60*, 309–365.

Effect size

A descriptive statistic that expresses the magnitude or strength of a relationship. There are three main types of effect sizes commonly employed in applied linguistics. When researchers are interested in comparing mean scores, a standardized mean difference effect size (usually **Cohen's *d***) is most appropriate. This effect size index expresses the difference between two mean scores in **standard deviation** units, thus enabling d values to be compared across studies as well as combined via **meta-analysis**. Toth and Guijarro-Fuentes (2013), for example, compared **pretest**, **posttest**, and **delayed posttest** scores for an instructed and control group and found, among other results, a difference of $d = .83$ between groups for one set of target features. This difference was also statistically significant ($p = .03$). However, whereas the **p-value** here indicates the probability of obtaining a significant difference when one does not actually exist, it provides little information about the magnitude or **practical significance** of that difference. In this case, the d value of .83 indicates a relatively large effect. Though not often viewed as such, **correlation** coefficients (e.g., Pearson's r) are another type of effect size, indicating the strength of a relationship between two measured variables. A third type, or family of, effect sizes used in applied linguistics includes R^2 and **eta²**, which express shared variance and variance accounted for, respectively. The use of these and other effect sizes is critical in enabling researchers to move beyond the dichotomous approach embodied by p-values and **Null Hypothesis Significance Testing.** For this very reason, and due to the requirements of at least six applied linguistics journals* (starting with Ellis, 2000), the reporting of effect sizes has increased dramatically in recent years (Plonsky, 2014). Largely absent in the field, however, are meaningful interpretations of such quantitative results. In an attempt to guide future efforts in this area, Plonsky and Oswald (2014) synthesized the d values and correlation coefficients extracted from 346 primary studies and 91 meta-analyses of L2 research. Based on their results, a tentative set of field-specific benchmarks for interpreting d and r values are put forth (see Table 9). The authors also caution against blind application of such benchmarks, discussing a number of additional considerations for interpreting effect sizes in applied linguistics.

*The six journals we know of that now require effect sizes are: *Language Learning*; *Language Learning & Technology*; *Modern Language Journal*; *Studies in Second Language Acquisition*; *TESOL Quarterly*; *Foreign Language Annals*.

Table 9 General guidelines for interpreting effect sizes in applied linguistics research

Effect Size	Small-ish	Medium-ish	Large-ish
Mean difference between groups (d)	.40	.70	1.00
Mean difference within groups (d)	.60	1.00	1.40
Correlation (r)	.25	.40	.65

E

Ellis, N. C. (2000). Editorial statement. *Language Learning, 50,* xi–xiii.

Norris, J. M., Plonsky, L., Ross, S. J., & Schoonen, R. (2015). Guidelines for reporting quantitative methods and results in primary research. *Language Learning, 65,* 470–476.

Plonsky, L. (2014). Study quality in quantitative L2 research (1990-2010): A methodological synthesis and call for reform. *Modern Language Journal, 98,* 450–470.

Plonsky, L. (2015). Statistical power, *p* values, descriptive statistics, and effect sizes: A "back-to-basics" approach to advancing quantitative methods in L2 research. In L. Plonsky (Ed.), *Advancing quantitative methods in second language research* (pp. 23–45). New York: Routledge.

Plonsky, L., & Oswald, F. L. (2014). How big is "big"? Interpreting effect sizes in L2 research. *Language Learning, 64,* 878–912.

Toth, P. D., & Guijarro-Fuentes, P. (2013). The impact of instruction on second-language implicit knowledge: Evidence against encapsulation. *Applied Psycholinguistics, 34,* 1163–1193.

Eigenvalue (see Factor analysis)

Elicited imitation test

A data elicitation method in which participants hear sentences and are asked to repeat them. Sometimes the sentences are grammatically correct; however, learners can be given incorrect sentences, which they are asked to repeat correctly. The accuracy of the repeated utterance is then analyzed and scored in comparison to the original stimulus sentence. Generally, participants are awarded one point for correct production of a sentence, and no points for incorrect production or avoidance of a pre-specified linguistic structure. In addition, participants often perform some type of comprehension response before repeating the sentence, in an attempt to focus attention on meaning and prevent memorization of the stimulus sentence. Elicited imitation tests have been used in an attempt to measure implicit L2 knowledge, because they arguably make it difficult for participants to draw on explicit L2 knowledge when reproducing the sentences (Erlam, 2006). An argument in favor of using elicited imitation tests is that they are arguably reconstructive in nature. That is to say, learners hold the semantic content in their heads, but they do not remember the specific linguistic forms that were used in the sentence. Thus, learners have to draw on their own knowledge to reconstruct the sentences. In this view, learners will have to draw on their implicit, proceduralized knowledge to reconstruct the sentence because it is difficult to draw on explicit knowledge in real-time language production. Because the imitation task is oral, learners cannot keep the sentence in front of them. It may be possible for learners to hold the sentence in their phonological short-term memory, but in many instances, researchers attempt to prevent memorization by the inclusion of comprehension activities after learners hear a sentence but before they repeat it. For example, learners may be asked to indicate if they think a sentence is true or not. Thus, by focusing on the semantic content of the sentence, it is argued that learners cannot keep the linguistic items in their short-term memory.

Though attractive as a potentially useful and relatively simple-to-administer proxy for L2 proficiency (see Tracy-Ventura, McManus, Norris, & Ortega, 2014), elicited imitation tests have been criticized. Jessop, Sazuki, and Tomita (2007), for example, contend that elicited imitation tests are not reconstructive in nature, but rely on repetition.

Erlam, R. (2006). Elicited imitation as a measure of L2 implicit knowledge: An empirical validation study. *Applied Linguistics, 27*, 464–491.

Jessop, L., Sazuki, W., & Tomita, Y. (2007). Elicited imitation in second language acquisition research. *The Canadian Modern Language Review, 64*, 215–238.

Tracy-Ventura, N., McManus, K., Norris, J., & Ortega, L. (2014). "Repeat as much as you can": Elicited imitation as a measure of oral proficiency in L2 French. In P. Leclercq, A. Edmonds, & H. Hilton (Eds.), *Measuring L2 proficiency: Perspectives from SLA* (pp. 143–166). Bristol: Multilingual Matters.

Emic

A term used in **qualitative research** to describe an insider perspective. As such, it contrasts with an outsider, or **etic**, perspective. The goal of much qualitative research is to understand how the participants in the research make sense of the context themselves, rather than how researchers interpret the context. An example of this perspective is found in **conversation analysis (CA)**, which examines talk in interaction, and tries to interpret the discourse based on the participants' responses to previous turns. Thus, there are no external categories or concepts that researchers bring with them to the discourse to try to help them interpret it. In fact, CA eschews the use of external categories, even those that may be characteristic of the participants (e.g., gender, L1 status), unless these **constructs** appear in the discourse and are treated as relevant by the participants.

Haugh, M. (2007). Emic conceptualisations of (im)politeness and face in Japanese: Implications for the discursive negotiation of second language learner identities. *Journal of Pragmatics, 39*, 657–680.

E

Epistemology

Ways of knowing and perceiving knowledge. In one sense, epistemologies are the lenses through which researchers see the world. Epistemological stances are not always considered in applied linguistics research, even though they are closely related to the different paradigms within which applied linguists work. In a **positivist** or **postpositivist** paradigm, for example, researchers often assume that objectively true knowledge is not only possible but desirable. Researchers in critical theory and **constructivist** paradigms, by contrast, accept the subjectivity of knowledge, recognizing the values they bring to their research, their data, and the interpretations thereof. Given such different paradigmatic stances, it is not surprising to find that researchers from different epistemological points of view engage in different methodological practices. Positivists generally conduct **quantitative research** in an effort to find reliable and generalizable evidence of objective reality. In contrast, constructivists often engage in **qualitative research** in an effort to gain insights into specific contexts and conditions. Finally, closely related to one's understanding of the nature of knowledge and knowing (i.e., epistemology) is one's understanding of the nature of the reality around them (i.e., **ontology**).

Lincoln, Y. S., & Guba, E. G. (2000). Paradigmatic controversies, contradictions, and emerging confluences. In N. K. Denzin & Y. S. Lincoln (Eds.), *Handbook of qualitative research* (2nd ed., pp. 163–188). Thousand Oaks, CA: Sage.

Ortega, L. (2005). Methodology, epistemology, and ethics in instructed SLA research: An introduction. *Modern Language Journal, 89*, 317–327.

Richards, K. (2003). *Qualitative inquiry in TESOL*. New York: Palgrave Macmillan.

Eta^2 (see Eta-squared)

Eta-squared

An **effect size** that expresses the amount of variance in the **dependent variable** that can be accounted for by the **independent variable**(s). Eta-squared (also written eta^2 or η^2) is most often associated with **ANOVA** and its variants (e.g., **ANCOVA**). As implied by their names, these analyses examine whether and to what extent a sample's scores differ across groups (e.g., native vs. non-native speakers; control vs. experimental group). The eta^2 value associated with the analysis then indicates the percentage of variance in the dependent variable that can be explained by or attributed to participants' group membership. In addition to eta-squared, which indicates all of the variance accounted for by the independent variables, it is also possible to calculate partial eta-squared, which indicates the amount of unique variance accounted for by one independent variable. Granena and Long (2013), for example, ran a series of ANOVAs comparing early- and late-learners' L2 performance. In phonology, the difference between group scores was found to be statistically significant ($p < .001$) with a partial eta-squared value of .748, indicating that a great amount (nearly 75%) of the variance in phonology scores was due to group membership (i.e., early vs. late learner).

Though not often viewed as such, eta-squared is actually very similar—both conceptually and arithmetically—to R^2. Both effect size indices are concerned primarily with explaining variance. However, whereas eta-squared expresses variance due to a **categorical variable**, R^2 indicates covariance or shared variance between two or more **continuous variables** and is, for this reason, often reported along with regression results.

Granena, G., & Long, M. H. (2013). Age of onset, length of residence, language aptitude, and ultimate L2 attainment in three linguistic domains. *Second Language Research, 29*, 311–343.

Ethics (see Research ethics)

Ethnography
A method within **qualitative research** in which researchers spend considerable time within a specific social context in order to gain a rich and full understanding of the context and the individuals within it. For example, Han (2014) examined the lives of two Chinese immigrants in Canada. She reports on the global, national, and local contexts that her participants found themselves in. In addition, over the course of a year, Han regularly interviewed her participants, as well as other individuals who figured prominently in their lives. She also conducted observations of the participants in their home, work, church, and other social settings. Ethnographies generally attempt to present an **emic** perspective in which the researcher explores the **constructs** that are important to the participants rather than those that are important to the researcher. As such, researchers often do not begin an ethnographic study with preconceived **research questions**. Rather, researchers may begin with a more general focus. One way of uncovering the perspectives of the participants is by the researcher engaging in **participant observation**, in which she or he becomes a member of the community that is being investigated.

Han, H. (2014). Accessing English and networks at an English-medium multicultural church in east Canada: An ethnography. *The Canadian Modern Language Review/La Revue canadienne des langues vivantes, 70,* 220–245.

Modiba, M., & Stewart, S. (2014). Understanding classroom practice: Ethnographic reflection as a methodological tool for professional development. *Ethnography and Education, 9,* 140–152.

Mukul, S., & Martin-Jones, M. (2013). Multilingual resources in classroom interaction: Ethnographic and discourse analytic perspectives. *Language and Education, 27,* 285–297.

Pople, I., & Cain, L. Manchester life and language: British cultural ethnography for international students. *Innovation in Language Learning and Teaching, 4,* 93–99.

Zheng, C. (2012). Understanding the learning process of peer feedback activity: An ethnographic study of exploratory practice. *Language Teaching Research, 16,* 109–126.

Etic
A term used to describe an outsider perspective in research. As such, it contrasts with an insider, or **emic**, perspective. In many types of research, particularly in quantitative studies, the researcher approaches the research context with a particular set of variables in mind that he or she wants to test. As such, researchers bring their own perspectives to bear on the research context. One argument against this approach is that researchers might not conceive of the context/**construct** in the same way that the participants do, and thus, researchers may not be getting an accurate picture of the context, because they are imposing their own perspectives on the data or participants. An example of this may occur when researching psychological constructs such as motivation or anxiety. Researchers may

view the constructs in a particular way, which may or may not align with the experience or beliefs of the participants. However, because experimental and quasi-experimental research is generally concerned with making comparisons among multiple contexts or groups, it is necessary to ensure that the object of investigation is being measured reliably across all contexts. Consequently, the use of etically determined constructs allows for more consistent analysis of the variable(s) in question.

Experimental design

A research method that involves researchers in intentional manipulation of variables. As such, experimental design differs from descriptive designs in which researchers observe a specific context rather than intervene in it. In experimental designs, there is generally a **dependent variable** (or series of dependent variables) that represents what the researcher is examining for change. Then there are one or more **independent variables** that the researcher systematically manipulates to determine their effects on the dependent variable. The researcher may include or exclude specific independent variables, or vary the intensity of the variables. In order to determine the effects of independent variables on dependent variables, researchers generally engage in **pretesting** and **posttesting**, with the treatment coming between the testing sessions. In addition to treatments and testing, experimental design includes: (a) random assignment of participants to groups, and (b) a control group. Many research studies in SLA are not truly experimental, but rather, are **quasi-experimental** in nature because they often lack random group assignment, relying instead on convenience sampling. In addition, many applied linguistics studies include comparison groups, but not true control groups. For example, Ammar and Spada (2006) used intact classes to investigate the effects of two different types of corrective feedback. In addition to the two treatment groups, they included a comparison group that completed the treatment activities but did not receive any corrective feedback. However, no control group, which was not manipulated in any way, was included.

Ammar, A., & Spada, N. (2006). One size fits all? Recasts, prompts, and L2 learning. *Studies in Second Language Acquisition, 28*, 543–574.

Shadish, W. R., Cook, T. D., & Campbell, D. T. (2002). *Experimental and quasi-experimental designs for generalized causal inference.* Boston, MA: Houghton Mifflin.

Experimental group

The group (or groups) in experimental or quasi-experimental research that receives the **treatment**. Thus, in a study of the effects of a specific type of instruction on L2 learning, the experimental group is the one that is taught using the specified method. In contrast to experimental groups, there are comparison and control groups. **Comparison groups** generally participate in the research activities, but do not receive any treatment. Control groups, on the other hand, only undergo **pretesting** and **posttesting**, with no exposure to the intervening activities, and instead, continue with their regular activities. In addition, native speakers are sometimes used as a control group or baseline group. In some cases, a research study may have only an experimental group, but in such cases, it is difficult to attribute any effects found in the study to the treatment and not to some other, random, intervening variable. Other studies may have two or more experimental groups, which allow comparison of the different types of treatment in relation to each other, but do not provide information about what does or does not happen to a group without treatment. Consequently, it is important to have a comparison group and/or control group in order to most clearly determine the effects of the treatment.

Exploratory factor analysis (see Factor analysis)

External validity (see Generalizability, Validity)

Extraction (see Factor analysis)

Eye tracking

A type of research method that allows researchers to measure and record participants' eye movements. Participants are placed in front of a computer screen, and there is a camera that tracks their eye as they read or look at the screen. There are several different configurations for obtaining eye tracking data, but central to all is the data that the method provides, and what information that data can provide. Eye tracking records primarily two types of data—eye fixations and eye movements. Eye fixations occur when the eye focuses on a specific image; the eye tracker then records the length of that fixation in milliseconds. In addition, eye-tracking technology measures saccades, which are the movements of the eyes from fixation to fixation. Eye tracking is used to investigate a variety of **research questions**. For example, it can be used in reading studies to measure how participants process a text. It can tell how long individuals fixate on specific words, and how individuals process the text, whether they progressed forward without returning to previous words or moved back and forth in the text.

Eye tracking can also be used in a visual-world paradigm, in which participants hear words and are asked to look at the corresponding images on the screen. The time that it takes for learners to hear a word and to look at the image can provide information about the anticipatory effects that a

E

word might bring about. Some studies that have used this paradigm have investigated L2 learners' knowledge of gender agreement in languages such as Spanish. It has been found that native speakers will use the gendered article as a cue for which picture to look at, and thus they may start looking at a picture representing a masculine noun as soon as they hear the article *el* (Lew-Williams & Fernald, 2010).

Another way that eye tracking can be used is to generate heat maps, which indicate how long individuals look at a specific part of the screen. More numerous and longer fixations are represented by more intense colors, and thus indicate greater or less attention to different areas. In an application of this aspect of eye tracking, Smith (2012; see Figure 10) used heat maps to investigate the extent to which L2 learners noticed corrective feedback provided during written synchronous computer-mediated communication.

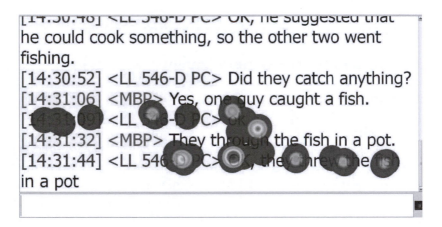

Source: Taken from Smith (2012, p. 64).

Figure 10 Heat map

Figure 11 is a representation of how an individual reads a sentence. The circles represent fixations, and the larger the circle, the longer the fixation time. The lines with arrows represent saccades and indicate the directional movement of the eye from fixation to fixation.

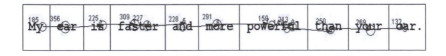

Figure 11 Gazes and fixations from an eye tracker

Lew-Williams, C., & Fernald, A. (2010). Real-time processing of gender-marked articles by native and non-native Spanish speakers. *Journal of Memory and Language, 63*, 447–464.

Smith, B. (2012). Eye tracking as a measure of noticing: A study of explicit recasts in SCMC. *Language Learning & Technology, 16*, 53–81.

Winke, P., Godfroid, A., & Gass, S. M. (2013). Introduction to the special issue: Eye-movement recordings in second language research. *Studies in Second Language Acquisition, 35*, 205–212.

E

Face validity

The **validity** that a test or treatment has in the eyes of those who are participating in it or administering it. In other words, do test-takers, as well as administrators who rely on test results, view the test as a good measurement of the **construct** under consideration? For example, TOEFL and IELTS are tests with fairly strong face validity because those who take them and those who interpret the resulting scores generally accept the claim that they are relatively good measures of English language proficiency. In contrast, pair work and conversational interaction may have little face validity as classroom activities for L2 learners who view L2 learning as acquiring rules and metalinguistic knowledge about language. In their study of the effectiveness and validity of planning time in speaking tests, Wigglesworth and Elder (2010) found that participants expressed a preference for having planning time when taking a speaking test. The authors argue that this desire is worth noting, and potentially incorporating, for the sake of face validity. Face validity is, of course, just one aspect of validity, and is generally not viewed as being as important as **construct validity** or **reliability**.

Wigglesworth, G., & Elder, C. (2010). An investigation of the effectiveness and validity of planning time in speaking test tasks. *Language Assessment Quarterly, 7*(1), 1–24.

Factor analysis

A set of structure-analyzing statistical procedures used to investigate the underlying **correlations** in a set of observed variables in order to group them in related clusters. Factor analysis is also a data reduction technique. There are two general types of factor analyses: confirmatory and exploratory. The former is used when researchers want to determine if a data set contains the number and composition of factors that theory or other research has already determined. Thus, researchers are comparing their data to a hypothesized model to see how well those data conform to that model. On the other hand, exploratory factor analysis is used when there may be little previous research or theoretical guidance to specify factors. There are numerous steps in conducting a factor analysis, with the primary decisions revolving around the type of factor extraction and rotation. Factor extraction pertains to how many clusters of variables (referred to as factors or components) to retain from the data set. This decision can be based on theoretical reasons for a confirmatory factor analysis, or on statistical indicators that the analysis provides (referred to as eigenvalues) for exploratory factor analysis. Once extracted, the factors are generally rotated in order to maximize the relationship of the variables within a factor, and maximize the differences between factors. Two general methods of rotation, orthogonal and oblique, are used when it is expected that the factors will be either unrelated or related to each other, respectively. Because the factors in applied linguistics research are generally related in some way, oblique rotation is usually the better method to employ. The results of the rotation are presented with each variable in the analysis having a factor loading score. Loadings of .30 or .40 are generally considered high. When interpreting the results, researchers look at which variables loaded highly on a factor, in order to help them interpret that factor. The stronger the loadings, the more central that variable is to the factor. Factor analysis can be used with **survey** data in an attempt to reduce the number of items. For example, if several items have high loadings on one factor, they can be considered to represent the same **construct**, and the researcher may wish to retain only the items with the highest loadings on the factor. Alternatively, one item might have high loadings on more than one factor, in which case, the item is referred to as a complex variable. Because a complex variable does not represent one clear factor, it can be helpful to remove it from the **questionnaire.** Examining the communalities (i.e., the amount of variance in a variable that is common to all the other variables as well) can provide information about how the item relates to the overall questionnaire, and items with low communalities can be excluded from the analysis. Factor analysis is also used to examine the common underlying relationships in a questionnaire. For example, in Table 10, abbreviated from Loewen et al. (2014), the factors were interpreted as: 1 = common inferential statistics

Table 10 Sample results from a factor analysis

	Component		
	1	**2**	**3**
p-value	.944	−.263	.054
ANOVA	.933	−.114	.031
Post hoc tests	.882	.042	−.059
Rasch Analysis	−.109	.856	.119
Structural equation modeling	.131	.800	−.054
Median	−.070	−.025	.906
Mean	.021	−.091	.872

Source: Based on Loewen et al. (2014).

knowledge, 2 = advanced statistics knowledge, and 3 = basic descriptive statistics knowledge, as indicated by the shaded scores.

It is also possible to calculate factor scores for each individual participant in the data set. Thus, in the data from Loewen et al., each participant can be given a score on each factor, based on how they responded to each item within that factor. In this way, a researcher could run inferential statistics on just three **independent variables**, rather than the 28 original questionnaire items.

A good factor analysis should account for a considerable amount of the variance in the data set, from 60% and upward.

In an analysis of their 51-item metacognitive awareness listening questionnaire, Vandergrift, Goh, Mareschal, and Tafaghodtari (2006) used an exploratory factor analysis to investigate the degree to which language learners were aware of the L2 listening comprehension process. Results indicated that 44.5% of the total variance was explained by five factors: (1) person knowledge, (2) mental translation, (3) directed attention/concentration, (4) planning, and (5) problem-solving.

Loewen, S., & Gonulal, T. (2015). Exploratory factor analysis and principal components analysis. In L. Plonsky (Ed.), *Advancing quantitative methods in second language research* (pp. 182–212). New York: Routledge.

Loewen, S., Lavolette, E., Spino, L., Papi, M., Schmidtke, J., Sterling, S., & Wolff, D. (2014). Statistical literacy among applied linguists and second language acquisition researchers. *TESOL Quarterly, 48,* 360–388.

Plonsky, L., & Gonulal, T. (2015). Methodological synthesis in quantitative L2 research: A review of reviews and a case study of exploratory factor analysis. *Language Learning,* 65, Supp. 1, 9–36.

Vandergrift, L., Goh, C. C. M., Mareschal, C. J., & Tafaghodtari, M. H. (2006). The metacognitive awareness listening questionnaire: Development and validation. *Language Learning, 56*(3), 431–462.

Factor loading (see Factor analysis)

Factorial analysis of variance (see Analysis of variance)

F

Field notes

Researchers' personal writings or recordings that aim to document and describe the events under consideration in observational **qualitative research**. As such, researchers try to record as objectively and descriptively as possible the things that they are observing; however, they may also record their opinions, impressions, and interpretations of the events as well. Field notes, then, become one source of data that can be analyzed for larger trends and themes. In a critical ethnographic **case study** of designer immigrant students at an English-medium school in Singapore, De Costa (2015) collected field notes from classroom excursion and general school observations. These notes contained examples of the community's expectations that these designer immigrants perform as scholars, which the author showed to be a source of language learning anxiety for one of the students.

In one sense, field notes may have become less important with the advent of audio and video recording, which provide a more permanent record of events; however, there are still instances where it may be impossible or inappropriate to conduct such recordings, so researchers must rely on what they are able to write down. For example, some teachers may not wish to have recording equipment in the classroom due to its potentially disruptive qualities, but teachers might not object to being observed. In such cases, field notes can be taken unobtrusively during the observation. Another function of field notes may be as an addition to recordings, in order for researchers to add additional information that is not captured by the recordings, such as their impressions or interpretations of an event.

De Costa, P. I. (2015). Re-envisioning language anxiety in the globalized classroom through a social imaginary lens. *Language Learning, 65*(3), 504–532.

Fixed effects

The investigation of a variable in **quantitative research** in which all possible categories of interest to the researcher are included. For example, the type of **treatment** provided in a research study can be considered a fixed effect because the researcher presumably includes all the relevant treatment types. Fixed effects cannot be generalized beyond a specific study. In contrast, **random effects** can be generalized and include only a subset of possible conditions of interest to a researcher. In academic research, most variables are treated as fixed effects. Additionally, some statistical programs, such as **SPSS**, allow researchers to designate a variable as a random or fixed effect.

Cunnings, I., & Finlayson, I. (2015). Mixed effects modeling and longitudinal data analysis. In L. Plonsky (Ed.), *Advancing quantitative methods in second language research* (pp. 159–181). New York: Routledge.

fMRI (see Functional magnetic resonance imaging)

Forest plot

A graphic technique used to display meta-analytic effects for a sample of studies. As shown in Figure 12, a sample forest plot from Berlim, Eynde, Tovar-Perdomo, and Daskalakis (2014), the **effect size** contributed by each study in the **meta-analysis**, an **odds ratio** in this case, is presented numerically on the left-hand side of the figure along with other relevant data (e.g., *p*-value). The effect size is also indicated visually, in the form of a square on the x axis, by its location in the right-hand side of the figure. The larger the square, the larger the sample (or other index used to weight the effect size). The error associated with each point estimate is also provided

F

Study name	Statistics for each study					Remitters/total		Relative weight
	Odds ratio	Lower limit	Upper limit	z	P	Active rTMS	Sham rTMS	
George et al. (1997)	2.538	0.085	75.765	0.538	0.591	1/7	0/5	1.99
Berman et al. 2000	3.316	0.120	91.601	0.708	0.479	1/10	0/10	2.08
Boutros et al. (2002)	0.727	0.039	13.452	-0.214	0.831	1/12	1/9	2.70
Padberg et al. (2002)	4.200	0.197	89.609	0.919	0.358	3/20	0/10	2.45
Koerselman et al. (2004)	1.000	0.019	52.362	0.000	1.000	1/26	1/26	1.47
Rossini et al. (2005)	21.596	1.205	387.150	2.086	0.037	14/37	0/17	2.76
Su et al. (2005)	21.000	1.085	406.551	2.014	0.044	10/20	0/10	2.61
Avery et al. (2006)	8.000	0.926	69.078	1.891	0.059	7/35	1/33	4.94
Loo et al. (2007)	1.594	0.235	10.817	0.477	0.633	3/19	2/19	6.26
O'Reardon et al. (2007)	2.853	1.228	6.633	2.436	0.015	22/155	8/46	32.27
Stern et al. (2007)	14.467	0.659	317.545	1.695	0.090	3/10	0/15	2.41
Mogg et al. (2008)	2.889	0.664	12.560	1.415	0.157	7/28	3/29	10.63
George et al. (2010)	3.061	1.046	8.960	2.041	0.041	13/92	5/98	19.90
Blumberger et al. (2012)	0.905	0.053	15.492	-0.069	0.945	1/22	1/20	2.85
Bakim et al. (in press)	7.071	0.774	64.575	1.733	0.083	9/23	1/12	4.69
	3.298	2.042	5.325	4.881	0.000	96/516	23/459	

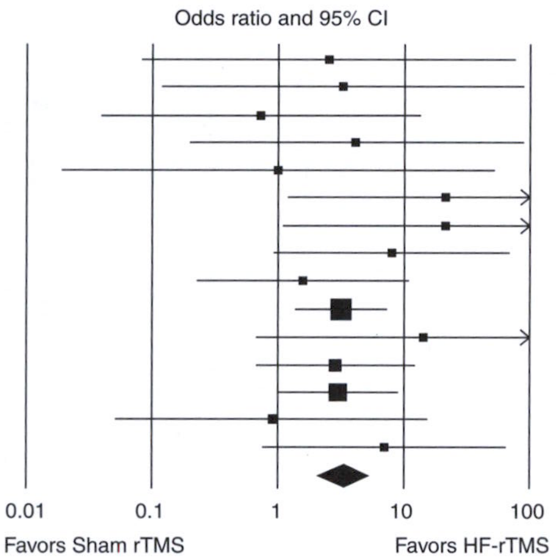

Odds ratio and 95% CI

Favors Sham rTMS   Favors HF-rTMS

Source: Berlim, Eynde, Tovar-Perdomo, and Daskalakis (2014): p. 233.

Figure 12 Forest plot

visually in the form of "arms" extending to the left and right of the square. The shorter the arms, the more precise or stable the estimate. The first study in the sample, for instance, has an odds ratio of 2.538. It is perhaps a somewhat unstable point estimate, however, as indicated by the length of the arms extending from it. The results for O'Reardon et al., by contrast, though similar in magnitude, may be more trustworthy based on both the shorter arms and the larger sample, indicated by the larger square. One final yet crucial piece to a forest plot is the overall meta-analytic result, which appears at the bottom of the plot and is typically represented by a diamond. In the sample, we can see by the location of the diamond that the overall (meta-analytic) effect for this sample of studies is an odds ratio of 3.298.

Forest plots can be made using software designed for meta-analysis, such as *Comprehensive Meta-analysis* (Borenstein, Hedges, Higgins, & Rothstein, 2005). They can also be made using less specialized programs such as Excel, but it is considerably more difficult to do so. Consequently, forest plots have not been used frequently in applied linguistics (although see Jeon & Yamashita, 2014), but they are a potentially useful technique for displaying the **range** and summary of effects across a meta-analytic sample (see Anzures-Cabrera & Higgins, 2010).

See also **Funnel plot**.

Anzures-Cabrera, J., & Higgins, J. P. T. (2010). Graphical displays for meta-analysis: An overview with suggestions for practice. *Research Synthesis Methods, 1*, 66–80.

Berlim, M. T., Eynde, F. v. d., Tovar-Perdomo, S., & Daskalakis, Z. J. (2014). Response, remission and drop-out rates following high-frequency repetitive transcranial magnetic stimulation (rTMS) for treating major depression: A systematic review and meta-analysis of randomized, double-blind and sham-controlled trials. *Psychological Medicine, 44*, 225–239.

Borenstein, M., Hedges, L., Higgins, J., & Rothstein, H. (2005). *Comprehensive meta-analysis*, Version 2. Engelwood, NJ: Biostat.

Jeon, E. H., & Yamashita, J. (2014). L2 reading and its correlates: A meta-analysis. *Language Learning, 64*, 160–212.

F

Frequency

A descriptive statistic that tallies the occurrence of the variable under consideration. It is the primary statistic used with categorical data, because it is possible only to count the number of instances of each category. For example, researchers may tally the number of speakers of various L1s in their data set. Frequency counts can be used as **dependent variables** in primarily one inferential statistical test, namely **chi-square**, in which the number of observations in each category is compared to the number that would be expected by chance or if there were no relationship between two variables.

Friedman's ANOVA

A type of analysis of variance that is used when the assumption of **normal distribution** is violated for more than two related groups. As such, Friedman's ANOVA is the **non-parametric** equivalent of a repeated measures ANOVA, and instead of calculating statistical differences based on mean scores, it uses ranked data. If there is a statistically significant result, it is possible to follow up with a **post hoc test**, such as the **Wilcoxon signed-rank test**, which will conduct pairwise comparisons on the data. For example, Robinson (2007) performed a Friedman's ANOVA with Wilcoxon signed-rank post hoc tests in his study of task complexity. English L2 speakers performed three tasks, each with increasing complexity, and the learners' oral production was analyzed for complexity, accuracy, and fluency. Among other findings, Robinson reported a significant difference for *words per turn* (df, 2, $\chi^2 = 9.32$, $p < .01$), with the significant difference occurring between the simple and medium task performance (Wilcoxon $z = -2.72$, $p < .01$).

Friedman's ANOVA is appropriate when one group of participants provides multiple datapoints (i.e., a within-groups design), such as with pretest, immediate posttest, and delayed posttest. However, in many cases, applied linguistics researchers wish to compare the effects of more than one group over time, and Friedman's ANOVA is not able to accommodate that type of research design.

Robinson, P. (2007). Task complexity, theory of mind, and intentional reasoning: Effects on L2 speech production, interaction, uptake and perceptions of task difficulty. *International Review of Applied Linguistics, 45*, 193–213.

Functional magnetic resonance imaging (fMRI)

A technology that allows real-time observation of brain activity associated with language input, processing, and production. More specifically, fMRI indicates the location of brain activity by detecting blood oxygen levels and any changes that occur over time and in response to different stimuli. The use of fMRI in applied linguistics has been concentrated primarily in the domains of psycholinguistics, neurolinguistics, and bilingualism, helping researchers to address questions related to lexical and sentential processing. Another area that has been studied using fMRI is cognitive control, the notion that bilinguals may possess cognitive advantages over monolinguals. Support for such an advantage stems in part from fMRI findings of activation (increased blood oxygen levels) within the same regions required for both cognitive control tasks and language control tasks (e.g., Abutalebi & Green, 2007).

Abutalebi, J., & Green, D. W. (2007). Bilingual language production: The neurocognition of language representation and control. *Journal of Neurolinguistics, 20*, 242–275.
de Bot, K. (2008). The imaging of what in the multilingual mind? *Second Language Research, 24*, 111–133.

Sabourin, L. (2009). Neuroimaging and research into second language acquisition. *Second Language Research, 25*, 5–11.

Sabourin, L. (2014). fMRI research on the bilingual brain. *Annual Review of Applied Linguistics, 34*, 1–14.

Funnel plot

A data visualization technique used to plot **meta-analysis** results and to inspect them for publication bias. The funnel plot is a scatterplot wherein the effect size of each study is plotted on the x axis, with the mean effect usually marked with a vertical line (see Figure 13). An indicator of the precision of the effect size measurement, typically the sample size, is plotted on the y axis. Studies with larger samples should contain less **sampling error**, and should, therefore, be found close to the population mean. On the other hand, studies with smaller samples generally contain greater sampling error and will therefore likely spread out at the bottom of the figure. If the meta-analyzed studies contain publication bias toward statistically significant findings, however, the spread of effects at the bottom of the figure will not be even. Specifically, few small-sampled studies with small effects (bottom left) will be found in comparison to those with a small sample and large effects (bottom right). A lack of symmetry in the plot can also indicate the presence of systematic moderators present in the sample. Figure 13 was adapted from the funnel plot in Lee, Jang, and Plonsky's (2015) meta-analysis of the effects of pronunciation instruction. As expected, there

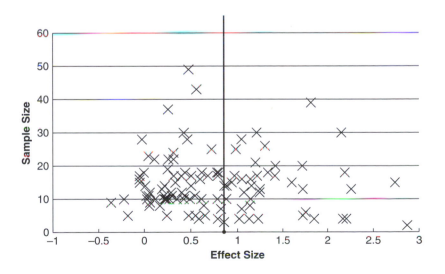

Source: Adapted from Lee et al. (2015).

Figure 13 Funnel plot

is much greater variability in effect sizes lower on the plot (i.e., with smaller samples). That is, studies with smaller samples produce a larger range of effects, likely due to increased sampling error. We also see, however, a greater spread of scores in the bottom right (small samples, larger effects) than in the bottom left (small samples, small effects), which the authors interpreted as a sign of bias in favor of publishing statistically significant results. For additional examples of funnel plots in applied linguistics, see Li (2010), Norris and Ortega (2000), and Plonsky (2011).

See also **Forest plot**.

Anzures-Cabrera, J., & Higgins, J. P. T. (2010). Graphical displays for meta-analysis: An overview with suggestions for practice. *Research Synthesis Methods, 1*, 66–80.

Lee, J., Jang, J., & Plonsky, L. (2015). The effectiveness of second language pronunciation instruction: A meta-analysis. *Applied Linguistics, 36*, 345–366.

Li, S. (2010). The effectiveness of corrective feedback in SLA: A meta-analysis. *Language Learning, 60*, 309–365.

Norris, J. M., & Ortega, L. (2000). Effectiveness of L2 instruction: A research synthesis and quantitative meta-analysis. *Language Learning, 50*, 417–528.

Plonsky, L. (2011). The effectiveness of second language strategy instruction: A meta-analysis. *Language Learning, 61*, 993–1038.

F

Gg

Gain score

A **dependent variable** that is often calculated in experimental and quasi-experimental research to measure the difference in participants' performance from **pretest** to **posttest**, or from immediate posttest to delayed posttest. Gain scores are calculated by subtracting the pretest scores from the posttest scores. Gain scores can be subjected to **inferential statistics** to determine the effect of a treatment, either for a single treatment group or across multiple groups. By comparing the gain scores of several groups, researchers can determine if one or more groups improved significantly more than other groups. For example, in a study of written corrective feedback, Lundstrom and Baker (2009) analyzed gain scores from pretest to posttest for two treatment groups: one who only gave written feedback and one who only received written feedback. They found a higher gain score for the givers, which the authors interpreted as a more significant improvement in the quality of writing for those who provided rather than received feedback.

In addition to comparing gain scores, researchers can also compare raw pretest and posttest scores, generally using repeated measures or mixed design **analysis of variance**. However, in cases where there are significant differences between groups on the pretest, using gain scores can provide information about absolute improvement regardless of the participants' starting point.

Lundstrom, K., & Baker, W. (2009). To give is better than to receive: The benefits of peer review to the reviewer's own writing. *Journal of Second Language Writing, 18*, 30–43.

General linear model (GLM)

A family of statistical procedures that encompasses almost all quantitative techniques employed in applied linguistics, such as **t-test**, **ANOVA**, **correlation**, **multiple regression**, **factor analysis**, and **structural equation modeling**. Underlying all of these procedures is an interest in linear relationships among variables. In the case of correlation and regression analyses, this interest is quite clear; these procedures provide quantitative estimates of shared **variance** between two or more variables. Likewise, t-tests and ANOVAs are used to estimate the amount of variance in a dependent or criterion variable that can be accounted for by group membership.

An understanding of this broad notion as applied to the many statistics that fall under the GLM also makes clearer the hierarchical relationships between them. For example, ANOVA can be seen as a special case of **multiple regression** in which only a single categorical predictor variable is included in the model. Extending this line of thinking just one step further, even an independent samples *t*-test can be considered a special case of regression (or correlation), wherein we examine the correlation between two sets of scores. (We've saved you the formulae-heavy explanation here. To test this yourself, though, try running an independent samples *t*-test. Then, run a correlation between the independent and dependent variables. The *p*-values will be identical.) And all of these procedures can be considered special and more basic cases of structural equation modeling (see Graham, 2008).

These relationships between GLM statistics are not often discussed in applied linguistics research methods texts and, consequently, they are not likely to be familiar to most researchers in the field (Plonsky, 2014). A quick perusal of 10 applied linguistics research methods texts shows that none provide a full discussion of the inner workings of the GLM and only three even mention it (see Table 11). This point is worth noting because, as argued in Cohen's now-classic (1968) paper and demonstrated in Skidmore and Thompson's (2010) review of statistical analyses in education, an understanding of the relationship between these statistics may lead researchers to move toward regression models that explain variance in a dependent variable rather than focusing so heavily on mean differences.

Brown, J. D. (1988). *Understanding research in second language learning: A teacher's guide to statistics and research design.* Cambridge: Cambridge University Press.

Cantos Gomez, P. (2013). *Statistical methods in language and linguistic research.* Bristol, CT: Equinox.

Table 11 The GLM in applied linguistics research methods texts

Book	Coverage of GLM
Brown (1988)	None
Hatch & Lazaraton (1991)	Mentioned briefly
Mackey & Gass (2005)	None
Rasinger (2008)	None
Larson-Hall (2010)	None
Porte (2010)	None
Richards, Ross, and Seedhouse (2012)	Mentioned briefly
Cantos Gomez (2013)	None
Turner (2014)	None
Plonsky (2015)	Mentioned briefly

Cohen, J. (1968). Multiple regression as a general data-analytic system. *Psychological Bulletin, 70*, 426–443.

Graham, J. M. (2008). The general linear model as structural equation modeling. *Journal of Educational and Behavioral Statistics, 33*, 485–506.

Hatch, E., & Lazaraton, A. (1991). *The research manual: design and statistics for applied linguistics*. Rowley, MA: Newbury House.

Larson-Hall, J. (2010). *A guide to doing statistics in second language research using SPSS*. New York: Routledge.

Mackey, A., & Gass, S. M. (2005). *Second language research: Methodology and design*. Mahwah, NJ: Lawrence Erlbaum.

Plonsky, L. (2014). Study quality in quantitative L2 research (1990–2010): A methodological synthesis and call for reform. *Modern Language Journal, 98*, 450–470.

Plonsky, L. (Ed.) (2015). *Advancing quantitative methods in second language research*. New York: Routledge.

Porte, G. K. (2010). *Appraising research in second language learning: A practical approach to critical analysis of quantitative research* (2nd ed.). Amsterdam: John Benjamins.

Rasinger, S. (2008). *Quantitative research in linguistics: An introduction*. New York: Continuum.

Richards, K., Ross, S. J., & Seedhouse, P. (2012). *Research methods for applied language studies*. New York: Routledge.

Skidmore, S. T., & Thompson, B. (2010). Statistical techniques used in published articles: A historical review of reviews. *Educational and Psychological Measurement, 70*, 777–795.

Turner, J. L. (2014). *Using statistics in small-scale language education research: Focus on nonparametric data*. New York: Routledge.

Generalizability

How well the results of a specific research study can be applied to different contexts or **populations**. Also referred to as external **validity**, generalizability is primarily a concern of **quantitative research**. It is based on the idea that taking a sample from a larger population will allow researchers to make inferences about that population. Researchers often take specific steps to try to increase the generalizability of their work. For example, **random selection** of participants increases generalizability because the sample is ideally not biased by any unintended selection criteria; however, random selection is not a common practice in applied linguistics research. In addition, sample size is important for generalizability. If data from only a few cases are observed, then they may not be typical of the larger population. This is one reason why generalizability is a concern of quantitative and not necessarily **qualitative research**, which generally investigates smaller numbers of participants, engaging in more context-specific analyses. In addition, quantitative research generally follows a postpositivist paradigm, which attempts to investigate objective reality. Qualitative research, on the other hand, is more concerned with situatedness and contextualization than with generalizability. In the end, however, a single research study will always be somewhat limited in its generalizability, regardless of whether it is quantitative or qualitative, which is why **replication** and **research synthesis** are necessary for gaining a wider perspective on a specific topic.

G

GJT (see Grammaticality judgment test)

GLM (see General linear model)

Goodness of fit

A statistical term referring to how well a specific model accounts for the data. Often, the goodness of fit is determined by comparing the results that would be expected for frequency counts, based on the data sampling, with the results that were actually observed. Some **inferential statistics**, such as **logistic regression**, calculate a specific goodness of fit value. In addition, there is a goodness of fit **chi-square** test that is used to compare the observed frequencies of a single nominally measured variable with what might be expected by chance.

Grammaticality judgment test (GJT)

A type of data collection **instrument** that asks participants to provide their assessment of the grammaticality of a set of sentences. Technically, these are sometimes referred to as acceptability judgments, because participants are providing their opinions, while grammaticality refers to the inherent qualities of the sentences. The use of grammaticality judgment tests (GJTs) in applied linguistics can be traced back to formal linguistics research where they were used to provide information about linguistic competence and the boundaries of human language, especially from a Universal Grammar perspective in which language was viewed as an innate human characteristic. Currently, GJTs are often used to assess L2 learners' proficiency on linguistic structures. One advantage of GJTs is that they are able to target specific linguistic structures that might be difficult to elicit using other methods. However, GJTs involve conscious processes in which participants are focused on linguistic items, and as such, often encourage the use of explicit linguistic knowledge. GJTs can be designed in several different ways. Participants may simply indicate their judgments, or they may also be asked to provide corrections of any incorrect sentences. Participants may also be asked to indicate their level of certainty in their responses as well as the type of knowledge they used to make their judgments (e.g., a rule, intuition). Participants may have an unlimited period of time to make their responses, or they may have some time limit imposed on them. Finally, GJTs may be delivered in writing or aurally.

Gutiérrez, X. (2013). The construct validity of grammaticality judgment tests as measures of implicit and explicit knowledge. *Studies in Second Language Acquisition, 35*(3), 423–449.

Ionin, T., & Zyzik, E. (2014). Judgment and interpretation tasks in second language research. *Annual Review of Applied Linguistics, 34*, 37–64.

Loewen, S. (2009). Grammaticality judgment tests and the measurement of implicit and explicit L2 knowledge. In R. Ellis, S. Loewen, R. Erlam, J. Philp, C. Elder, & H. Reinders (Eds.), *Implicit and explicit knowledge in second language learning and teaching* (pp. 94–112). Clevedon: Multilingual Matters.

Schütze, C. T., & Sprouse, J. (2014). Judgment data. In R. J. Podesva, & D. Sharma (Eds.), *Research methods in linguistics* (pp. 27–50). Cambridge: Cambridge University Press.

Graphic representation of data

One way to better understand a data set is by creating visual representations of the data itself or of the patterns found therein. Thus, while it is possible to interpret data based on descriptive statistics such as the **mean** and **standard deviation**, it is also possible to do so using charts and graphs. In fact, some researchers have argued in recent years that graphic representations of the data should be used more frequently and in more effective ways in conjunction with statistical analyses (Larson-Hall, 2015; Larson-Hall & Plonsky, 2015). Examples of graphic representations include:

- bar graphs
- box-and-whisker plots
- forest plots
- funnel plots
- histograms
- line graphs
- pie charts
- P–P and Q–Q plots
- stem and leaf plots

Hudson, T. (2015). Presenting quantitative data visually. In L. Plonsky (Ed.), *Advancing quantitative methods in second language research* (pp. 78–105). New York: Routledge.

Larson-Hall, J. (2015). *A guide to doing statistics in second language research using SPSS and R* (2nd ed.). New York: Routledge.

Larson-Hall, J., & Herrington, R. (2010). Improving data analysis in second language acquisition by utilizing modern developments in applied statistics. *Applied Linguistics, 31*, 368–390.

Larson-Hall, J., & Plonsky, L. (2015). Reporting and interpreting quantitative research findings: What gets reported and recommendations for the field. *Language Learning, 65*, Supp. 1, 127–159.

Grounded theory

An inductive approach to generating and supporting theoretical constructs and relationships. Grounded theory is particularly useful when theory is not available to explain a particular phenomenon or experience. Though not a necessarily or exclusively qualitative approach, grounded theory is almost invariably employed with qualitative data resulting, for example, from interviews or observations.

The process embodied by grounded theory is largely bottom-up. The researcher may begin to analyze an interview or transcript in a line-by-line fashion, keeping track of interesting or noteworthy observations. Additional passes through the same text might seek to flesh out these observations, examine possible patterns between them, and/or identify relationships between a participant's context and his/her perceptions therein. The process is highly iterative, with the researcher returning to the data multiple times. True to the approach taken by this and many other qualitative techniques, grounded theorists also arrive at and make arguments for theoretical and empirical findings in a context that recognizes the researchers' experience, background, and patience as all part of the process (Hadley, 2015).

Charmaz, K. (2006). *Constructing grounded theory. A practical guide through qualitative analysis.* London: Sage.

Corbin, J. A., & Strauss, A. (2008). *Basics of qualitative research* (3rd ed.). Thousand Oaks, CA: Sage.

Dillon, D. R. (2012). Grounded theory and qualitative research. In C. Chapelle (Ed.), *The encyclopedia of applied linguistics.* Malden, MA: Wiley Blackwell.

Glaser, B. G. (2001). *The grounded theory perspective: Conceptualization contrasted with description.* Mill Valley, CA: Sociology Press.

Hadley, G. (2015). *English for academic purposes in neoliberal universities: A critical grounded theory.* New York: Springer.

G

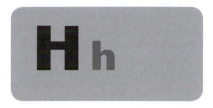

Hierarchical linear modeling (see Mixed effects modeling)

Histogram

A type of data display in which the frequency or occurrence of different values is represented by bars on a graph. The y axis of the graph represents the **frequency**, while the x axis represents points on the scale used to measure the data. In Figure 14, the x axis represents **standard deviations** from the mean, which is represented by zero. The y axis shows how many cases occur at each standard deviation (i.e., distance from the mean score). Thus, nearly 30 cases have a standard deviation of just over zero, while only one or two cases have a standard deviation of 3 or –3. A histogram provides useful information about the distribution of the data. Results may show a **bell curve**, as in the example, with most of the data occurring in the middle of the scale, or histograms may indicate **skewness** in the data, if counts are more

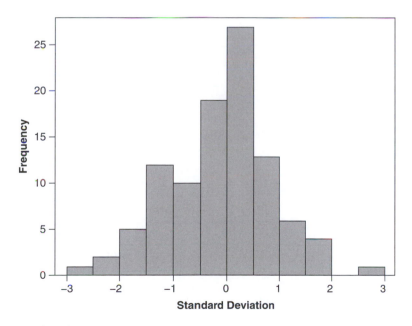

Figure 14   Histogram

frequent towards one end of the scale. Histograms may also show a **bimodal distribution** with two peaks across the scale. A histogram is similar to a **bar graph**; however, typically the x axis in a histogram is a continuous scale, while in a bar graph it consists of categories. Consequently, the columns in bar graphs do not usually touch each other, whereas in histograms, they do. However, these differences are not always maintained.

Homogeneity of variance

An **assumption** of **parametric** statistical tests, such as ***t*-tests** and **analysis of variance (ANOVA)**, that compare the means of two or more groups. Homogeneity of variance assumes that the distribution of data is similar for the groups that are being compared. One method of investigating homogeneity of variance is through visual displays of the data, such as **boxplots**. For example, Figure 15 presents results of a hypothetical study investigating the errors made by native (NSs) and heritage speakers (HSs) of Spanish in identifying mistakes in gender and number. As might be expected, the two groups differed greatly with respect to their mean and variance: NS mean = 4.2, variance = 4.0; HS mean = 10.8, variance = 23.9. In other words, there were very few errors made by NSs in identifying grammatical mistakes; and

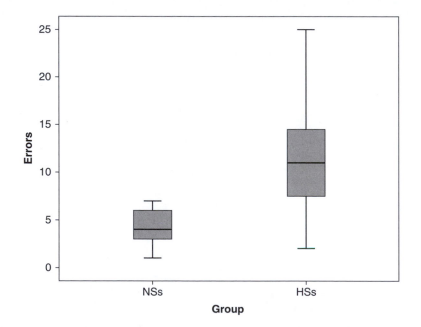

Figure 15 Box-and-whiskers plot showing a lack of homogeneity of variance

as a group, these participants were quite uniform as shown in their low variance and narrow whiskers on the boxplot. In contrast, the whiskers on the HS boxplot are relatively wide. Based on this information, the data would not be considered to have met the assumption of homogeneity of variance.

In addition to examining the descriptives and a graphic representation of the data, homogeneity of variance can also be formally assessed using **Levene's test**. If Levene's test is not significant ($p > .05$), then the researcher can assume that there is no statistical difference in the variance of the two groups. Conversely, if Levene's test is significant ($p < .05$), then the **null hypothesis** that there is no difference in variance between the groups should be rejected, meaning the assumption of homogeneity of variance has been violated. Running Levene's test on the example data from above yields a statistically significant p-value, thus confirming our assessment, based on the descriptives and visuals, of a lack of homogeneity of variance between groups. However, Levene's test is sensitive to large sample sizes, and may return a significant result even if the difference in variance among the groups is not very large. One way to address the violation of the assumption of homogeneity of variance is to apply transformational processes to the data, in which specific statistical procedures are applied equally to all datapoints. In addition, having an equal number of participants in each group can minimize the negative impact of violating this assumption. For ANOVA, it is possible to use Welch or Brown–Forsythe procedures to address heterogeneity of variance.

Hypothesis (see Research hypothesis)

H

Imputation (of data)

A method of data cleaning in statistical analysis in which values are assigned to missing datapoints. In many cases, researchers are not able to obtain complete data sets in which every participant contributes data for every variable. For example, participants may choose not to answer every question on a survey or questionnaire. Because missing data can have a negative influence on statistical analyses, researchers must decide how to address this issue. One possibility is to remove any participants who are missing data, a procedure referred to as "listwise deletion." However, this option can lead to a substantial reduction in the number of participants. Another option is to impute values to replace the missing data, by estimating what those values might have been. One of the more common methods of imputing data is to use the mean score. By so doing, the researcher is left with a more complete data set. This approach will result in a slightly more homogenous view of the sample, however. It is also possible to use other statistical calculations to arrive at replacement values. Nevertheless, all methods of data imputation have their shortcomings, which can affect the accuracy of the analysis. Consequently, data imputation is not common in applied linguistics research. However, Wolf and Jenkins (2014) reanalyzed their workplace literacy data using several different imputation methods, and they provide detailed information regarding this process.

Wolf, A., & Jenkins, A. (2014). Do "learners" always learn? The impact of workplace adult literacy courses on participants' literacy skills. *British Education Research Journal, 40,* 585–609.

Independence (of data)

A characteristic of data whereby each observation comes from a different individual, and one person's data do not affect another's. In contrast, dependent data are related to each other in some way. For example, if a **survey** is given to a group of individuals, each individual should contribute only one survey, and as a result, each person's responses on the survey will be unaffected by the responses of other participants. However, if one individual fills out two surveys, then those data are dependent, because there is a strong probability that the individual will respond to the two surveys in a related way. Independence of data is an **assumption** of several **inferential statistics**. For example, independent samples *t*-tests and one-way **analysis**

of variance both assume that the data are independent. Chi-square is another test that assumes that the data are independent. When the data are not independent, then it is possible to run a paired samples *t*-test or a repeated measures analysis of variance, both of which take into account the dependent or correlated nature of such data sets. Sometimes the term **between-groups** analysis is used for analyzing independent data, while **within-groups** analysis refers to dependent data.

Independent variable

A variable that is investigated for its effects on the **dependent variable**. In other words, it is the variable that is expected to have some impact on the target **construct** in question. Therefore, the independent variable (or variables) is manipulated in some way in order to test its effects. For example, a researcher may wish to test the effects of a specific type of classroom instruction on learning. The researcher would designate the independent variable, such as type of corrective feedback, and then investigate the effects of that independent variable on a dependent variable, such as L2 proficiency. There may be multiple independent variables in a given research study.

Inferential statistics

Statistics that allow researchers to make generalizations about the processes or phenomena that they are studying. Inferential statistics assume that rather than analyzing an entire **population** (e.g., all beginner-level students of Spanish as a foreign language in the United States), it is possible to select a sample that will be representative of the entire population (e.g., beginner-level students of Spanish at Michigan State University). The results of inferential statistics, which are based on the sample, may then be generalized to the broader population if: (a) the sample is sufficiently large (i.e., has sufficient **statistical power**), and (b) it is representative of the population. Inferential statistics contrast with **descriptive statistics** in that the latter only describe what is observed in a data set and do not attempt to go beyond that description. There are many types of inferential statistics, including *t*-tests, **analysis of variance**, **regression**, and **chi-square**.

Informed consent

The idea that participants have the right to know what they are getting into when they agree to participate in a research study. Informed consent is one of the pillars of modern **research ethics** involving human subjects. Thus, it is not considered ethical to have people take part in research studies without their knowledge or agreement. Usually informed consent is obtained before the beginning of a research study. The researcher typically explains the goals and procedures to prospective participants and invites them to participate. Often participants will sign a consent form indicating that they agree to take part in the experiment. In some cases, if prior knowledge of the goals of the research study may affect participants' performance, it is possible to either: (a) describe the general, rather than specific, goals of the research study, or (b) gain informed consent after the data has been collected. The former might involve a researcher conducting a descriptive study of corrective feedback in the classroom, stating that the goal of the research is to examine L2 classroom interaction without mentioning that corrective feedback is the primary focus. In the case when informed consent is obtained at the end of the research, participants are given the opportunity to withdraw their data from the project; such delayed consent is not general practice in applied linguistics research.

Sterling, S. (2015). *Informed consent forms in ESL research: Form difficulty and comprehension.* Unpublished doctoral dissertation. Michigan State University.

Institutional review board (IRB)

An organization, usually at a university, that oversees **research ethics** and approves research projects involving human subjects. Because of abuses committed by researchers in the past, which involved experimenting on people without their knowledge or consent, researchers must now submit their research projects to an IRB, which assesses the ethical nature of the proposed research. Researchers must obtain approval from the IRB before they can begin conducting a research study with human participants. Although IRB is a common designation for this organization in North America, other terms include independent ethics committee or ethical review board. The existence and nature of such boards varies substantially from country to country.

Instrument

A general term referring to data elicitation devices used in empirical research. In other words, instruments are the tools used by researchers to collect data. Instruments may be **surveys**, **questionnaires**, tests, and **interview** protocols, all of which directly elicit data. In addition, other tools such as reading passages, oral texts, or task activities that may not involve direct data elicitation are also considered to be instruments. When reporting research, a description of all instruments used in the study—including their source, development, and piloting procedures—should be included in the Method section (see Derrick, in press). Sometimes the instruments are presented along with the procedures, in an effort to convey simultaneously what was used in the study and how it was used.

Derrick, D. J. (in press). Instrument reporting practices in second language research. *TESOL Quarterly.*

Intact class

A class that is not constituted specifically for research purposes. One of the hallmarks of experimental research is **random sampling**, in which partici-pants are selected randomly to participate in research. However, in applied linguistics research, particularly in classroom contexts, **random selection** is often not practiced because of its unfeasibility. In fact, in many cases, intact classes are used for research purposes, meaning that a researcher observes or provides a treatment to a class that has already been consti-tuted by the educational institution, and the researcher makes no attempt to manipulate the grouping of individuals who are in the class. For example Ammar and Spada (2006) investigated the differential effects of corrective feedback (prompts versus recasts) in three intact grade 6 ESL classes. One class received recasts, one received prompts, and the final class served as a comparison group, which participated in the treatment activities but did not receive corrective feedback. Using intact classes can be a threat to the **validity** of a study, because the sample may be biased in certain ways. For example, by choosing to recruit a morning class rather than an afternoon class, researchers may have students with different individual characteris-tics, who select morning or afternoon classes based on their motivation or other factors. However, using intact classes in research has high **ecological validity**, because research is being conducted on classes as they exist in real life. In some cases, researchers use **pretests** to ensure that intact classes are statistically similar on the construct that is being investigated.

Ammar, A., & Spada, N. (2006). One size fits all? Recasts, prompts, and L2 learning. *Studies in Second Language Acquisition, 28*, 543–574.

Interaction effect

A type of statistical result produced in factorial ANOVAs (and other procedures with two or more independent variables) in which a combined influence of the independent variables on the dependent variable is observed. It is possible to have two-way interaction effects, three-way interaction effects, and so on, depending on the number of independent variables. However, the most common interaction effects in applied linguistics research are two-way, with larger interaction effects being harder to interpret. One of the more com-monly observed cases of interaction effects is found in quasi-experimental research investigating the effects of L2 instruction on multiple groups over time. In such cases, researchers want to know if there is a differential effect

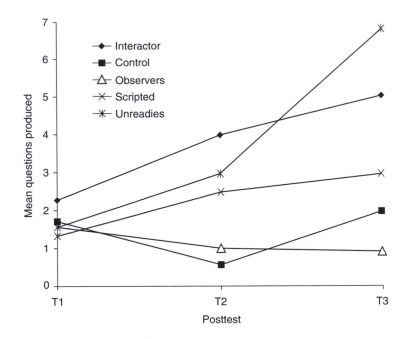

Source: Mackey (1999, p. 573; Figure 3).

Figure 16   Line graph showing an interaction effect

for instruction, a result which is indicated by the presence of a statistically significant interaction effect. Similarly, different levels of proficiency might respond to experimental treatments differently. In this case, we would say that there is an interaction between the independent variables of proficiency and treatment condition.

In addition to reporting the statistical results, it is often helpful to use line graphs to visualize the relationship between the two variables. Parallel lines indicate a lack of interaction, while non-parallel lines indicate an interaction effect. For example, in a study of corrective feedback provided to several different groups of L2 learners, Mackey (1999) found a marginally significant interaction between the variables Group and Time [$F(8, 58) = 1.99$, $MSE = 5.89, p = .080$], indicating that not all groups increased equally from Test 1 to Test 2 and Test 3. Mackey used a line graph to show that while some groups' scores decreased or remained steady over time, other groups' scores increased (Figure 16).

See also **Main effect.**

Mackey, A. (1999). Input, interaction and second language development: An empirical study of question formation in ESL. *Studies in Second Language Acquisition, 21,* 557–587.

Internal validity (see Validity)

Interquartile range (IQR)

A measure of **dispersion** in a given set of values, indicating the spread of the scores. More specifically, the interquartile range (IQR) specifies the scores that constitute the lower and upper bounds of the 25th and 75th **percentile**, respectively. The IQR as a measure of dispersion can also be seen in **boxplots**, where the lower and upper edges of the box represent the 25th and 75th percentiles, respectively. The boxplots in Figure 17, adapted from Plonsky and Oswald (2014), provide a visual representation of **correlation** coefficients collected from 175 primary studies and 20 meta-analyses. Although the **median** values of the two data sets are very similar (close to $r = .40$, as shown by the bar across the middle of each box), their IQRs are different, as illustrated by the size of the boxes; the IQR of the meta-analytic correlations is clearly somewhat larger, ranging from roughly $r = .25$ to .65, compared with the IQR of primary study correlations, which ranges from $r = .25$ to just over .50. The IQR may be a more appropriate indicator of variability, particularly when working with a non-normal distribution in which the median is determined to be a more appropriate measure of **central tendency.** In contrast, **variance**

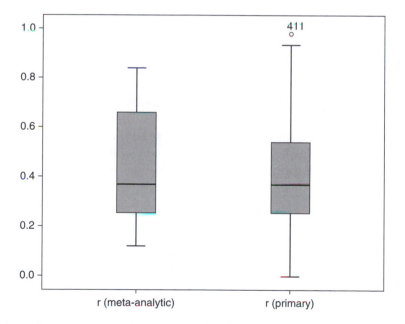

Source: Adapted from Plonsky & Oswald (2014).

Figure 17 Boxplots of correlation coefficients (*r*) from meta-analytic and primary study data sets

or **standard deviation** is generally reported along with the **mean** when the data have a **normal distribution**.

Plonsky, L., & Oswald, F. L. (2014). How big is 'big'? Interpreting effect sizes in L 2 research. *Language Learning, 64,* 878–912.

Inter-rater reliability

The consistency in coding that exists when data are analyzed by more than one individual. In many cases, coding categories may be somewhat subjective, so in order to ensure that the coding accurately follows the rubric, researchers may have one or more additional individuals code all or a portion of the data. For this process, the second rater is trained to use the coding rubric and is then given data to code. Inter-rater reliability may be calculated as a simple **percentage** agreement; however, **Cohen's kappa** can also be used, which is a more conservative measure of reliability because it helps correct for chance agreement. There is no fixed cutoff for considering inter-rater reliability to be acceptable, but the higher the agreement, the better. Often a percentage agreement of 80–90% is considered acceptable. In an effort to determine the normal range of estimates of inter-rater reliability (as well as internal consistency and intra-rater reliability) in L2 research, Plonsky and Derrick (under review) meta-analyzed 2,244 reliability coefficients from 532 studies. The median (50th percentile) observed for inter-rater reliability estimates was .92. The authors also suggested that the 25th percentile in the sample, .83, might be considered a minimally acceptable level of inter-rater agreement.

In cases where there is disagreement between raters, there are several remedies. One is for raters to consult with each other, and to come to a consensus through negotiation regarding the discrepancies in coding. Another option is for the disputed data to be removed from the analysis. Finally, an additional rater can be brought in to provide another perspective.

Another issue in inter-rater reliability is how much data should be double-coded. If the data set is not all that large, both raters might code all the data; however, in analyses with large amounts of data, a subset of the data is often coded. In general, between 10–20% of the data is considered adequate, especially if there is a high level of agreement. The amount of data coded and the minimal level of agreement required also depends somewhat on the nature of the variable being coded. Some variables are low inference, meaning that coding is fairly objective and easy. For example, the presence or absence of a student response after the provision of corrective feedback might be considered fairly low inference. However, with high inference categories, which may be more subjective, a larger amount of data may need to be double-coded to make sure that the categories are being interpreted similarly by both individuals. For example, the successfulness of the student responses following corrective feedback might be more of a high inference category. An example of inter-rater reliability is presented in Simpson-Vlach and Ellis' (2010) study of academic formulaic language, in which they employed Cronbach's alpha to investigate the level of agreement in raters' responses to three surveys. Survey A measured whether raters thought phrases were fixed expressions: inter-rater $\alpha = .77$; Survey B measured whether raters thought phrases had a cohesive meaning: inter-rater $\alpha = .67$; Survey C measured whether raters thought the phrases were worth teaching: inter-rater $\alpha = .83$. The results indicated that Survey C had the highest level of rater agreement, while Survey B had the lowest.

See **Intraclass correlation**.

Plonsky, L., & Derrick, D. J. (under review). A meta-analysis of reliability coefficients in second language research. Manuscript under review

Simpson-Vlach, R., & Ellis, N. C. (2010). An academic formulas list: New methods in phraseology research. *Applied Linguistics, 31*, 487–512.

Interval variable

Another term for a **continuous variable**.

Interview

A type of data collection in which the researcher uses questions to elicit responses from one or more research participants. Interviews are an important component of **qualitative research**, in which the researcher attempts to understand the perspective of another individual. Interviews are particularly useful in gaining insight into non-observable phenomena: attitudes, beliefs, and cognitive processes such as noticing. There are several types of interviews that range in terms of their flexibility. In a structured interview, the least flexible type, the researcher develops a set of questions before the interview, and then asks a number of individuals the same set of questions in order to see how each person responds to identical stimuli. Subsequently, the researcher can compare responses related to specific topics. Structured interviews are comparable to **questionnaires** or **surveys** with a fixed set of questions. Semi-structured interviews also include a set of predetermined questions; however, the researcher has the freedom to follow up on specific topics, and to ask additional questions. Finally, unstructured interviews, the most flexible type of interview, do not have a predetermined number or set of questions. Instead, the researcher follows the course of the interview, following up on interesting topics and encouraging the interviewee to say more.

In addition to asking questions, researchers may use other oral or written stimuli to elicit participants' responses. For example, in a **stimulated recall** interview, participants may be shown a video clip of a previous classroom encounter and asked what they were thinking at the time of the action. Other types of interviews might present individuals with novel stimuli, in order to elicit their thoughts and opinions about them.

Interviews allow researchers to investigate phenomena that might not otherwise be accessible. In addition, interviews can allow participants to express their own views and raise topics that are important to themselves rather than simply responding to topics identified by the researcher. Interviews also allow researchers to follow up on vague or unclear responses, something that is not usually possible in a written **survey** or **questionnaire**.

There are also several disadvantages of interviewing. First, it is time-consuming, thereby limiting the number of participants that may be included. Consequently, interview data are generally analyzed qualitatively, with the purpose of gaining a deeper understanding of a few individuals and contexts, rather than trying to make broad generalizations by gathering data from numerous participants. Interviewers must also be careful to minimize their influence on the interviewee, by avoiding leading questions or indicating that some responses are better than others. Yet another downside of interviews is that they do not generally allow the interviewee the anonymity that might be possible using questionnaire- or survey-based approaches.

One type of interview that involves multiple participants is a focus group, in which two or more individuals are gathered together by the researcher and are asked to respond to questions about and to discuss a specific topic.

Hyland, K., & Zuengler, J. (Eds.) (2011). Qualitative interviews in applied linguistics: Discursive perspectives [Special Issue]. *Applied Linguistics, 32*(1).

Miller, E. R. (2011). Indeterminacy and interview research: Co-constructing ambiguity and clarity in interviews with an adult immigrant learner of English. *Applied Linguistics, 32*, 43–59.

Intraclass correlation (ICC)

A measure of **inter-rater reliability** or consistency across raters. The ICC is particularly useful in cases where more than two raters are involved and/or raters do not all rate the same samples. In this sense, ICC is more flexible than other indices for inter-rater reliability, such as **Cronbach's alpha**. However, ICC can also be more complicated, because there are three different types or models of ICC coefficients, each of which makes different assumptions about the data and the raters. Model 1, for example, is only appropriate when a set of raters are selected at random to assess subjects from the population of raters. This model rarely applies in applied linguistics. In Model 2, raters have been selected at random again, but all samples are rated by all raters. Model 3 shares with Model 2 the condition that all samples are rated by all raters, but it differs in that the sample of raters equals the population of raters of interest. There are also subtypes within each of these models, derived on the basis of the formula used to calculate the reliability estimate. All can be calculated using **SPSS**.

One area of applied linguistics where intraclass correlations are commonly found is in research on L2 pronunciation. Isaacs and Trofimovich (2012), for example, asked three experienced ESL teachers to rate 30 speaking samples on a nine-point comprehensibility scale. Simply averaging the raters' scores for each sample might have mistakenly assumed consistency across raters' and, indeed, even though the scores provided by raters 1 and 2 were sufficiently correlated, less of a consensus was found when rater 3's scores were included. If one of the raters diverges substantially from the other two, for example, the researchers may choose to exclude his or her ratings or to engage in further rater training/calibration. Finally, compared to other indices used to estimate inter-rater reliability, ICC generally provides a slightly more generous view of agreement (Plonsky & Derrick, under review).

Field, A. P. (2005) Intraclass correlation. In B. S. Everitt, & D. C. Howell (Eds.), *Encyclopedia of statistics in behavioral sciences*. Chichester, England: Wiley.

Isaacs, T., & Trofimovich, P. (2012). Deconstructing comprehensibility: Identifying the linguistic influences on listeners' L2 comprehensibility ratings. *Studies in Second Language Acquisition, 34*, 475–505.

McGraw, K. O., & Wong, S. P. (1996). Forming inferences about some intraclass correlation coefficients. *Psychological Methods, 1*, 30–46.

Plonsky, L., & Derrick, D. J. (under review). A meta-analysis of reliability coefficients in second language research. [Manuscript under review].

Shrout, P. E., & Fleiss, J. L. (1979) Intraclass correlations: Uses in assessing rater reliability. *Psychological Bulletin, 2*, 420–428.

Intra-rater reliability

A method of dual coding of data to ensure that the coding categories or scores are being used in a consistent manner. However, instead of another individual coding part of the data, intra-rater coding involves the researcher coding the data again after some period of time. In other words, the researcher establishes his or her coding categories (or scale) and at that time codes the data. Sometime later, often after several weeks, the researcher goes back to the data, and without looking at the previous results, recodes the data. Then the researcher calculates the degree of agreement between the coding at time one and time two. For example, Riazantseva (2012) double-coded 15% of all the writing samples in her study on the effects of written corrective feedback, although she did not specify the amount of time between coding sessions for characteristics such as grammatical and lexical errors. She had an intra-rater reliability rate of 96%. A **percentage** agreement of 80–90% is desirable; however, lower rates of agreement may be acceptable, especially if the study is exploratory. Because they are based on the decisions of a single individual, estimates of intra-rater reliability can also be expected to be higher than inter-rater reliability estimates (see Plonsky & Derrick, under review). Intra-rater reliability coding is not as common in applied linguistics research as is **inter-rater reliability**.

Plonsky, L., & Derrick, D. J. (under review). A meta-analysis of reliability coefficients in second language research. [Manuscript under review.]

Riazantseva, A. (2012). Outcome measure of L2 writing as a mediator of the effects of corrective feedback on students' ability to write accurately. *System, 40*, 421–430.

IQR (see Interquartile range)

IRB (see Institutional review board)

IRIS database

A resource developed in the early 2010s, the IRIS database is a free, online repository of research **instruments** and materials. Researchers may upload any such materials that they have used in previously published studies, making them available for anyone to download. One aim of IRIS is to make **replication** of research studies simpler by allowing researchers easy access to previously used materials.

IRIS: A digital repository of data collection instruments for research in second-language learning and teaching. Available from http://www.iris-database.org/iris/app/home/index

Marsden, E., Mackey, A., & Plonsky, L. (in press). Breadth and depth: The IRIS repository. In A. Mackey & E. Marsden (Eds.), *Instruments for research into second languages: Empirical studies advancing methodology*. New York: Routledge.

Item response theory

An approach to assessment that seeks to understand the psychometric properties of test items. Item response theory (IRT) is often discussed in contrast to classical test theory, which considers tests at the level of analysis rather than items. Indeed, estimates of **reliability** such as **Cronbach's alpha** provide information about the test in general. By contrast, IRT and the larger approach embodied by Latent Trait Models focus on item-level analysis and are able to make generalizations about underlying constructs beyond the sample. Interest among applied linguistics in IRT and many-facet Rasch measurement has increased substantially in recent years (McNamara & Knoch, 2012).

Ellis, D. P., & Ross, S. J. (2014). Item response theory in language testing. In A. J. Kunnan (Ed.), *The companion to language assessment*. Malden, MA: Wiley. DOI: 10.1002/9781118411360.wbcla016

Knoch, U., & McNamara, T. (2015). Rasch analysis. In L. Plonsky (Ed.). *Advancing quantitative methods in second language research* (pp. 279–308). New York: Routledge.

McNamara, T. (1996). *Measuring second language performance*. London & New York: Longman.

McNamara, T., & Knoch, U. (2012). The Rasch Wars: The emergence of Rasch measurement in language testing. *Language Testing, 29*(4), 553–574.

Wright, B. D. (1992). Raw scores are not linear measures: Rasch vs. Classical Test Theory CTT comparison. *Rasch Measurement Transactions, 6*(1), 208.

κ (see Cohen's kappa)

Kolmogorov–Smirnov test
A test that determines whether a data set meets the **assumption** of having a **normal distribution**. The Kolmogorov–Smirnov test compares the distribution of the actual data against a hypothetical, and normally distributed, set of data using the same **mean** and **standard deviation** as the real data. If the results of the test are non-significant, it means that there is no difference between the two distributions, and the researcher can state that the assumption of a normal distribution has been met. However, if the test result is statistically significant, then the data can be assumed to have a non-normal distribution. The Kolmogorov–Smirnov test is similar to the **Shapiro–Wilk test**, but the latter has more power to detect non-normal distributions and can be more appropriate for use with sample sizes of around 50 or smaller. However, both tests are sensitive to sample size and may be more likely to return a significant result for a large sample size, even though the violation may be slight. Consequently, it is important to use multiple methods, including **skewness** and **kurtosis** values, and visual inspection of data to investigate the assumption of the normal distribution of data.

Kruskal–Wallis test
A **non-parametric** test used to compare scores from three or more groups. The Kruskal–Wallis test, which is equivalent to a parametric one-way **ANOVA,** assumes that the data are **independent**, but it does not assume that the data are normally distributed. Instead of using mean scores to investigate differences between the groups, it uses the rank order of the data to make comparisons. Oliver (2002) used Kruskal–Wallis tests to investigate the negotiation patterns of children when interacting with interlocutors who varied according to L1, age, L2 proficiency, and gender. Among other results, Oliver found statistically significant differences in the number of negotiation strategies based on the L1 composition of the **dyads**, with non-native speaker pairs having greater amounts of negotiation than mixed native/non-native pairs or native speaker pairs. She reported the Kruskal–Wallis results for the comprehension checks as χ^2 (2, N = 141), 19.17, p < .0001 (p. 103).

Oliver, R. (2002). The pattern of negotiation for meaning in child interactions. *Modern Language Journal, 86*, 97–111.

Kurtosis

A problem with numeric data in which the peak of a **normal distribution** is either too high or too low, thereby adversely affecting the results of **parametric statistics**. Kurtosis values much larger than 3 imply a high peak (a leptokurtotic distribution; see Figure 18), while values much smaller than 3 imply a flat or platykurtotic distribution (see Figure 19). Kurtosis values close to 3 imply a normal distribution without kurtosis. Although statistical software packages such as **SPSS** provide measures of kurtosis, it is not an assumption that is frequently checked or reported in applied linguistics research.

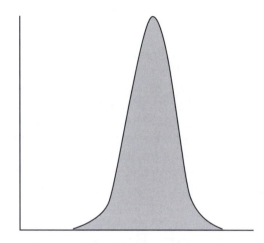

Figure 18 Leptokurtotic distribution

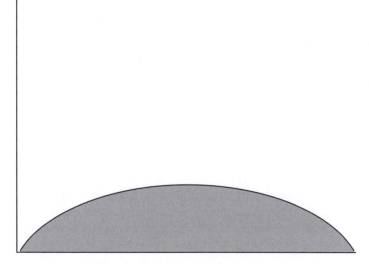

Figure 19 Platykurtotic distribution

Laboratory-based research

Research that is conducted in a researcher-controlled environment to which participants are brought. Much **quantitative research** is conducted in laboratories because it is easier to manipulate the topic of investigation and limit the influence of extraneous variables. As a result of the greater experimental control available, larger effects are often observed in lab-based research (e.g., Li, 2010; Plonsky & Oswald, 2014; cf. Gass, Mackey, & Ross-Feldman, 2005). In addition, lab research can be particularly useful in the context of quantitative research, which is generally interested in a close analysis of specific variables rather than a holistic interpretation of a larger context. One concern about laboratory studies is their **generalizability** to other contexts. For example, in the area of instructed SLA, there is disagreement about the applicability of laboratory-based studies to the classroom, with some researchers suggesting that instructed SLA research should happen primarily in the classroom and not the lab (e.g., Nunan, 1991). Proponents of lab-based instructional studies argue that the messiness of conducting classroom research and the difficulty of controlling extraneous variables means that it is difficult to draw conclusions about specific variables because there are too many intervening variables. For these reasons, it may be advisable to test and verify (quasi-)experimental effects in lab contexts before any such attempts in classrooms. This approach is also more ethical in the sense that valuable class time is less likely to be wasted on treatments that have yet to be confirmed under highly controlled conditions.

Foster, P. (1998). A classroom perspective on the negotiation of meaning. *Applied Linguistics, 19*, 1–23.

Gass, S., Mackey, A., & Ross-Feldman, L. (2005). Task-based interactions in classroom and laboratory setting. *Language Learning, 55*, 575–611.

Hulstijn, J. (1997). Second language acquisition research in the laboratory: Possibilities and limitations. *Studies in Second Language Acquisition, 19*, 131–143.

Li, S. (2010). The effectiveness of corrective feedback in SLA: A meta-analysis. *Language Learning, 60*, 309–365.

Nunan, D. (1991). Methods in second language classroom-oriented research: A critical review. *Studies in Second Language Acquisition, 13*, 249–274.

Plonsky, L., & Oswald, F. L. (2014). How big is 'big'? Interpreting effect sizes in L2 research. *Language Learning, 64*, 878–912.

Yang, L. R., & Givón, T. (1997). Benefits and drawbacks of controlled laboratory studies of second language acquisition: The Keck second language learning project. *Studies in Second Language Acquisition, 19*, 173–193.

Latent variable

A term often used in **factor analysis** and **structural equation modeling** to refer to variables that are not directly measured but instead, are identified inductively by analyzing a combination of the observed variables measured in the study. Also referred to as underlying **constructs**, latent variables are considered to be more fundamental or basic than other variables. For example, Loewen et al. (2009), in their factor analytic study of learner beliefs about grammar and error correction, asked the following **research question**: *What underlying constructs [latent variables] are present in L2 learners' responses to a questionnaire regarding their beliefs about grammar instruction and error correction?* (p. 93). The factor analysis reduced the researchers' 28-item questionnaire to six factors, which the researchers identified as latent variables, such as Efficacy of Grammar, Negative Attitudes to Error Correction, and Priority of Communication, based on the observed questionnaire items that loaded on each factor.

> Loewen, S., Li, S., Fei, F., Thompson, A., Nakatsukasa, K., Ahn, S., & Chen, X. (2009). Second language learners' beliefs about grammar instruction and error correction. *Modern Language Journal, 93*, 91–104.

Latin square design

A type of counterbalanced research design in which values are placed in a **contingency table** that is the size of the number of categories (i.e., 2 × 2 for two categories, 3 × 3 for three categories): each value appears in only one row and one column. A Latin square design is sometimes used in studies with multiple data collection **instruments** and sessions in order to avoid finding an effect based on differences in the instruments or order of data collection. For example, a researcher may wish to administer a **pretest**, immediate **posttest**, and **delayed posttest**, resulting in three categories. One way to minimize a test effect in which participants get better simply because they are familiar with the test items is to have multiple versions of the test, A, B and C (three categories), so that a participant has different but equivalent items on each testing occasion. However, the order of the presentation of the tests might affect participant performance, so having some participants take each version of the test on each testing occasion helps minimize the effect of order of presentation. Table 12 indicates the design that a researcher could use in such a scenario, with a third of the research participants each taking the tests in a different order.

Table 12 Latin square design

Pretest	Immediate Posttest	Delayed Posttest
A	B	C
B	C	A
C	A	B

Levene's test

A test used to assess the **assumption** of **homogeneity of variance**, which is an assumption of tests comparing **means**, such as *t*-tests and **ANOVAs**. Levene's test assumes that there is no difference in the variance of two groups; consequently, a statistically significant *p*-value indicates that the assumption has been violated, while a non-significant value indicates that the assumption of homogeneity of variance has been met. For example, Uggen (2012) reported that Levene's test indicated that the assumption of homogeneity of variance was not met ($p = .032$) in her data set; therefore, she used non-parametric tests, which do not assume homogeneity of variance, to analyze her data.

Levene's test is sensitive to sample size, so that even a small difference in variances may produce a statistically significant result with a large sample size. Homogeneity of variance can also be inspected visually, using **box-and-whisker plots**.

Uggen, M. S. (2012). Reinvestigating the noticing function of output. *Language Learning, 62*, 506–540.

Likert scale

A numeric scale that is used to assess the strength of participants' responses to specific questions or statements. For example, in a **survey** or **questionnaire**, participants may be asked to indicate how strongly they agree or disagree with a statement by choosing a number between a certain range. Often that range is from 1 to 5, but it may vary anywhere from a three-point scale (1–3) and up. In L2 pronunciation research, for example, Likert scales with seven or even nine points are often used to indicate raters' perceptions of L2-speaker comprehensibility (e.g., Saito & Lyster, 2012). In addition to providing a numeric response for participants, there are often descriptors provided to accompany numeric ratings. Sometimes only the poles of the scale are labeled, such as *strongly agree/strongly disagree*; in other cases, each individual choice is labeled. A potential issue to consider in designing a Likert scale is whether to have an odd or even number of possible responses. The advantage of having an even number is that it forces respondents to express some agreement or disagreement, even if only slight. In contrast, an odd number of responses allows participants to indicate that they have no preference in either direction. Technically, Likert scale data are ordinal because the values do not represent true numeric distinctions; however, Likert scale data are often treated as continuous and are subjected to analyses using **means** and **standard deviations**. The advantages of using a Likert scale are that it is easy for participants to respond to, and the data are easy to analyze. However, disadvantages include possible uncertainty in assuming that the respondents interpreted the questions and responses in the same manner as each other and as the researcher.

The following questions from Loewen et al. (2014, p. 384) show a six-point Likert scale with descriptors on each end of the scale but none between points.

1. To what extent do you identify yourself as a researcher? (circle one)
   Not at all   Exclusively
   1   2   3   4   5   6
2. To what extent do you conduct *quantitative* research? (circle one)
   Not at all   Exclusively
   1   2   3   4   5   6
3. To what extent do you conduct *qualitative* research? (circle one)
   Not at all   Exclusively
   1   2   3   4   5   6

In contrast, the questions in Table 13 from Winke (2013, p. 266) show Likert scales with five, individually labeled points.

Table 13   Likert scale items

Section II. LISTENING In ENGLISH ...	Not at all	With much difficulty	With some difficulty	With very little difficulty	Easily
1. I can understand simple questions in social situations such as "How are you?", "Where do you live?", and "How are you feeling today?"	1	2	3	4	5
2. I can understand someone who is speaking slowly and who is giving me directions on how to walk to a nearby location.	1	2	3	4	5
3. I can understand headline news broadcasts on the radio.	1	2	3	4	5
4. I can understand a recorded message that is left for me on my cell phone or answering machine.	1	2	3	4	5

Dörnyei, Z., with Taguchi, I. (2010). *Questionnaires in second language research: Construction, administration, and processing* (2nd ed.). London: Routledge.

Loewen, S., Lavolette, B., Spino, L., Papi, M., Schmidtke, J., Sterling, S., & Wolff, D. (2014). Statistical literacy among applied linguists and second language acquisition researchers. *TESOL Quarterly, 48*, 360–388.

McDonough, K., & Mackey, A. (Eds.) (2013). *Second language interaction in diverse educational contexts* (pp. 247–268). Philadelphia: John Benjamins.

Saito, K., & Lyster, R. (2012). Effects of form-focused instruction and corrective feedback on L2 pronunciation development of /r/ by Japanese learners of English. *Language Learning, 62*, 595–633.

Winke, P. (2013). The effectiveness of interactive group orals for placement testing. In K. McDonough & A. Mackey (Eds.), *Second language interaction in diverse educational contexts: Language learning & language teaching* (pp. 247–268). Amsterdam: John Benjamins.

Line graph

A graph in which datapoints are illustrated with a line going from point to point. Line graphs, found by Hudson (2015) to be the most commonly used visual display of data in a sample of articles from five applied linguistics journals, are frequently used to present changes observed over time, as found, for example, in results from quasi-experimental studies that have multiple groups with **pretest** and **posttest** scores. The slope of the line from pretest to posttest provides a clear visual representation of participants' performance over time. In addition, comparing the slopes of two or more groups can provide information about any two-way **interaction effects** that are present in the data. In many instances, line graphs are followed up with **inferential statistics** in order to determine the magnitude and importance of any differences exhibited in the graphs.

In Figure 20, Derwing, Munro, Thomson, and Rossiter (2009) illustrate the difference in fluency ratings of Mandarin and Slavic groups at three different

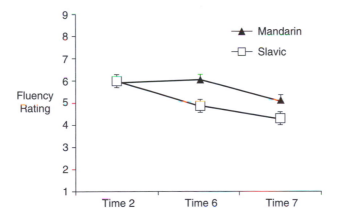

Source: Derwing, Munro, Thomson & Rossiter (2009, p. 544).

Figure 20 Line graph [mean fluency ratings for Mandarin and Slavic groups (1 = extremely fluent, 9 = extremely disfluent)]

time periods. The line graph shows that overall, both groups decreased; however, Mandarin speakers decreased only from time 6 to time 7, while the Slavic group decreased each time. Though easy to interpret, one downside to most line graphs is that they generally do not include information about the dispersion around the mean scores they present (see Larson-Hall & Plonsky, 2015; Weissgerber, Milic, Winham, & Garovic, 2015).

Derwing, T., Munro, M., Thomson, R., & Rossiter, M. (2009). The relationship between L1 fluency and L2 fluency. *Studies in Second Language Acquisition, 31*, 533–557.

Hudson, T. (2015). Presenting quantitative data visually. In L. Plonsky (Ed.), *Advancing quantitative methods in second language research* (pp. 78–105). New York: Routledge.

Larson-Hall, J., & Plonsky, L. (2015). Reporting and interpreting quantitative research findings: What gets reported and recommendations for the field. *Language Learning, 65*(Supp. 1), 125–157.

Weissgerber, T. L., Milic, N. M., Winham, S. K., & Garovic, V. D. (2015). Beyond bar and line graphs: Time for a new data presentation paradigm. *PLoS One Biology, 13*, e1002128.

Linear regression

A statistical procedure that, like **correlation**, examines the strength of the relationship between two measured variables. Linear regression differs from correlation, however, in its predictive ability. Whereas a correlation can only indicate the extent to which two variables move up or down in tandem, a regression can be used to predict the values of one variable, such as reading comprehension, based on the values of another variable, such as vocabulary size. A regression with only one dependent (also called *criterion* or *outcome*) variable and one predictor variable is referred to as a univariate regression. Linear regression models also differ from correlation in that they can integrate multiple predictor variables. In doing so, researchers are able to produce predictions for their criterion variable that take additional factors and measures into account based on theoretical and/or practical considerations. Expanding on the example variables from above, this type of multivariate (or multiple) regression might allow researchers to make a prediction about a learner's score on a test of reading comprehension based on scores for different variables such as L1 reading level, as well as L2 lexical and grammatical knowledge. The output of a linear regression analysis, whether univariate or multivariate, provides R^2 values, which indicate the amount of variance in the criterion variable that can be accounted for by the predictor variables, both individually and collectively. Beta values are also provided for each predictor, which enable the researcher to estimate values of the criterion variable.

See also **Multiple regression**.

Jeon, E. H. (2015). Multiple regression. In L. Plonsky (Ed.), *Advancing quantitative methods in second language research* (pp. 131-158). New York: Routledge.

Loess line

A line applied to **scatterplots** in **correlations** and **regressions** that is based on small subsets of the data rather than the entire data set. Often a regression line is added to a scatterplot to investigate the **assumption** of linearity in the data. The regression line is a straight line that is placed in such a way as to best account for the relationship between the two variables being examined. However, a regression line may not provide the most faithful or fitting representation of the relationship between the two measured variables. A Loess line, by contrast, provides a more accurate representation of the data because it is not required to be straight and may indicate a **curvilinear** relationship. The two scatterplots below include both a regression line (the straight, dotted line) and a Loess line (the curved, solid line). In Figure 21, the Loess and regression lines are similar, indicating that the data have a linear distribution. However, in Figure 22, the Loess line varies considerably from the regression line and indicates that the data are curvilinear, rather than linear.

Larson-Hall, J., & Herrington, R. (2010). Improving data analysis in second language acquisition by utilizing modern developments in applied statistics. *Applied Linguistics, 31*, 368–190.

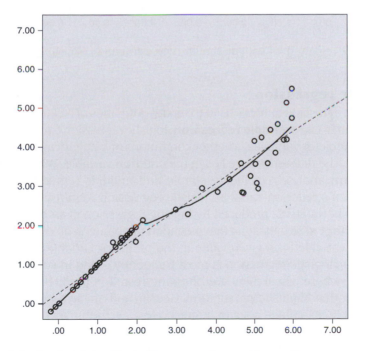

Figure 21   Scatterplot with similar regression and Loess lines

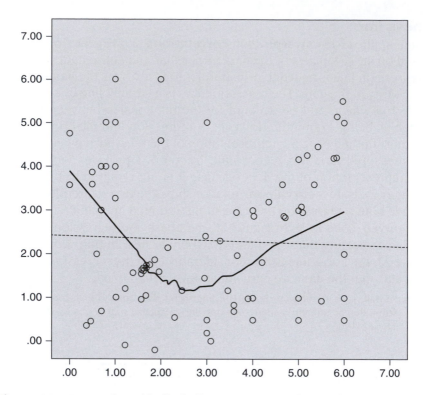

Figure 22   Scatterplot with dissimilar regression and Loess lines

Logistic regression

A type of regression analysis used to model outcomes of a categorical criterion variable. Like **multiple regression**, logistic regression can be used with several predictor variables, whether continuous or categorical, to predict an outcome. The difference here lies in the criterion variable. Whereas **linear regression** analyses, including simple and multiple regression, involve a continuous criterion variable, logistic regression requires a categorical one. One key statistic produced by logistic regression is an **odds ratio**: a type of **effect size** indicating the likelihood of obtaining an outcome in the criterion variable for a given value in the predictor variable(s). In applied linguistics, logistic regression is most frequently found in sociolinguistics research, where researchers are often interested in predicting the use of one or another linguistic variant form. Geeslin and Guijarro-Fuentes (2008), for example, examined a set of linguistic (e.g., +/-animacy) and extralinguistic (e.g., level of education, age) predictors of the use of *estar* (vs. *ser*) in bilingual and monolingual speakers of Spanish. Logistic regression was appropriate because the criterion variable, the presence or absence of *estar*, is a categorical variable. A number of variables such as predicate type and adjective class, were found to be significant predictors of the speakers' choice of copula. In addition, these predictors varied across the participants' language backgrounds.

See also **VARBRUL**.

Geeslin, K. L., & Guijarro-Fuentes, P. (2008). Variation in contemporary Spanish: Linguistic predictors of estar in four cases of language contact. *Bilingualism: Language and Cognition, 11*, 365–380.

Logit

A standardized measure of a given score (e.g., test-taker ability) relative to other factors, such as item difficulty and rater severity. The use of logit scores carries with it several benefits that are particularly useful in the context of language assessment. First, because logits are standardized values, they can be treated as **interval scale** data, which assumes that the difference between any two consecutive values is identical (e.g., the difference between 1 and 2 is the same as between 4 and 5). Further, and perhaps more importantly, when used in **Rasch analysis**, logits place all variables on a common logit scale, thereby facilitating a greater understanding of the relationships between them. For example, if a test-taker and a given item on a test fall at the same logit value, regardless of what that value may be, then that test-taker has an equal chance of correctly or incorrectly answering the item (Knoch & McNamara, 2015). Winke, Gass, and Myford (2014), for example, mapped and compared logit scores on a scale of -6 to +6 for a number of variables related to test-takers' scores, such as rater severity and task difficulty. A general aim of the study was to uncover sources of potential rater bias, such as rater familiarity with the L1s of test-takers. In the absence of such bias, the logit scores for test-taker L1 and for raters would be expected to be uniformly close to zero.

Knoch, U., & McNamara, T. (2015). Rasch analysis. In L. Plonsky (Ed.), *Advancing quantitative methods in second language research* (pp. 279–308). New York: Routledge.

McNamara, T. (1996). *Measuring second language performance.* London & New York: Longman.

McNamara, T., & Knoch, U. (2012). The Rasch Wars: The emergence of Rasch measurement in language testing. *Language Testing, 29*(4), 553–574.

Winke, P., Gass, S., & Myford, C. (2014). Raters' L2 background as a potential source of bias in rating oral performance. *Language Testing, 30*, 231–252.

Wright, B. D. (1992). Raw scores are not linear measures: Rasch vs. Classical Test Theory CTT comparison. *Rasch Measurement Transactions, 6*(1), 208.

Longitudinal design

A type of research that occurs over a period of time. There is no agreed upon length of time, but generally in applied linguistics research, studies conducted over one or two weeks, or longer, are considered longitudinal;

however, in some cases, longitudinal studies are conducted over a period of years. In many cases, because of the long-term nature of the research, longitudinal research involves only a small number of individuals or cases. A benefit of conducting longitudinal research is that it can show how language develops over time within specific individuals. In contrast, **cross-sectional** research relies on sampling learners at different proficiency levels to make inferences about those proficiency levels. Derwing and Munro (2013) undertook a seven-year examination of the speaking skills of L2 learners of English from participants with Mandarin and Slavic L1 backgrounds. In addition to the L1 differences observed, the longitudinal data revealed the non-linear development of pronunciation skills that took place over time. For example, the only major gains for Slavic speakers' accents took place during their first two years in the target language environment. Another example of a longitudinal investigation is Schmitt's (1998) study of vocabulary development in three adult learners of English with advanced proficiency. True to the depth-over-breadth focus often found in longitudinal designs, Schmitt used a number of different measures to examine the participants' knowledge—and change in knowledge over the course of a year—of 11 target words.

Longitudinal research is often qualitative in nature and includes case studies and ethnographies, which often aim to provide thick and rich description of a context, rather than providing only numeric representations of **constructs**. For example, Wolff (2015) followed four MA-TESOL students during their first two semesters of study. Using journal entries, observations, and **interviews**, Wolff documented the changes that took place in the participants' identities as L2 teachers, as a result of their involvement in coursework and a teaching practicum.

However, as in the example studies by Derwing and Munro (2013) and Schmitt (1998), it is certainly possible for **quantitative research** to be longitudinal as well. One of the more common types of quantitative, longitudinal design involves a **delayed posttest**, often two weeks or more, after an experimental **treatment**. In the case of quantitative analyses, several unique challenges arise, such as the handling of data dependencies and modeling non-linear change over time. Fortunately, a number of statistical tools, in addition to repeated measures t-tests and ANOVAs, have been developed for such situations, including multilevel modeling and latent growth curve modeling. See Barkaoui (2014) for an overview of these procedures as well as a more general review of the types of longitudinal research that have been carried out in applied linguistics.

Barkaoui, K. (2014). Quantitative approaches for analyzing longitudinal data in second language research. *Annual Review of Applied Linguistics, 34*, 65–101.

Cunnings, I., & Finlayson, I. (2015). Mixed effects modeling and longitudinal data analysis. In L. Plonsky (Ed.), *Advancing quantitative methods in second language research* (pp. 159–181). New York: Routledge.

Derwing, T. M., & Munro, M. J. (2013). The development of L2 oral language skills in two L1 groups: A 7-year study. *Language Learning, 63,* 163–185.

Ortega, L., & Byrnes, H. (Eds.). (2008). *The longitudinal study of advanced L2 capacities.* New York, NY: Routledge.

Ortega, L., & Iberri-Shea, G. (2005). Longitudinal research in second language acquisition: Recent trends and future directions. *Annual Review of Applied Linguistics, 25,* 26–45.

Schmitt, N. (1998). Tracking the incremental acquisition of second language vocabulary: A longitudinal study. *Language Learning, 48,* 281–317.

Wolff, D. (2015). *All in the same boat? – Native and non-native English speaking teachers' emerging selves in a U.S. MATESOL program.* Unpublished doctoral thesis. Michigan State University.

L

Main effect

A type of statistical result produced in factorial **ANOVA**s (and other procedures with two or more independent variables) in which the influence of an independent variable on the dependent variable is calculated. If main effects are statistically significant, it indicates that there are overall differences on the variable under consideration in relation to the dependent variable. For example, main effects are reported in mixed design ANOVAs from quasi-experimental studies that investigate the effects of different types of L2 instruction on a pretest and posttests: in these cases, instructional group and testing time are the independent variables that produce main effects. A main effect for group indicates that overall, across all testing times, there are differences between the groups. In other words, one or more groups are consistently higher or lower on all tests. Similarly, a main effect for testing time reveals that the test performance of all groups differed across the tests, which generally indicates that all groups improved equally on the different tests. For example, Saito and Wu (2014) investigated the effects of pronunciation training, with and without error correction, on Cantonese L1-speakers' ability to perceive Mandarin tones. The results, shown in Figure 23, indicate there were significant main effects for the T1–T2 and the T2–T4 pairings [$F(1, 38) = 6.23$, $p = .017$ and $F(1, 38) = 6.23$, $p = .006$, respectively], which means that for these two conditions, all three groups significantly reduced their number of errors, but there was no differential reduction, as indicated by the downward pointing arrows for all groups. In contrast, there was a significant **interaction effect** for the T1–T4 pairing [$F(2, 38) = 9.81$, $p < .001$], with the line graph indicating a sharp reduction in errors for the FFI-only group, while the control group actually increased in their number of errors.

In addition to reporting the statistical results, it is often helpful to use line graphs to visualize the relationship between the two variables. Parallel lines indicate a lack of interaction, while non-parallel lines indicate an interaction effect.

In many instances, researchers are not primarily interested in main effects because they do not provide information about the differential effects of any instructional treatment; rather, researchers are often more concerned with interaction effects.

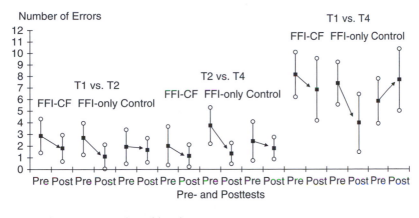

Saito & Wu (2014, p. 665; Figure 3).

Figure 23   Main and interaction effects of learners' pre- and posttest scores

Saito, K., & Wu, X. (2014). Communicative focus on form and second language suprasegmental learning: Teaching Cantonese learners to perceive Mandarin tones. *Studies in Second Language Acquisition, 36*, 647–680.

MANCOVA (see Multivariate analysis of covariance)

Mann–Whitney *U* test

A non-parametric statistical procedure in which two independent groups are compared by rank-ordering, from lowest to highest, the participants' scores in each group and then calculating a rank-sum score. If the rank-sum scores for the two groups are sufficiently similar, then there is no statistically significant difference between them; however, if the rank sum scores differ considerably, then a statistically significant difference may be found, much as for an independent samples *t*-**test**. The lower the rank-sum score, the lower the rankings of the group, while a high rank-sum score reflects higher group rankings. The Mann–Whitney test is appropriate to use when the **assumption** of **normal distribution** has been violated, and when there are two groups comprised of different individuals (e.g., independent samples). When reporting the results of a Mann–Whitney test, the test statistic, which is represented by *U*, should be reported, along with the **medians**, **interquartile ranges**, corresponding **z-score**, significance value, and **effect size**. An example of the use of the Mann–Whitney *U* test comes from Uggen's (2012) study of the noticing function of L2 learners' written production. Uggen compared the pretest differences between an experimental group and a control group, which she reported as non-significant ($U = 8.00$, $p = .12$, $r = -.23$). The Mann–Whitney test is equivalent to the **Wilcoxon**

rank-sum test, which also compares the rankings of two independent groups that are not normally distributed.

Uggen, M. S. (2012). Reinvestigating the noticing function of output. *Language Learning, 62*, 506–540.

MANOVA (see Multivariate analysis of variance)

Mean

A measure of **central tendency** that is calculated by summing all scores in a data set and then dividing by the number of scores. Also known as the average, the mean is frequently used in applied linguistics research because it takes into account every score in the data, and many **parametric statistics**, such as *t*-tests and **ANOVAs**, are based on the mean. One disadvantage of the mean is that it is particularly sensitive to extreme scores; consequently, in samples with a wide **range** of scores, including several **outliers**, it may be better to use the **median** or **mode** as a measure of central tendency and to conduct **non-parametric statistics**.

In addition to using the mean to understand the composition of a data set, it is also important to consider the **dispersion** of scores, often represented by the **standard deviation** or **variance**. Relying only on the mean and failing to consider the dispersion of scores can give an incorrect impression of the uniformity of the data. Presenting the standard deviation, along with the mean, also enables research consumers and secondary researchers (e.g., meta-analysts) to calculate the **effect size** resulting from a comparison of mean scores.

Median

A measure of **central tendency** in which the data is divided into two sections and the middle score taken. If the group has an even number of items, then the midpoint between the two center scores is taken. Regardless, 50% of participants fall on either side of the median. The median is not sensitive to extreme scores, and it is therefore useful when **outliers** are present in the data or when the data are not normally distributed. The median is not especially useful for conducting **inferential statistics**; thus, preference is often given to the **mean** as a measure of central tendency in applied linguistics research. However, the median is used when computing some non-parametric statistical analyses, such as the **Mann–Whitney *U* test**, when the **assumption** of **normal distribution** of the data is violated. Table 14 presents both mean and median L2 proficiency scores. In this data set, the two scores are generally equal, indicating the absence of outlying scores. As with the mean, it is important to consider the dispersion of scores around

Table 14 Mean and median sores

Proficiency	Mean	SD	Min	Max	Median
Speaking	55	10.3	31	98	59
Reading	75	14.1	44	99	77
Writing	64	8.6	43	78	65

the median. Though not present in Table 14, such dispersion is often represented by and reported as the **interquartile range**, which, like the median and unlike the standard deviation, does not assume a normal distribution.

See also **Mode**.

MEM (see Mixed effects modeling)

Member-checking
A process whereby a research participant is asked to verify the perceptions that a researcher has drawn from collected observations, **interviews**, **field notes**, and so forth, involving the participant. Member-checking involves engaging with participants in a kind of meta-talk, asking them directly and openly whether the researcher's interpretations align with and accurately reflect their own views. In some cases, the participants themselves may actually engage in some level of data analysis. Member-checking is especially common for interviews which are "co-constructed discourse events" and, as such, cannot be considered "direct windows on the minds of interviewees" (Block, 2000, p. 758). There are several rationales for member-checking. On a very basic level, a researcher may be interested in verifying the accuracy of certain factual information. Involving participants in studies after data are collected can also reduce the perception of a one-way give–take relationship between researchers and participants. Perhaps most importantly, member-checking is a means to validate interpretations made by the researcher, thereby leading to more authentic, accurate, and transferable conclusions. Yang and Kim (2011) collected a variety of different types of data from two study-abroad learners, including interviews, journal entries, autobiographies, and **stimulated recall** protocols. The researchers then induced themes from these data sources regarding the participants' beliefs about and experiences during their study abroad, as well as regarding their language learning more generally. The participants were asked to confirm these interpretations in the process of member-checking. Finally,

M

member-checking is frequently, but not exclusively, found in **qualitative research** in applied linguistics as well as sociolinguistics, anthropology, and elsewhere (see Gu, 2014); it is also emblematic of non-positivist **ontologies** that accept the role of subjectivity and multiple perspectives on the same event.

Block, D. (2000). Problematizing interview data: Voices in the mind's machine? *TESOL Quarterly, 34*, 757–763.

Gu, Y. (2014). To code or not to code: Dilemmas in analysing think-aloud protocols in learning strategies research. *System, 43*, 74–81.

Yang, J-.S., & Kim, T. Y. (2011). Sociocultural analysis of second language learner beliefs: A qualitative case study of two study-abroad ESL learners. *System, 39*, 325–334.

Meta-analysis

In its narrow form, meta-analysis consists of the averaging of **effect sizes** across a set of primary studies in a given research area. More broadly, though, meta-analysis embodies an entire set of procedures designed to yield a view of the domain in question that is more objective, transparent, and systematic than traditional literature reviews. Many of these procedures are identical to those undertaken in **research synthesis,** of which meta-analysis is a type (see Plonsky & Oswald, 2015). What distinguishes the latter is simply the aggregation of effect sizes, which is not always found in the former.

Most applied linguists were first introduced to meta-analysis by Norris and Ortega (2000), whose seminal study synthesized and meta-analyzed findings on the effects of L2 instruction. Since then, the use of meta-analysis in the field has expanded dramatically; as of this writing, approximately 100 meta-analyses have been presented and/or published in applied linguistics (Plonsky & Oswald, 2014), a sample of which are shown in Table 15 along with their respective domains of inquiry. The majority have examined the effects of different treatments or interventions, such as corrective feedback or explicit instruction, on L2 learners' knowledge of grammar, pragmatics, pronunciation, and vocabulary. Other meta-analyses have, however, synthesized research on associational relationships such as the correlates of reading comprehension and working memory. In addition to the proliferation of research adopting a meta-analytic approach, interest and maturity in the use of meta-analysis in applied linguistics is also evident in the publication of articles discussing meta-analytic methods in the field (e.g., In'nami & Koizumi, 2010; Norris & Ortega, 2007; Plonsky, 2012; Plonsky & Brown, 2015).

Finally, despite the benefits of synthesizing research via meta-analysis in comparison to the less systematic approach inherent in traditional reviews, meta-analysis is by no means immune to researcher subjectivity or other threats to **validity** common in traditional, qualitative reviews. On the contrary, meta-analyses involve numerous judgments on the part of the

Table 15 Sample of meta-analyzed topics in applied linguistics*

Main area	Sub-area	Authors (year)
L2 instruction		
	Grammar	Norris and Ortega (2000)
	Pragmatics	Jeon and Kaya (2006)
	Vocabulary	Won (2008)
	Pronunciation	Lee, Jang, and Plonsky (2015)
Assessment		
	Test format effects	In'nami and Koizumi (2010)
	Self-assessment	Ross (1998)
Individual differences		
	Working memory	Linck, Osthus, Koeth, and Bunting (2013)
	Aptitude	Li (2015)
	Motivation	Masgoret and Gardner (2003)
	Strategies	Plonsky (2011)
Computer-assisted language learning		
	Game-based learning	Chiu, Kao, and Reynolds (2012)
	Hypertext glosses	Yun (2011)
	Synchronous computer-mediated communication	Ziegler (in press)
Interaction and Feedback		
	Interaction	Keck, Iberri-Shea, Tracy-Ventura, and Wa-Mbaleka (2006)
	Feedback	Li (2010)
	Interaction + feedback	Mackey and Goo (2007)

*This table provides only a sample of topics and meta-analyses that have been carried out in the field. For a more complete list, and for full citations, see Plonsky's online bibliography.

researcher, nearly all of which require an intimate understanding of both the substantive domain in question and the techniques being employed (see Oswald & Plonsky, 2010).

Chiu, Y.-H., Kao, C.-W., & Reynolds, B. L. (2012). The relative effectiveness of digital game-based learning types in English as a foreign language setting: A meta-analysis. *British Journal of Educational Technology, 43*, E104–E107.

In'nami, Y., & Koizumi, R. (2010). Database selection guidelines for meta-analysis in applied linguistics. *TESOL Quarterly, 44*, 169–184.

Jeon, E. H., & Kaya, T. (2006). Effects of L2 instruction on interlanguage pragmatic development: A meta-analysis. In J. M. Norris & L. Ortega (Eds.), *Synthesizing research on language learning and teaching* (pp. 165–211). Philadelphia: John Benjamins.

Keck, C. M., Iberri-Shea, G., Tracy-Ventura, N., & Wa-Mbaleka, S. (2006). Investigating the empirical link between task-based interaction and acquisition: A meta-analysis. In J. M. Norris & L. Ortega (Eds.), *Synthesizing research on language learning and teaching* (pp. 91-131). Philadelphia: John Benjamins.

Lee, J., Jang, J., & Plonsky, L. (2015). The effectiveness of second language pronunciation instruction: A meta-analysis. *Applied Linguistics, 36*, 345–366.

Li, S. (2010). The effectiveness of corrective feedback in SLA: A meta-analysis. *Language Learning, 60*, 309–365.

Li, S. (2015). The associations between language aptitude and second language grammar acquisition: A meta-analytic review of five decades of research. *Applied Linguistics, 36*, 385–408.

Linck, J. A., Osthus, P., Koeth, J. T., & Bunting, M. F. (2013). Working memory and second language comprehension and production: A meta-analysis. *Psychonomic Bulletin & Review, 21*, 861–883.

Mackey, A., & Goo, J. (2007). Interaction research in SLA: A meta-analysis and research synthesis. In A. Mackey (Ed.), *Conversational interaction in second language acquisition: A collection of empirical studies* (pp. 407–451). New York: Oxford University Press.

Masgoret, A.-M., & Gardner, R. C. (2003). Attitudes, motivation, and second language learning: A meta-analysis of studies conducted by Gardner and associates. *Language Learning, 53*, 123–163.

Norris, J. M., & Ortega, L. (2000). Effectiveness of L2 instruction: A research synthesis and quantitative meta-analysis. *Language Learning, 50*, 417–528.

Norris, J. M., & Ortega, L. (2007). The future of research synthesis in applied linguistics: Beyond art or science. *TESOL Quarterly, 41*, 805–815.

Oswald, F. L., & Plonsky, L. (2010). Meta-analysis in second language research: Choices and challenges. *Annual Review of Applied Linguistics, 30*, 85–110.

Plonsky, L. (2011). The effectiveness of second language strategy instruction: A meta-analysis. *Language Learning, 61*, 993–1038.

Plonsky, L. (2012). Replication, meta-analysis, and generalizability. In G. Porte (Ed.), *Replication research in applied linguistics* (pp. 116–132). New York: Cambridge University Press.

Plonsky, L., & Oswald, F. L. (2014). How big is 'big'? Interpreting effect sizes in L2 research. *Language Learning, 64*, 878–912.

Plonsky, L., & Brown, D. (2015). Domain definition and search techniques in meta-analyses of L2 research (Or why 18 meta-analyses of feedback have different results). *Second Language Research, 31*, 267–278.

Plonsky, L., & Oswald, F. L. (2015). Meta-analyzing second language research. In L. Plonsky (Ed.), *Advancing quantitative methods in second language research* (pp. 106–128). New York: Routledge.

Ross, S. (1998). Self-assessment in second language testing: A meta-analysis and analysis of experiential factors. *Language Testing, 15*, 1–20.

Won, M. (2008). *The effects of vocabulary instruction on English language learners: A meta-analysis*. Unpublished doctoral dissertation. Texas Tech University, Lubbock, TX.

Yun, J. (2011). The effects of hypertext glosses on L2 vocabulary acquisition: A meta-analysis. *Computer Assisted Language Learning, 24*, 39–58.

Ziegler, N. (in press). Synchronous computer-mediated communication and interaction: A meta-analysis. *Studies in Second Language Acquisition*.

M

Missing data

Data that are not available for analysis for one reason or another. Generally, missing data is an issue for quantitative rather than qualitative analyses. Missing data may occur for a number of reasons. There may have been problems with the data collection process. In some cases, the technology used to record the data—a computer program, audio/video recorder, eye tracker—may not have functioned properly, thereby causing data not to be captured or captured in such a way as to be unusable. Other times, missing data can be due to participant error. If participants do not fully understand the procedures of the research study, they may complete the data collection process incorrectly; thus rendering any data unusable. Finally, there may be missing data due to participant absenteeism or **attrition**, which is particularly problematic for longitudinal studies in classroom contexts. For example, a student may be present for a **pretest**, and part of the classroom **treatment**, but then be absent for other treatment sessions and/or the **posttest**. As a result, the researcher is not able to determine the full effect of the treatment for such individuals because of the missing data.

There are several methods for dealing with missing data. One option is to entirely exclude any participants with only partial data, and thus only participants with complete data will be included in the data set. This method is called "listwise" or "casewise deletion." However, recruiting large numbers of participants can be difficult, so even partial data from subjects can be valuable. In some instances, therefore, it may be acceptable to include participants' data, even if it is not complete. For example, if a student took a pretest and **delayed posttest**, but was absent for the immediate posttest, the student's data could be included in the analyses that involve the two tests for which they were present. A similar issue may occur on a **survey** or **questionnaire**, in which a participant answers only some of the questions. The researcher may choose to include the participant's data, with the limitation that it is not complete. This method is called pairwise deletion. A number of different techniques for **imputation** of data (i.e., estimating and replacing missing values) are also possible.

There are some types of analyses that are more sensitive to missing data than others: for example, **correlations** and **factor analysis** can be skewed by missing data because the analysis examines the relationships between all the variables. However, t-tests and ANOVAs may be less sensitive to missing data, particularly if there is a large sample size. Additionally, it is important for the researcher to consider whether data are missing at random. The absence of any datapoints is undesirable; however, even more problematic are data that may be systematically missing. In longitudinal studies, for example, there may be a relationship between a participant's performance and his/her likelihood to attrite. In other words, those students who are less interested or motivated to learn may also be more likely to have lower scores and to choose not to complete the study. Such a situation would present a threat to the internal **validity** of the study because the remaining sample may provide a biased level of performance. Data not missing at random may also be present when participants avoid particularly difficult items on a test. If many students fail to respond to these items, and the researcher only counts those scores with responses, group scores are likely to be upwardly biased. In such circumstances, it is the researcher's ethical responsibility to examine and determine whether or not data are missing at random and whether to respond via imputation of data or other means (see Enders & Gottschall, 2011). Fortunately, there are a number of well-developed procedures for such situations (see Cheema, 2014 for a review). Somewhat surprisingly, however, this issue is rarely given explicit consideration in reports of applied linguistics research.

Cheema, J. R. (2014). A review of missing data handling methods in education research. *Review of Educational Research, 84*, 487–508.

Enders, C. K., & Gottschall, A. C. (2011). The impact of missing data on the ethical quality of a research study. In A. T. Panter, & S. K. Sterba (Eds.), *Handbook of ethics in quantitative methodology* (pp. 357–381). New York: Psychology Press.

Little, R. J. A., & Rubin, D. B. (2002). *Statistical analysis with missing data*. Hoboken, NJ: Wiley.

Pichette, F., Béland, S., Jolani, S., & Leśniewska, J. (2015). The handling of missing binary data in language research. *Studies in Second Language Learning and Teaching, 5*, 153–169.

Mixed design analysis of variance (see Analysis of variance)

Mixed effects modeling (MEM)

A statistical approach that is able to simultaneously account for (i.e., model) both fixed and random effects. Recall that **fixed effects** are those independent variables that may contribute to the variance observed in a given data set, whereas **random effects** help explain variance in the population. Viewing independent or predictor variables in this manner is not common in applied linguistics. It is, however, gaining momentum in certain areas (psycholinguistics and assessment; e.g., Barkaoui, 2010, 2013; Tremblay, Derwing, Libben, and Westbury 2011) and among certain camps of researchers (Stefan Gries and colleagues; e.g., Gries, 2013, 2015).

One reason for an increased interest in mixed effects modeling (MEM) is that it provides quantitative researchers with an analytical framework that is robust to many of the assumptions that plague linear models. MEMs are also quite flexible, allowing both categorical and continuous predictor and criterion variables.

Perhaps the strongest case in favor of MEMs stems from their ability to account for the hierarchical (i.e., dependent, correlated) nature of many data sets. It is not uncommon in applied linguistics for researchers to analyze groups and subgroups (and even sub-subgroups) that are nested within each other. A single classroom teacher, for example, may provide the treatment for multiple classes in a quasi-experimental study. Other classes that participate in the study may be taught by different teachers but may be found at the same institution. Still other groups participating in the study may be at a different institution or even in a different country. Hierarchical linear modeling (HLM), a type of regression model and a type of MEM, provides researchers with a set of analyses for accounting for the shared variance within and between each level or grouping (e.g., teacher, institution, city, country). HLM is also frequently used when analyzing data from **longitudinal designs** with repeated data collection periods. As an application of MEM, this approach, also referred to as "growth curve analysis," does not require or assume linear development to occur over time. For an example of HLM analysis in the context of L2 research, see Moeller, Theiler, and Wu (2012).

MEMs are generally carried out using **R**, SPSS, and other statistical software packages. For a guide to conducting MEM using **R**, see Cunnings and Finlayson (2015).

Baayen, R. H., Davidson, D. J., & Bates, D. M. (2008). Mixed-effects modeling with crossed random effects for subjects and items. *Journal of Memory and Language, 59*, 390–412.

Barkaoui, K. (2010). Explaining ESL essay holistic scores: A multilevel modeling approach. *Language Testing, 27*, 515–535.

Barkaoui, K. (2013). Using multilevel modeling in language assessment research: A conceptual introduction. *Language Assessment Quarterly, 10*, 241–273.

Cunnings, I. (2012). An overview of mixed-effects statistical models for second language researchers. *Second Language Research, 28*, 369–382.

Cunnings, I., & Finlayson, I. (2015). Mixed effects modeling and longitudinal data analysis. In L. Plonsky (Ed.), *Advancing quantitative methods in second language research* (pp. 159–181). New York: Routledge.

Gries, S. Th. (2013). Sources of variability relevant to the cognitive sociolinguist and corpus as well as psycholinguistic methods and notions to handle them. *Journal of Pragmatics, 52*, 5–16.

Gries, S. Th. (2015). The most underused statistical method in corpus linguistics: Multi-level (and mixed-effects) models. *Corpora, 10*, 95–125.

Moeller, A. J., Theiler, J. M., & Wu, C. (2012). Goal setting and student achievement: A longitudinal study. *Modern Language Journal, 96*, 153–169.

Tremblay, A., Derwing, B., Libben, G., & Westbury, C. (2011). Processing advantages of lexical bundles: Evidence from self-paced reading and sentence recall tasks. *Language Learning, 61*, 569–613.

M

Mixed methods design

Research that combines different paradigms and research traditions in an effort to arrive at a more complete understanding of the object under investigation. Most often mixed methods refers to the combination of **qualitative** and **quantitative research** methods. There are a number of benefits of collecting and integrating both types of data in a single study. For one, though quantification may introduce greater systematicity and objectivity into a study, the majority of the variables that applied linguists are interested in are qualitative in nature. For instance, there is nothing inherently numerical about motivation, explicit instruction, learner beliefs, classroom dynamics, test validity, or linguistic complexity. A mixed methods approach, therefore, provides the researcher with the objectivity of quantitative measurement and statistics while studying these phenomena in a way that preserves much of their natural state. These and other potential benefits have led a number of scholars in applied linguistics to argue in favor of the use of mixed methods (e.g., Brown, 2014; Dörnyei, 2007). This direction largely mirrors a similar movement toward acceptance and encouragement of mixed methods in the broader social and educational sciences (e.g., Creswell & Plano Clark, 2007; Greene, 2007). Of course, mixed methods research is not without its own set of corresponding challenges. It is often difficult to reconcile, for example, the distinct epistemological stances of quantitative and qualitative approaches (see findings of Hashemi & Babaii's, 2013, systematic review of mixed methods research in applied linguistics). In addition, fully integrating results from two data sets, rather than treating them sequentially, can be challenging, and may even lead to findings that are opaque compared to those that are based on just one type of data (Riazi & Candlin, 2014). Despite these and other challenges, there is certainly potential in the future of mixed methods in applied linguistics.

Brown, J. D. (2014). *Mixed methods research for TESOL*. Edinburgh: University of Edinburgh Press.

Creswell, J. W., & Plano Clark, V. L. (2007). *Designing and conducting mixed methods research*. Thousand Oaks, CA: Sage.

Dörnyei, Z. (2007). *Research methods in applied linguistics: Quantitative, qualitative and mixed methodologies*. Oxford: Oxford University Press.

Greene, J. C. (2007). *Mixed methods in social inquiry*. San Francisco, CA: Jossey–Bass.

Hashemi, M. R. (2012). Reflections on mixing methods in applied linguistics research. *Applied Linguistics, 32*, 206–212.

Hashemi, M. R., & Babaii, E. (2013). Mixed methods research: Toward new research designs in applied linguistics. *Modern Language Journal, 97*, 828–852.

Jang, E. E., Wagner, M., & Park, G. (2014). Mixed methods research in language testing and assessment. *Annual Review of Applied Linguistics, 34*, 123–153.

Riazi, A. M., & Candlin, C. N. (2014). Mixed-methods research in language teaching and learning: Opportunities, issues and challenges. *Language Teaching, 47*, 135–173.

Mode

A measure of **central tendency** that consists of the most frequently occurring value in a data set. Mode is not affected by **outliers** or extreme values; however, mode does not provide any information about other values in the data. In the example data shown in Table 16, the mode for age of arrival is 14, because it is the most frequently occurring value in the data set. In contrast, the **median** score is 19, and the mean is 19.3. Another disadvantage of the mode is that it may reflect **bimodal distribution** if there is an equal **frequency** of two or more values. Because of these limitations, the mode does not usually provide the best representation of the entire data set; consequently, it is seldom reported in applied linguistics research. Instead, median and mean are generally preferred measures of central tendency.

Table 16 Sample scores for determining the mode

Age of arrival
14
19
14
20
25
14
29

Multicollinearity

A condition in which two **continuous variables** correlate highly with each other. Multicollinearity can be a problem for several types of analysis; therefore, the absence of multicollinearity is an **assumption** of several inferential statistical techniques, such as **multiple regression** and multiple analysis of variance (MANOVA). For instance, Webb, Newton, and Chang (2013), in a study investigating the effects of multiple exposures to collocations, examined their data for multicollinearity before conducting a MANOVA. No violation of the assumption was found. One way to avoid multicollinearity is to check the **correlation** coefficients for strong correlations of .80 or higher. In addition, a variance inflation factors (VIF) score can be calculated to detect multicollinearity. A VIF score greater than 10 indicates multicollinearity is present in the data set. If there are highly correlated variables, researchers should consider omitting one of the variables or combining them in some way. **Factor analysis** or **principal components analysis** are methods for addressing multicollinearity, because they group similar variables together on separate factors or components. Researchers can then create factor scores, which are mathematical composites of all the items that loaded on the factor. Alternatively, researchers may choose to retain one or two of the most representative items and remove the other items from future analyses.

Webb, S., Newton, J., & Chang, A. (2013). Incidental learning of collocation. *Language Learning, 63*, 91–120.

Multidimensional analysis

A set of procedures designed to examine co-occurrence patterns of linguistic features in different registers (see Biber, 1988). Underlying multidimensional analysis is the **assumption** that the situational characteristics and purposes of different registers are associated with each other and with the **frequency** patterns of different linguistic and discoursal features found in them. There are several steps involved in this approach. First, the researcher collects a set of texts and their associated register (e.g., academic writing; speaking) and, if relevant, sub-register (e.g., journal articles; service encounters). As in all **corpus**-building, and in sampling more generally, the researcher must take great care in choosing texts to ensure that the sample is representative of the **population** (i.e., the register of interest; see Egbert, Biber, & Gray, forthcoming). Each text in the corpus is then **tagged** for a set of linguistic features, the use of which is anticipated to be correlated within and to vary across registers. Such features may be morphological, syntactic, lexical, pragmatic, and so forth. Once the texts are tagged, the main statistical technique used in multidimensional analysis, **factor analysis**, is run. Linguistic features are treated as items or measures and their correlational patterns are extracted into a set of factors or dimensions. The dimensions are usually bipolar descriptors determined by the researcher, such as "involved vs. informational production," where the former might be characterized by more frequent use of first-person pronouns or private verbs and the latter by nouns or passive constructions. Other examples of dimensions include "narrative vs. non-narrative concerns" and "elaborated vs. situation-dependent reference." Based on the results of the factor analysis, each text can then be assigned a score on each dimension and these can be used for a variety of subsequent analyses. Biber, Conrad, Reppen, Byrd, and Helt (2002), for example, conducted a multidimensional analysis on written and spoken language use in university contexts. Their corpus, the TOEFL 2000 Spoken and Written Academic Language Corpus (T2K-SWAL), consisted of a total of 423 spoken and written texts comprising numerous sub-registers and approximately 2.7 million words of academic discourse. As a follow-up to the primary multidimensional analysis, the researchers compared the registers' dimension scores using a series of one-way **ANOVAs**. Other follow-up techniques used to build on the findings of multidimensional analyses include **discriminant function analysis** (Biber, 2003) and **cluster analysis** (Biber & Gray, 2013).

Biber D. (1988). *Variation across speech and writing.* Cambridge: Cambridge University Press.

Biber, D. (2003). Variation among university spoken and written registers: A new multidimensional analysis. In C. Meyer, & P. Leistyna (Eds.), *Corpus analysis: Language structure and language use* (pp. 47–70). Amsterdam, Netherlands: Rodopi.

Biber, D., Conrad, S., Reppen, R., Byrd, P., & Helt, M. (2002). Speaking and writing in the university: A multidimensional comparison. *TESOL Quarterly, 36,* 9–48.

Biber, D., & Gray, B. (2013). *Discourse characteristics of writing and speaking responses on the TOEFL iBT.* Princeton, NJ: Educational Testing Service.

Egbert, J., Biber, D., and Gray, B. (forthcoming). *Designing and evaluating language corpora.* Cambridge: Cambridge University Press.

Multiple regression

A type of **linear regression** which, as the name implies, includes more than one predictor variable. Multiple regression, like many other statistics in the **general linear model**, is primarily concerned with explaining or accounting for variance. More specifically, multiple regression provides a quantitative measure of variance in the criterion variable that can be explained individually and collectively by a set of categorical and/or continuous predictor variables. Multiple regression can also be considered as an extension of **correlation**, where multiple variables are examined with respect to their relationship to a given dependent (or criterion) variable simultaneously. Multiple regression is particularly useful in contexts where, based on theory and/or previous research, relationships between a **dependent variable** and a number of independent or predictor variables are expected. Jin and Barley (2013), for example, were interested in the respective contributions of several subskills to L2 Chinese-learners' overall (holistically scored) speaking performance. The authors therefore conducted a multiple regression with speaking performance as the criterion variable and the subskills as predictor variables. Four of the seven predictors were found to add significantly to the multiple regression model's ability to account for variance in speaking ability: target-like syllables, grammatical accuracy, and word tokens and types. And overall, this model was able to explain nearly 80% of the variance in the criterion variable. Although somewhat infrequent in applied linguistics research, multiple regression is a powerful procedure that has great potential to inform and test hypotheses in the field. Because it allows for multiple independent variables to be considered simultaneously, multiple regression can also reduce the need for numerous tests of **statistical significance**, thereby preserving experiment-wise **statistical power**. Returning to the above example, the authors could have simply run seven separate **correlations** and examined their statistical significance. However, this approach would have ignored correlations among predictor variables, leading to greater potential for **Type I errors**. Multiple regression, on the other hand, accounts for these correlations, thus reducing such errors. Finally, though not often viewed as such, one-way ANOVA can be considered a special case of regression with a single categorical predictor variable. And in fact, the R^2 that results from a multiple regression in this condition will be identical to the **eta^2** produced by an **ANOVA** using the same variables (see Cohen, 1968).

Cohen, J. (1968). Multiple regression as a general data-analytic system. *Psychological Bulletin 70*, 426–443.

Jeon, E. H. (2015). Multiple regression. In L. Plonsky (Ed.), *Advancing quantitative methods in second language research* (pp. 131–158). New York: Routledge.

Jin, T., & Barley, M. (2013). Distinguishing features in scoring L2 Chinese: How do they work? *Language Testing, 30*, 23–47.

Multivariate analysis of covariance (MANCOVA)

A type of analysis of variance (ANOVA) that includes two or more **dependent variables**, one or more **independent variables**, and a **covariate**. As such, MANCOVA is similar to **analysis of covariance (ANCOVA)**, which attempts to partial out the effects of a moderator variable that is not an object of investigation. MANCOVA involves a very similar process, statistically speaking, only with two or more dependent variables rather than just one as in the case of ANCOVA. MANCOVA is seldom used in applied linguistics research.

Multivariate analysis of variance (MANOVA)

A type of **analysis of variance (ANOVA)** that includes two or more **dependent variables**, as well as one or more **independent variables**. Other types of ANOVAs, such as one-way, repeated measures, and mixed design, have only one dependent variable. A benefit of conducting MANOVA is that it reduces the family-wise error rate, because it eliminates the need to run analyses for each dependent variable in a study. For example, one MANOVA with two dependent variables can take the place of two separate ANOVAs, one for each dependent variable. The fewer the number of statistical tests, the lower the likelihood of committing a **Type I error** in which **statistical significance** is incorrectly claimed. Another advantage of MANOVA is that it looks for interaction effects between the dependent variables, something that is not possible with other types of ANOVAs. If a statistically significant value is found for the initial **(omnibus)** MANOVA, then subsequent **post hoc tests**, including one-way ANOVAs, can be conducted in order to determine the exact location of the statistical differences. One potential problem with MANOVA is the possibility of high correlations between the dependent variables, which may weaken the power of the analysis. Webb (2007) provides an example of this procedure, which is rarely found in applied linguistics. The study tested vocabulary learning (the dependent variable) resulting from five different levels of frequency of exposure to target words (the independent variable). If a single posttest had been used, a single one-way ANOVA would have been sufficient. However, in an attempt to capture the multifaceted nature of vocabulary knowledge, this study included ten unique, dependent measures, and therefore compared the results for the five different conditions using a MANOVA. Following an overall statistically significant MANOVA, the author then conducted a number of post hoc tests to identify the precise location of differences between groups and types of vocabulary knowledge.

See also **Discriminant function analysis**.

Webb, S. (2007). The effects of repetition on vocabulary knowledge. *Applied Linguistics, 28*, 46–65.

Multivariate statistics

A set of statistical techniques that involve the analysis of multiple variables. Multivariate statistics are generally more complex than **univariate statistics**. Examples of multivariate statistics include:

- multiple regression
- factor analysis
- cluster analysis
- discriminant function analysis

Multivariate statistics are not found frequently in L2 research (Plonsky, 2013), and applied linguists generally do not report possessing great familiarity with these procedures (Loewen et al., 2014). There is nothing inherently inferior or superior about univariate or multivariate statistics. In fact, for any given study, the appropriateness and utility of each depends on its research questions and aims. The lack of use and knowledge of more multivariate procedures is somewhat concerning, however, considering that most of the constructs and relationships of interest in applied linguistics are multivariate in nature. That is, it is difficult to statistically model and to fully understand numerous relationships simultaneously when relying only on univariate statistics. A further consequence of the field's heavy preference toward univariate statistics in the face of multivariate relationships is the need for multiple (sometimes numerous) statistical tests, leading to an increased chance of **Type I error**. At the same time, there are also downsides to utilizing multivariate statistics. For example, greater analytical complexity and technical sophistication often come with further abstractions from the data and greater difficulty in interpretation. It is with this issue in mind that Wilkinson and the Task Force on Statistical Inference (1999), commissioned by the American Psychological Association, recommended the use of "minimally sufficient" statistics, a sentiment we agree with wholeheartedly. Other challenges associated with multivariate statistics include the requirements of large sample sizes and more stringent **assumptions** of the data.

Brown, J. D. (2015). Why bother learning advanced methods in L2 research. In Plonsky (Ed.), *Advancing quantitative methods in second language research* (pp. 9–20). New York: Routledge.

Fish, L. J. (1988). Why multivariate methods are usually vital. *Measurement and evaluation in counseling and development, 21*, 130–137.

Loewen, S., Lavolette, B., Spino, L., Papi, M., Schmidtke, J., Sterling, S., & Wolff, D. (2014). Statistical literacy among applied linguists and second language acquisition researchers. *TESOL Quarterly, 48*, 360–388.

Plonsky, L. (2013). Study quality in SLA: An assessment of designs, analyses, and reporting practices in quantitative L2 research. *Studies in Second Language Acquisition, 35*, 655–687.

Plonsky, L. (2015). Introduction. In L. Plonsky (Ed.), *Advancing quantitative methods in second language research* (pp. 3–8). New York: Routledge.

M

Wilkinson, L., & Task Force on Statistical Inference. (1999). Statistical methods in psychology journals: Guidelines and explanations. *American Psychologist, 54*, 594–604.

Mutual information score

A measure, used in corpus and vocabulary research, which represents the collocational strength of two or more words. In other words, mutual information scores can be viewed as a kind of **effect size** index that expresses the likelihood of finding word X in close proximity to word Y. One use of mutual information scores is to arrive at a better understanding of a particular word. This approach assumes that a word's "contextual company … can provide interesting insights" about its semantic properties (Sigley & Holmes, 2002, p. 150). It is no surprise, for example, that the collocations with the highest mutual information scores for the word *analysis* according to the academic register of the Corpus of Contemporary American English (COCA; Davies, 2010) are *cost-benefit* (MI = 8.84), *multivariate* (8.08), *regression* (7.71), and *statistical* (7.13). This index can also be used for pedagogical purposes, such as deciding which collocates and multi-word sequences to teach to L2 learners. In an English for Academic Purposes context, instructors or students themselves might use the same **corpus** to find that some of the adverbs most likely to modify *problematic* are *highly*, *particularly*, and *especially* (but not *very*). Despite these potential uses, mutual information scores have been criticized as a measure of collocational strength. Such critiques often focus on the fact that the formula for mutual information scores: (a) often ignores function words (as in the underlined words in <u>on the</u> other hand), and (b) accounts (i.e., adjusts) for overall **frequency** in its calculation of co-occurrences (see e.g., Biber, 2009).

Biber, D. (2009). A corpus-driven approach to formulaic language in English. *International Journal of Corpus Linguistics, 14*, 275–311.
Davies, M. (2010). The Corpus of Contemporary American English as the first reliable monitor corpus. *Literary and Linguistic Computing, 25*, 447–464.
Sigley, R., & Holmes, J. (2002). Looking at girls in corpora of English. *Journal of English Linguistics, 30*, 138–157.

M

N

Statistical notation representing the **sample** size in a study. Upper case *N* is generally used for either the size of the entire **population** or the size of the total number of participants in a study. In contrast, lower case *n* is used to refer to the size of specific groups within a study. Thus, a research study might have an overall sample size of $N = 100$, with four different treatment groups of $n = 25$ each. However, this distinction is not always maintained in applied linguistics literature.

Narrative research

A type of **qualitative research** consisting of **case studies** in which individuals relay stories, through oral **interviews** or written texts, from their lives that relate to the topic being researched. Narrative research is defined differently by different people; however, in general, it involves the researcher and participant(s) using stories to interpret and co-construct meaning from the narratives. These stories are then analyzed to identify the themes that are present in them. In addition, researchers may focus on temporal, geographical, and social aspects of participants' narratives. Researchers may be more or less implicated in the data collection process, depending on how actively they participate in the storytelling process. As individuals tell and retell stories from their lives, these stories help shape the interpretation of those events. Additionally, researchers will often share their interpretations of the data with the interviewees, in a type of **member-checking**, to get the participants' views of the research interpretations. In one article in a *TESOL Quarterly* special issue on narrative research, Johnson and Golombek (2011) investigate the stories of two English second-language teachers. They argue that narratives help individuals externalize and verbalize their experiences so that they can engage in a systematic evaluation of those experiences, an important component in teacher-education training and research.

Barkhuizen, G. (Ed.) (2013). *Narrative research in applied linguistics*. Cambridge: Cambridge University Press.

Benson, P. (2014). Narrative inquiry in applied linguistics research. *Annual Review of Applied Linguistics, 34*, 154–170.

Johnson, K. E., & Golombek, P. (2011). The transformative power of narrative in second language teacher education. *TESOL Quarterly, 45*, 486–509.

Nominal variable

A variable comprised of discrete categories, with no numerical properties among them. Nominal variables can also be referred to as **categorical variables**. Examples of common nominal variables in applied linguistics research include L1 background and target language, which are nominal because they have categories such as French, English, and Chinese. It is possible to tally the **frequency** of occurrence of each category within a nominal variable, and these frequencies can be used to conduct **chi-square** analyses in order to determine statistically significant associations in the data. However, it is not possible to compute means-based descriptive or **inferential statistics** with nominal variables.

Non-parametric statistics

Inferential statistics that can be used when the **assumption** of **normal distribution** of data has been violated and **parametric statistics** cannot be used. Non-parametric tests use the **median** scores and/or rank orders to determine whether differences in observed values are statistically significant. Table 17 provides several of the more prominent non-parametric tests and their parametric counterparts.

Due to non-normally distributed data, for example, McDonough (2004) used the Wilcoxon signed-rank test, instead of a paired samples t-test, to examine **pretest** to **posttest** differences in her participants' use of real conditionals in L2 English. Other commonly used non-parametric tests include Spearman's **correlation** and the **chi-square test** for categorical data. **Bootstrapping** provides yet another analytical option for researchers working with data that do not conform to a normal distribution.

McDonough, K. (2004). Learner-learner interaction during pair and small group activities in a Thai EFL context. *System, 32*, 207–224.

Turner, J. L. (2014). *Using statistics in small-scale language education research: Focus on non-parametric data*. New York: Routledge.

Table 17 Parametric and non-parametric counterparts of commonly used statistical tests

Non-parametric Test	Parametric Equivalent
Wilcoxon rank-sum test	Independent samples t-tests
Mann–Whitney U test	Independent samples t-test
Wilcoxon signed-rank test	Paired samples t-test
Kruskal-Wallis test	One-way analysis of variance
Friedman's ANOVA	Repeated measures analysis of variance
Spearman's correlation	Pearson's correlation

Normal distribution

A condition in which the majority of scores on a variable occur around the mean and the number of scores on either side of the mean taper off equally in a mathematically predictable manner. A normal distribution is also referred to as a Gaussian distribution or a **bell curve**. Normal distribution of data is assumed for many types of inferential statistics, such as *t*-**tests** and **ANOVAs**. Several statistical tests can be used to assess normal distribution, including **Kolmogorov–Smirnov** and **Shapiro–Wilk** tests. Data visualization techniques, such as **histograms, box-and-whisker plots**, and **stem and leaf plots**, can also provide information about the distribution of the data. If data are not normally distributed, they might be skewed, with scores occurring more frequently at one end of the scale rather than in the middle. For example, in the histogram in Figure 24, the data are bunched towards the left-hand side of the graph, indicating a positively skewed distribution. In Figure 25, the same positively skewed data are presented in a **box-and-whisker plot**, while Figure 26 illustrates a normally distributed **box-and-whisker plot**. A **bimodal distribution** is another type of non-normal distribution in which scores cluster around two different points on the scale. If data are not normally distributed, it may be necessary to compute **non-parametric statistics** or **robust statistics**, which do not assume a normal distribution. In addition, **data transformation**, in

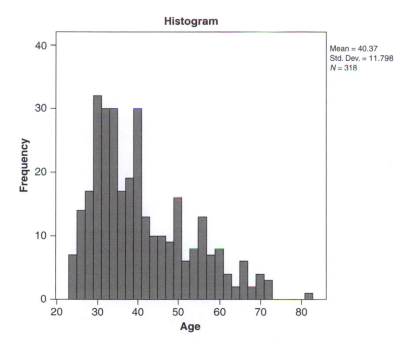

Figure 24   Histogram of positively skewed distribution

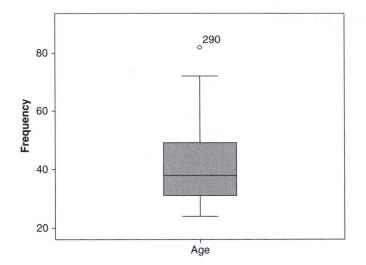

Figure 25   Box-and-whisker plot of positively skewed distribution

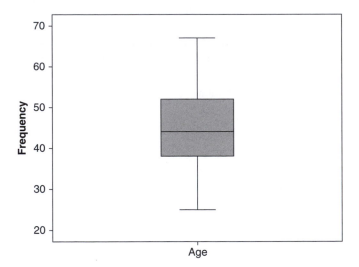

Figure 26   Box-and-whisker plot of normally distributed data

which mathematical procedures are applied equally to all datapoints, can sometimes be used to correct a non-normal distribution.

Null hypothesis

The basis of Null Hypothesis Significance Testing (NHST), the null hypothesis states that there is no difference or relationship between two observed phenomena. The null hypothesis, which is abbreviated to H_0, is investigated by using **inferential statistics** to calculate a test statistic and **p-value**. If the *p*-value is below the predetermined level for **statistical significance** (i.e., the **alpha level**), often set at .05, then researchers can reject the null hypothesis. However, if the *p*-value is greater than the alpha level, researchers must fail to reject the null hypothesis. In some scientific circles, NHST has been viewed as the standard approach to quantitative research; however, the overreliance on *p*–values, and the conceit that researchers truly expect to find no difference, has led to criticism of NHST. In applied linguistics, it is uncommon for researchers to explicitly state a null hypothesis along with their **research questions**. Instead, researchers are more likely to include directional research hypotheses that make predictions about the expected results of the research. One example of a null hypothesis comes from Scheffler's (2011) investigation into teachers' intuitions about grammatical rule difficulty and students' ability to use those rules. He proposed that there would be "no significant correlation between teachers' judgments and learners' performance" (p. 225). Because Scheffler found a statistically significant correlation, he rejected the null hypothesis.

Scheffler, P. (2011). Rule difficulty: Teachers' intuitions and learners' performance. *Language Awareness, 20*, 221–237.

NVivo

A computer-assisted qualitative data analysis software. Though many software packages exist to assist **quantitative researchers** with statistical analyses, NVivo provides one of the few platforms specifically designed for qualitative data. NVivo is particularly useful in that it allows researchers to both organize and analyze their data, tasks which are generally conducted separately using traditional or analogue methods. Researchers can: (a) enter text from **interviews** or **field notes**, (b) attach coding information to the texts, and (c) use the software to sort and group the data into "nodes" that can be used for further analysis. For example, Winke and Gass (2013), in their analysis of the effects of test-raters' accent familiarity on rating scores, used *NVivo 8* to group into themes the 260 qualitative data segments from their interviews with raters.

Other packages that provide tools similar to those available through *NVivo* include *ATLAS.ti* (http://atlasti.com/) and *MAXQDA* (http://www.maxqda.com/). For additional options and an extensive review of possibilities and procedures for analyzing qualitative data in applied linguistics, and in SLA in particular, see Baralt (2012).

Baralt, M. (2012). Coding qualitative data. In A. Mackey, & S. M. Gass (Eds.), *Research methods in second language acquisition: A practical guide* (pp. 222–244). Malden, MA: Wiley-Blackwell.

Winke, P., & Gass, S.M. (2013). The influence of second language experience and accent familiarity on oral proficiency rating: A qualitative analysis. *TESOL Quarterly, 47*, 762–789.

Observational research

Research that is non-interventionist and does not attempt to manipulate the context under investigation. Instead, in observational studies, researchers seek to describe a specific phenomenon or context, such as a classroom. In many cases, observational research is longitudinal in nature, with researchers collecting data over a period of days, weeks, or even years. Types of observational research include **ethnographies**, **case studies**, **conversation analysis**, **discourse analysis,** and others. The aim of observational research is generally to present a holistic, rich, and detailed description of the context or phenomenon under observation. Although observational research tends to be qualitative, it may also use **mixed methods** in which observations and descriptions occur with the goal of investigating certain phenomena. These phenomena can then be tallied and subjected to statistical analyses in order to determine their **frequency** in different contexts. This type of mixed methods research has been done with interactional features such as corrective feedback. For example, Ellis, Basturkmen, and Loewen (2001) observed English L2 classroom interaction, analyzing it for types of corrective feedback and uptake responses. The researchers also tallied the frequency with which certain types of feedback occurred with specific types of uptake.

Ellis, R., Basturkmen, H., & Loewen, S. (2001). Learner uptake in communicative ESL. *Language Learning, 51*, 281–318.

Odds ratio

An **effect size** that is used with **logistic regression**. Odds ratios indicate how much more or less likely a variable/phenomenon is to occur given a certain condition. An odds ratio greater than 1.0 indicates that the event is more likely to occur, while an odds ratio of less than 1.0 indicates that the outcome is less likely to occur. For example, an odds ratio of 2.0 would be interpreted as one outcome being twice as likely to occur, while an odds ratio of .5 would indicate that the outcome was half as likely to occur. Odds ratios are based on binary coding in order to determine the direction of the likelihood. In a study of successful uptake and accurate test scores, Loewen (2005) coded uptake as 0 = unsuccessful, 1 = successful, and test accuracy as 0 = inaccurate, 1 = accurate. Thus, the resulting odds ratios of 2.1 for successful uptake in relation to test accuracy was interpreted as learners being twice as likely to have accurate scores on the test when they had previously produced successful uptake on the targeted/tested structure.

Loewen, S. (2005). Incidental focus on form and second language learning. *Studies in Second Language Acquisition, 27,* 361–386.

Omnibus test

A statistical test that examines the overall relationships in a data set to initially determine whether there are any statistically significant differences (or associations), in which case, post hoc tests can be conducted to determine the exact nature and location of the statistical results. Types of omnibus tests include **analysis of variance** (ANOVA), **multiple regression**, and **chi-square**. One advantage of performing an omnibus test is that it reduces the chances of committing a **Type I error**, in which a statistically significant difference is found even when no such difference exists in the population at large. The risk of committing a Type I error increases with every statistical test that is conducted on a set of data. Performing an initial omnibus test reduces the number of statistical tests needed.

One-shot design

A type of research that involves only one instance of data collection. A one-shot design is generally associated with **quantitative research** methods, and it may occur, for example, when participants are given a language test or **survey** to which there is no follow-up. When examining L2 proficiency, one-shot designs are often **cross-sectional**, collecting data from different proficiency levels at the same time to give some indication of L2 development, rather than following learners over a period of time to achieve a **longitudinal** description of L2 development.

One-tailed hypothesis/test

A prediction of the directionality of a relationship, effect, or difference between groups (A > B or A < B). A one-tailed hypothesis can be contrasted with both a **null hypothesis**, which presupposes no relationship or difference between groups (A = B), and a **two-tailed hypothesis**, which predicts a relationship or effect without regard to the direction (e.g., A ≠ B). For instance, Hirata-Edds (2011) used a one-tailed test to determine that students in a Cherokee immersion program had a significantly higher proficiency in Cherokee than students in an English classroom. Hirata-Edds explained that "a one-tailed test was applied because children in the immersion group were expected to have more Cherokee language skills than those exposed only to English in the classroom" (p. 711). Thus, Hirata-Edd's **research hypothesis** presupposed greater effectiveness of one context over the other. With a one-tailed hypothesis, researchers investigate statistical significance in only one direction; however, in practice, applied linguists rarely follow this procedure, with

O

the result that one-tailed tests are uncommon in applied linguistics research. One argument in favor of using one-tailed tests is to limit the number of tests that need to be performed, thereby reducing the **Type I error** rate. As the field matures and theoretical predictions become more refined, the use of one-tailed hypotheses (and analyses) might be expected to increase.

Hirata-Edds, T. (2011). Influence of second language Cherokee immersion on children's development of past tense in their first language, English. *Language Learning, 61*, 700–733.

One-way analysis of variance (see Analysis of variance)

Ontology

A researcher's view about the nature of the world around us. The ontology of a **positivist** or postpositivist paradigm, for example, is that there is (likely) an objective truth or reality to be found even if our understanding of it is not likely to be complete. By contrast, a **constructivist's** ontology maintains that reality is more of a relative **construct** that is socially determined and constructed. As might be expected, different ontological perspectives will move researchers toward—if not necessitate—a number of other differences, particularly related to research methodology, throughout a study. These differences might include the types (or presence) of **research questions** being asked (restricted vs. open-ended and interpretable), the data collection **instruments** (formal measures of knowledge vs. less structured techniques), the types of data collected (e.g., quantitative vs. qualitative), and the outcomes and conclusions drawn based on the data.

See also **Epistemology**

Lincoln, Y. S., & Guba, E. G. (2000). Paradigmatic controversies, contradictions, and emerging confluences. In N. K. Denzin, & Y. S. Lincoln (Eds.), Handbook of qualitative research (2nd ed., pp. 163–188). Thousand Oaks, CA: Sage.
Richards, K. (2003). *Qualitative inquiry in TESOL*. New York: Palgrave Macmillan.

Operationalization

The way in which a larger **construct** that is the subject of investigation in a research study is measured. For example, there are many psychological constructs, such as anxiety, motivation, and personality type. However, it is not possible to measure these constructs directly or exhaustively; rather, a researcher must decide what measures will best represent the construct. Thus, for anxiety, researchers might decide to use a **survey** to operationalize the construct, or they might use a set of behaviors exhibited by learners in a specific context. These measures would constitute the way in which anxiety is operationalized in the study. Another common example of operationalization in SLA is the measurement of L2 proficiency: again, it is not possible to examine the level of language ability inside a learner's head, so proficiency must be represented in specific, measureable ways. For L2 proficiency, researchers often take an institutional placement level as an operationalization of proficiency. For example, in their study of eye tracking and grammaticality judgment tests, Godfroid et al. (2015) operationalized proficiency by reporting the placement level of their participants (Levels, 3, 4, and 5) at the English language center at which they were studying. Researchers might also use tests targeting specific linguistic areas, such as grammar or vocabulary, or tests of a more general nature, such as TOEFL or IELTS.

It is important to recognize that the way in which a construct is operationalized affects the interpretation of the data. For example, researchers might come to different conclusions if they use different measures of L2 proficiency. Although some methods of operationalization may be better than others because they have higher **construct validity**, there is generally no perfect method of operationalization. Every method will have some shortcoming, such as measuring only part of the construct. Thus, researchers should be clear on how they are operationalizing the construct, as well as the limitations inherent to their approach. To overcome such limitations, researchers often use more than one method of operationalization in order to triangulate and reach firmer conclusions about their data.

Godfroid, A., Loewen, S., Jung, S., Park, J., Gass, S., & Ellis, R. (2015). Timed and untimed grammaticality judgments measure distinct types of knowledge: Evidence from eye-movement patterns. *Studies in Second Language Acquisition, 37,* 269–297.

Ordinal variable

A variable in which individuals or objects are ranked in some way. Consequently, ordinal variables specify the order in which participants are categorized according to relative size or position, such as first, second, third. Likert scales found in questionnaire items asking for participant agreement on a scale of 1–5 are also often considered ordinal. Ordinal variables have—or may be assigned—numeric properties that are not found in **categorical variables**; however, the type of numeric information provided is more limited than that found in **continuous variables**. For example, L2 learners' scores on a proficiency test may be rank-ordered to indicate performance relative to other individuals. However, it cannot be assumed, based on such a ranking, that there is an equal distance between each point on the measurement scale. Thus, a researcher is not able to ascertain how much better the first-ranked student performed compared to the second- or third-ranked students. However, with a continuous scale, the researcher can calculate the mathematical distance between each student's score. In this way, ordinal data have limited utility for statistical analysis because they are not appropriate for calculating means-based descriptive and inferential statistics. As a result, ordinal variables are not used as commonly as continuous or interval variables in applied linguistics research.

However, ordinal data are used by some statistical procedures, especially non-parametric ones, such as Spearman's rho **correlations** and the **Mann–Whitney *U* test**, which use rank-ordering to investigate statistical differences in non-normally distributed data.

Outlier

A participant or value in a data set that is substantially above or below the **range** of the rest of the data. Often, the statistical cutoff procedure for determining outliers is whether they fall more than three **standard deviations** from the mean. Calculating this distance is fairly easy. Using **SPSS**, for example, the researcher simply creates a new variable wherein each value for the original variable is recoded as a ***z-score***. Outliers can be problematic for quantitative data analysis because they can affect statistical results in several ways. Furthermore, outliers may represent an individual or case that does not come from the same **population** as the rest of the group. For example, if researchers are examining the proficiency scores of intermediate L2 learners, they might find an average accuracy rate of 50%. However, they might notice that one person scored 95% on the test. On further investigation, the researchers may discover that this person was actually a native speaker; therefore, he or she does not come from the population under consideration, namely intermediate L2 learners. In such cases, it is best to exclude the outlier from the analysis. However, it is possible for outliers to come from the same population, but still not perform similarly to other participants. In these cases, an outlier will skew the average score and contribute to a non-normal distribution of the data. Several steps can be taken to address outliers in a data set. Instead of using mean scores, researchers can calculate **median** scores, which mitigate the influence of outliers by determining the middle score in the data, regardless of the **range**. However, many statistical tests cannot be computed using median scores. Another option is to remove outliers from the data set, particularly if there is good reason to suspect that they do not come from the target population. In a meta-analysis of comprehension-based and production-based L2 instruction, Shintani, Li, and Ellis (2013) identified and excluded from their analysis outliers that were more than 2.5 standard deviations from the mean. A total of 2 studies out of 35 were excluded from parts of the analysis as a result.

There are several ways to detect outliers in addition to the "greater than 3 standard deviations" rule. One is by examining **box-and-whisker plots**, which represent outliers by circles and asterisks outside the box and whiskers. There are also procedures in **multiple regression** for checking for outliers, such as calculating Cook's and Mahalanobis distances, because regression is a test that is particularly sensitive to outliers.

Shintani, N., Li, S., & Ellis, R. (2013). Comprehension-based versus production-based grammar instruction: A meta-analysis of comparative studies. *Language Learning, 63*, 296–329.

p (see p-value)

P–P plot

A graphic representation of the distribution of a data set used to assess the **assumption** of **normal distribution**. A P–P plot (probability–probability plot) charts the probability of a specific variable having a normal distribution by ranking the individual scores and converting them to standardized **z-scores**. The z-scores from the actual data set are plotted against the values that would be expected if the data were normally distributed. The

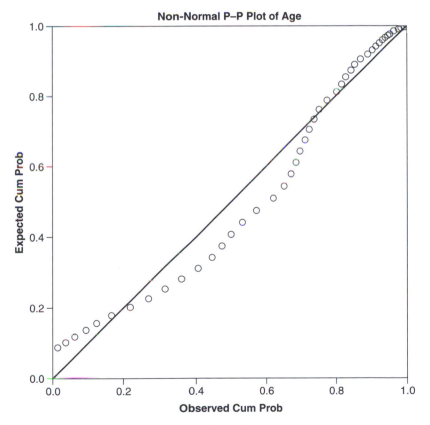

Figure 27 Non-normally distributed P–P plot

expected values (i.e., those anticipated assuming a normal distribution) are represented by a straight diagonal line, while the observed values are represented by individual dots. The closer the dots are to the diagonal line, the more normally distributed the dataset. In Figure 27, the trajectory of the dots varies considerably from the diagonal line, indicating a non-normal distribution. However, in Figure 28, the dots are much more closely aligned with the diagonal line, meaning that the data are more normally distributed.

P–P plots are similar to **Q–Q plots**; however, in Q–Q plots, the dots represent quantiles rather than individual scores. Because there are no specific criteria for deciding how similar the diagonal line (i.e., expected values) and the individual dots (i.e., observed values) must be in order for the data to be considered normally distributed, it is advisable to also conduct a **Kolmogorov–Smirnov** or **Shapiro–Wilk test** and examine a histogram of the data to investigate the assumption of normal distribution. However, a P–P plot can provide quick, visual information about the data.

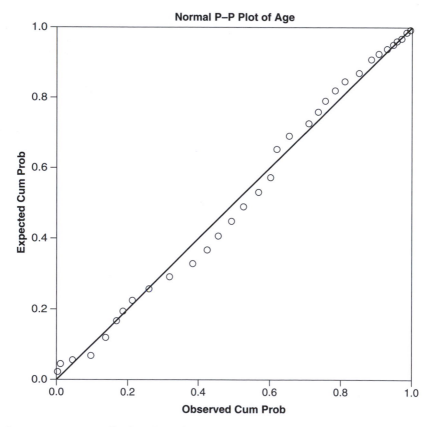

Figure 28 Normally distributed P–P plot

p-value

A number that indicates the level of **statistical significance** for the results of a statistical test. Thus, it is the number that researchers often refer to in order determine whether their results are significant. As such, the *p*-value is viewed in relation to the **alpha level** (*α*) and the probability of making a **Type I error**, in which a result is claimed to be significant but in reality is not. In many cases, an alpha level of .05 is set, indicating that the researcher can accept a 5% possibility that the results do not reflect a true effect. It is the *p*-value that then indicates such probability. In many cases, in **Null Hypothesis Significance Testing**, any *p*-value greater than .05 is considered to be non-significant; however, it is also possible for researchers to describe *p*-values that are close to the alpha level (such as *p* = .06 or .08) as approaching significance or indicating a tendency or trend towards significance. For example, in a self-paced reading study, VanPatten, Keating, and Leeser (2012) reported a trend toward significance for learner sensitivity to errors in verb phrases: *p* = .07 for the subject analysis and *p* = .093 for the item analysis.

Researchers are encouraged not to rely on *p*-values alone in determining the meaningfulness of their test results, in particular because *p*-values are affected by sample size. **Power** and **effect sizes** provide information about the presence and magnitude of effects in a data set, and these statistics should be reported in addition to *p*-values. In reporting the results of statistical tests, researchers should report exact *p*-values (e.g., *p* = .38 or *p* = .02) rather than relying on greater than (*p* > .05) or less than (*p* < .05) signs. Such exact reporting allows readers to see for themselves how close the *p*-value was to the alpha level. Readers' conclusions about the data might be different based on significant *p*-values of .001 or .04, as well as non-significant *p*-values of .06 versus .56.

See also **Statistical significance**.

Norris, J. M., Plonsky, L., Ross, S. J., & Schoonen, R. (2015). Guidelines for reporting quantitative methods and results in primary research. *Language Learning, 65,* 470–476.

VanPatten, B., Keating, G. D., & Leeser, M. J. (2012). Missing verbal inflections as a representational problem: Evidence from self-paced reading. *Linguistic Approaches to Bilingualism, 2,* 109–140.

Parameter (see Population parameter)

Parametric statistics

A type of inferential statistics that is based on the **assumption** of a **normal distribution** (also referred to as a Gaussian distribution or **bell curve**). Parametric tests include *t*-tests, **ANOVAs**, Pearson's **correlations**, as well as most other statistics in the **general linear model**. These are the most commonly used types of statistical tests in applied linguistics (Lazaraton, 2000). In cases when parametric statistics are deemed inappropriate due to a non-normal distribution, researchers can often turn to **non-parametric tests** or **robust statistics**. The non-parametric counterparts of the independent samples *t*-test and the Pearson's correlation, for example, are the **Mann–Whitney *U* test** and the Spearman's correlation, respectively.

Lazaraton, A. (2000). Current trends in research methodology and statistics in applied linguistics. *TESOL Quarterly, 34*, 175–181.

Partial correlation

A type of **correlation** that factors out the moderating influence of a third variable. Thus, if researchers want to investigate how well two variables relate to each other, while holding a third variable constant, they can perform a partial correlation. In addition, partial correlations can be used in multiple regression analyses to indicate the unique contribution of individual variables to the overall model. A partial correlation still produces a correlation coefficient of *r*. For instance, in a study on incidental vocabulary acquisition, Vidal (2011) reported partial correlation coefficients in order to determine the relationship for each variable, when the effects of the other variables were removed. She reported partial correlations for the following variables: frequency of occurrence ($r = .687$), predictability from word form ($r = .636$), type of word elaboration ($r = .605$), and type of word ($r = 448$). Based on these results, Vidal concluded that frequency of occurrence had the highest unique contribution to the model, while type of word had the lowest. Partial correlations are not commonly used in applied linguistics research.

Vidal, K. (2011). A comparison of the effects of reading and listening on incidental vocabulary acquisition. *Language Learning, 61*, 219–258.

Partial eta-squared (see Eta-squared)

Participant

A person who is the object of investigation, and therefore participates in a research project. Together the participants make up the **sample**. Sometimes participants are also called subjects; however, in some contexts, the latter term is viewed somewhat negatively. Participants in applied linguistics research come in all shapes and sizes, and in some cases, they possess characteristics that are being directly investigated in a research study, while at other times, some characteristics are incidental to the study. One primary distinction concerning participants in SLA research is between first language and second language speakers. Other participant characteristics, such as gender, age, language aptitude, and L2 proficiency level, are sometimes primary and sometimes incidental in a study. In all reports of research studies, there should be a section that describes the participants. In quantitative studies, this description can sometimes be rather general, under the assumption that the influence of many of the incidental participant characteristics will be rendered non-consequential by the sample size. For instance, VanPatten and Smith (2015) described their 49 participants in four sentences, covering basic demographic information such as knowledge of Japanese, education level, and L1 background. However, in **qualitative research**, the participants' characteristics are often described in much more detail, in part because there are often only a few participants in the study, and more importantly because the goal of the study is to provide rich and **thick description** of the participants and their contexts. As an example, De Costa (2015) devotes several pages to the description of his one participant.

De Costa, P. I. (2015). Re-envisioning language anxiety in the globalized classroom through a social imaginary lens. *Language Learning, 65*(3), 504–532.

VanPatten, B., & Smith, M. (2015). Aptitude as grammatical sensitivity and the initial stages of learning Japanese as a L2. *Studies in Second Language Acquisition, 37*, 135–165.

Participant observation

A type of **qualitative research** in which the researcher is involved in conducting descriptive research in a specific context, but instead of remaining uninvolved in the social setting, the researcher is actually one of the participants in the research context. In general, researchers prefer to remain separate from the research context, in an attempt to make more unbiased observations and exert minimal influence on the context. However, the observer's paradox means that all observation involves some altering of the research context, whether intentional or not. Participant observation may reduce the effects of the observer's paradox, as the participants become accustomed to the researcher's involvement in the research setting. In addition, participant observation simply acknowledges the effects of the researcher's presence, and indeed, some research would not be possible if the researcher were not a part of the research context. Researchers can also conduct non-participant observations, in which they are present in the research context; however, they do not interact with the participants nor participate in any activities.

Participant observation can be a common technique in ethnographic work. For example, Kulavuz-Onal and Vásquez (2013) conducted an ethnography in an online community of English teachers, participating in community events such as workshops and chat sessions. In contrast, Sauro and Smith (2010) observed the interactions of L2 German learners in an online chat, but did not participate in the chat themselves. This behavior is characterized as non-participant observation.

P

Kulavuz-Onal, D., & Vásquez, C. (2013). Reconceptualising fieldwork in an ethnography of an online community of English language teachers. *Ethnography and Education, 8*(2), 224–238.

Sauro, S., & Smith, B. (2010). Investigating L2 performance in text chat. *Applied Linguistics, 31*, 554–577.

Percentage

A common mathematical calculation that shows what proportion of the entire sample or set of observations is represented by a specific segment. Percentages are especially helpful in **descriptive statistics** when the number of items within variables differs, and thus does not allow for direct comparison of raw frequencies. By calculating percentages, a researcher can get a better idea of the proportions of categories within variables, even if the denominators are different. A percentage is calculated by dividing the total number of items in a variable by the number of items in a specific category, and then multiplying by 100.

Percentages are often used to describe linguistic features in a text or in a conversation. Gass and Varonis (1985), for example, were interested in comparing the **frequency** of repairs in interactions involving participants in three groups: native speakers, lower level learners, and more advanced learners. Because the total number of interactions differed across the groups, the authors calculated the proportion of repairs found in the data as percentages. Percentages are also often used to report test accuracy rates. If one test has a total of 50 items, and another has 100 items, a percentage score allows researchers to make easy comparisons between them, even though the raw scores are not equal. In general, it is better to run inferential statistics on raw frequencies rather than percentages when possible.

Though not often viewed as such, percentages can also be considered a kind of **effect size**, in that they offer a kind of "standard" score that can be compared and even combined across studies. And in fact, Brown (in press) meta-analyzed percentages of different types of feedback (e.g., recast, metalinguistic) and errors that received feedback (e.g., vocabulary, grammar, pragmatics) based on observational data from a number of classroom-based studies. Among other results, Brown found 57% and 30% of all feedback moves in primary studies observing different types of feedback were recasts and prompts, respectively. Looking across the sample, he also found grammar errors to receive feedback more often than other types of errors, such as pronunciation.

Brown, D. (in press). The type and linguistic foci of oral corrective feedback in the L2 classroom: A meta-analysis. *Language Teaching Research.*

Gass, S. M., & Varonis, E. (1985). Variation in native-speaker speech modification to non-native speakers. *Studies in Second Language Acquisition, 7*, 37–57.

Percentile

A standardized method of indicating how specific scores or participants rank in relation to the rest of the data set. A percentile ranking indicates how many participants obtained lower scores than the participant in question: thus, if a participant is in the 90th percentile, then 90% of the participants had lower scores. Percentiles are commonly found in applied linguistics research in the form of **box-and-whisker plots**, which provide a visualization of the distribution of the data. The box represents the middle 50% of the data (i.e., the 25th to 75th percentiles), and the lower and upper whiskers represent the 0 to 25th and 75th to 100th percentiles, respectively. Finally, percentiles can be especially useful when the data do not conform to a **normal distribution,** because they provide information about the relative relationships of scores in the data and can be used to identify the center and spread of non-normally distributed data.

Phi

An **effect size** that measures the strength of an association between two categorical variables on a scale of 0 to (positive) 1, in which both variables contain only two levels, thereby creating a 2 × 2 **contingency table**. Consequently, phi is an appropriate effect size to use with chi-square analyses. Phi is the equivalent of the *r* value for a correlation, and the larger the value, the stronger the magnitude of the relationship. If conducting a chi-square with variables containing more than two categories, researchers should use **Cramer's V** as an effect size.

Pie chart

A circular graph with pie-shaped wedges representing various categories. The entire circle represents 100% of the cases or categories of the variable being illustrated, and the wedges represent the number of cases within each specific category: thus, the larger the wedge, the higher the number of observed cases relative to the other categories being represented.

P

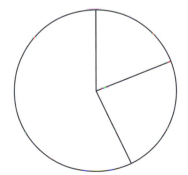

Figure 29   Pie chart

Pie charts are easy to produce and can be easy to interpret, assuming there are not too many categories included (see Hudson, 2015). For example, Figure 29 has three categories representing 60, 25 and 20 percent of the data.

Hudson, T. (2015). Presenting quantitative data visually. In L. Plonsky (Ed.), *Advancing quantitative methods in second language research* (pp. 78–105). New York: Routledge.

Pilot study

A small-scale study that is conducted before the main research study in order to ensure that the research **instruments** and procedures work as they are intended: for example, a pilot study might be used to ensure the **construct validity** of a test. A test that is designed to measure L2 learners' proficiency, but on which L1 speakers do poorly during a pilot study, might need to be revised. Similarly, researchers might administer a **questionnaire** in a pilot study to make sure that the questions are interpreted in the way that the researcher intends and/or that the instrument can be expected to perform at acceptable levels of internal consistency.

There are two different **populations** that researchers might draw on in a pilot study. The first group is a representative sample of the population for which the instrument or procedure is intended. Thus, if a researcher is targeting upper intermediate English-speaking learners of French, then it is important to include such learners in the pilot to make sure that any tests or procedures are suitable for that population. The second group that might be used in a pilot study is a baseline group. For example, researchers might give native speakers a questionnaire to make sure that they understand it before giving it to L2 speakers.

Generally, pilot studies are administered to a small number of people. For example if a group of 10 native speakers scores accurately on a proficiency test, there is probably no need to pilot the test further with that group. However, if the piloting reveals problems with the instrument, then additional participants might be needed. Such problems might also send the researcher back to the drawing board, after which he or she might conduct another pilot study to see if the changes in the research design have been effective.

In many cases, the data from a pilot study are not included in the final data set. The exception might be if the pilot shows that the instruments and procedures are acceptable as they stand and no further changes are necessary. Then, the data from the pilot study would be equivalent to the data gathered during the actual study and could be incorporated. Also, in many cases, the details of a pilot study are not reported in journal articles, although there might be mention of the existence of a pilot phase (Derrick, in press). In contrast, in research proposals or student theses and dissertations, there might be more explanation of the pilot process, and how the pilot affected the final design of the study. Kiss and Nikolov (2005) included a description of their pilot study in their validation study of an aptitude measure for young learners. The aims of their pilot study were:

1. *To check the appropriacy of the test tasks for the target population.*
2. *To gauge the difficulty of the test tasks.*
3. *To compare achievement on the different tasks within the test.*
4. *To compare achievement on the aptitude measure with achievements on an English-language proficiency measure* (p. 112).

A pilot test with 55 items in four components was administered to 36 twelve-year-old children in Hungary. Based on those results, one component of the test was completely revised, another component was revised slightly, and the other two tasks were retained but had several items removed. The revised aptitude test was administered to 398 sixth graders in several Hungarian schools.

Yet another motivation for pilot studies is to enable researchers to more accurately estimate the magnitude of the effect or relationship of interest (i.e., the **effect size**). With this information, they can then conduct a power analysis to determine the size of the sample they would likely need to observe a statistically significant relationship, if present.

See also **Statistical power.**

Derrick, D. J. (in press). Instrument reporting practices in second language research. *TESOL Quarterly.*

Kiss, C., & Nikolov, M. (2005). Developing, piloting, and validating an instrument to measure young learners' aptitude. *Language Learning, 55,* 99–150.

Population

The entire set of people, texts, and so forth that comprise the focus of a research study. In one sense, the field of applied linguistics is concerned with the entire population of language users, teachers, testers, and learners; however, in practice, the population under consideration in one research study is generally more specific than that. For example, researchers might determine that they are interested in university-level learners of Chinese. Such a population might be broken down further, perhaps according to proficiency level or institution. Although populations generally consist of people, it is also possible to investigate populations of educational institutions or texts. For example, a researcher might wish to examine the types of classes offered at private language schools in Australia. Alternatively, a researcher might wish to investigate the linguistic structures used to express stance in British newspapers. These contexts would constitute the population under consideration. In most cases, it is not possible to gather data from an entire population; therefore, **inferential statistics** are used to make inferences about a population based on a **sample** taken from that population. As a result, it is very important to ensure that a representative sample is chosen that will allow for valid and reliable generalizations to be made about the population as a whole.

See also **Participant**.

Population parameter

A characteristic of a **population** that can be used as a research **variable**. For example, if researchers are investigating the population of students studying Spanish as a foreign language at an American university, various parameters of that population would include first language, proficiency level, and length of study. It is important that researchers clearly define and accurately measure the parameters they are interested in. Doing so entails at least two main benefits. First, having clear population parameters allows readers to more readily assess whether and to what extent a study's findings might be applicable in their own contexts. Second, future researchers can more easily address the external **validity** and **generalizability** of the study's findings, particularly by closely replicating specific variables. Finally, population parameter can refer to any statistic, such as the **mean** or **standard deviation**, that is related to the population.

Positivism/Postpositivism

Empirical paradigms in which researchers strive for objectivity and truth through scientific means. These approaches, often representative of a specific worldview or **ontology**, are rather dominant in applied linguistics research and are characterized primarily, or at least traditionally, by researchers who strive for impartiality, test hypotheses, and usually base their findings on quantitative data and analyses. One of the primary differences between positivism and postpositivism is that the former is more confident about uncovering the truth of things, while postpositivism acknowledges that all observation and measurement is biased and error-prone (and not exclusively in the statistical/psychometric sense); consequently, multiple types of investigation, through **triangulation**, are needed to uncover the nature of the world around us. Because of the pervasiveness of the postpositive paradigm in applied linguistics, researchers working within that tradition may be less aware of other ontological and

epistemological perspectives. Researchers working in other paradigms within applied linguistics such as **constructivism**, on the other hand, may possess a greater awareness of their ontological and epistemological choices which, among other attributes, allow for subjectivity and dialog between all stakeholders involved in research. As might be expected, differences between researchers working in positivist (e.g., traditional or cognitivist SLA) and non-positivist (e.g. sociocultural theory) paradigms has been a source of tension in applied linguistics and elsewhere in the social sciences (i.e., the so-called paradigm wars). For example, there has been an often vigorous debate between researchers working within socio-cultural and cognitivist traditions of SLA (e.g., Firth & Wagner, 1997; Gass, Lee, & Roots, 2007; see also Ortega, 2005). However, more recently, there have been attempts to understand and bridge such divides (e.g., Atkinson, 2014; Hulstijn, 2013; Hulstijn et al., 2014) in order to identify the benefits that each perspective can bring to the study of SLA. Despite these efforts, many of the epistemological, ontological, and methodological differences between camps remain.

Atkinson, D. (2014). Language learning in mindbodyworld: A sociocognitive approach to second language acquisition. *Language Teaching, 47*, 467–483.

Firth, A., & Wagner, J. (1997). On discourse, communication, and (some) fundamental concepts in SLA research. *Modern Language Journal, 81*, 285–300.

Gass, S. M., & Lee, J., & Roots, R. (2007). New ideas or a new articulation. *Modern Language Journal, 91*, 788–799.

Hulstijn, J. (2013). Is the second language acquisition discipline disintegrating? *Language Teaching, 46*, 511–517.

Hulstijn, J., Young, R., Ortega, L., Bigelow, M., DeKeyser, R., Ellis, N., Lantolf, J., & Talmy, S. (2014). Bridging the gap: Cognitive and social approaches to research in second language learning and teaching. *Studies in Second Language Acquisition, 36*, 361–421.

Lincoln, Y. S., & Guba, E. G. (2000). Paradigmatic controversies, contradictions, and emerging confluences. In N. K. Denzin, & Y. S. Lincoln (Eds.), *Handbook of qualitative research* (2nd ed., pp. 163–188). Thousand Oaks, CA: Sage.

Ortega, L. (2005). Methodology, epistemology, and ethics in instructed SLA research: An introduction. *Modern Language Journal, 89*, 317–327.

Phillips, D. C., & Burbules, N. (2000). *Postpositivism and educational research*. Lanham, MD: Rowman & Littlefield Publishers.

P

Post hoc test

A statistical test that is run after an initial statistical analysis in order to investigate a specific result in more detail. In general, a post hoc test can refer to any type of test that is performed after an initial analysis. Post hoc tests are not generally part of the planned analysis addressing one of the study's research questions, but are conducted to follow up on interesting or puzzling results that need to be explored further and in more detail. For example, Crossley, Subitrelu, and Salsbury (2013) investigated factors that might affect L2 learners' oral production of vocabulary items. Their initial analysis found different influences on the production of nouns compared to verbs; consequently, Crossley et al. ran a post hoc analysis to investigate the lexical properties of nouns and verbs.

A more specific type of post hoc test refers to a set of statistical tests that can be run after an initial omnibus test, such as an **analysis of variance**. For example, in order to avoid a **Type I error**, researchers might wish to run an initial ANOVA to investigate the relationships between several **independent variables**. If the ANOVA results are statistically non-significant, then the researchers would not conduct any additional analyses. However, if the results were statistically significant, then the researchers could continue with post hoc tests to determine exactly where the significant differences occurred. There are several types of post hoc tests that can be conducted after a significant ANOVA, and although similar in many ways, they each carry their own set of characteristics and **assumptions**. For example, the Least Significant Differences (LSD) post hoc test is the most liberal. It does not control for Type I errors, and it is the same as conducting multiple *t*-tests. Other post hoc tests include Bonferroni, Scheffe, Tukey, and Games-Howell. Lyster (2004) followed a statistically significant mixed design ANOVA with Tukey post hoc tests to investigate the effects of form-focused instruction and corrective feedback on four different experimental groups.

Crossley, S. A., Subtirelu, N., & Salsbury, T. (2013). Frequency effects or context effects in second language word learning. *Studies in Second Language Acquisition, 35*, 727–755.

Lyster, R. (2004). Differential effects of prompts and recast in form-focused instruction. *Studies in Second Language Acquisition, 26*, 399–432.

Posttest

A feature of **experimental** and **quasi-experimental** research designs meant to measure the effects of a **treatment** or intervention that has been administered to the participants. There are several options to consider when conducting a posttest (see Plonsky & Gurzynski-Weiss, 2014). One important issue is the timing of the posttest. There are two general options employed in applied linguistics and throughout other areas of education and psychology: immediate and **delayed posttests**. Immediate posttests are sometimes administered directly following the treatment, although sometimes a posttest is termed immediate even though it may occur a day or two after the treatment. There can be even more variability in the timing of a delayed posttest, which can occur anywhere from several days to several years after the treatment. However, in applied linguistics research, the delay is usually one or two weeks. One criticism of L2 research is that it does not always investigate the long-term effects of treatments by including posttests, especially delayed ones. For example, only 38% of the studies in Plonsky's (2013) sample of primary studies included a delayed posttest in their design. Nevertheless, administering delayed posttests can be important, because some types of L2 development may not be evident immediately after the treatment. Consider, for example, the results of Mackey and Goo's (2007) meta-analysis of the effects of L2 interaction: whereas vocabulary gains were larger than grammar gains on immediate posttests, the delayed post-tests showed an overall advantage for grammar over vocabulary.

One consideration in determining the amount of delay relates to how easy it will be to control for intervening variables affecting the posttest results. For example, if a posttest is held several months after an intervention, it may be the case that learners receive other instruction or practice with the targeted structures. Thus, the posttest results are not indicative of the treatment's effect by itself.

Another issue to consider is what instruments to use for the posttest. In many cases, researchers use the same instrument for the **pretest** and any posttests. However, without a control group it is not possible to determine if improvement from pretest to posttest is due to the treatment or simply due to a test practice effect. In other words, the learners may do better the second time they take a test simply because they have already completed the test once. To avoid a test effect, sometimes different versions of the test are made, and these are then rotated so that some participants take Test A as the pretest and Test B as the posttest, while other participants take the tests in the reverse order. When using different tests for pretesting and posttesting, it is important to demonstrate the tests are equivalent. If the items on one test are easier than those on another test, then any increase or decrease in scores from pretest to posttest will be an artifact of the test design rather than the treatment.

Another issue to consider when designing a posttest is whether the items on the posttest were used during the treatment or are new to the learners. Sometimes researchers will include new test items to determine if participants are able to generalize the treatment effects to a new context.

Mackey, A., & Goo, J. (2007). Interaction research in SLA: A meta-analysis and research synthesis. In A. Mackey (Ed.), *Conversational interaction in second language acquisition: A collection of empirical studies* (pp. 407–449). Oxford: Oxford University Press.

Plonsky, L. (2013). Study quality in SLA: An assessment of designs, analyses, and reporting practices in quantitative L2 research. *Studies in Second Language Acquisition, 35*, 655–687.

Plonsky, L., & Gurzynski-Weiss, L. (2014). Research methods. In C. Fäcke (Ed.), *Manual of language acquisition* (pp. 31–49). Berlin: De Gruyter.

P

Power analysis (see Statistical power)

Practical significance

The degree to which a research study has real-world implications. In **quantitative research**, much is made of **statistical significance**, particularly in **Null Hypothesis Significance Testing** (NHST). Researchers want to know whether any differences or relationships found as a result of statistical analyses are greater than what would be expected due to chance or other random factors. Often, an **alpha** level of .05 is set, and values greater than that are considered non-significant, while values below .05 are considered significant. However, there has been a reaction against the emphasis that NHST places on statistical significance based on a single, arbitrary cutoff point. For example, *p*-**values** of .04 and .06 have a difference of only .02; however, in traditional NHST, the former would be considered statistically significant while that latter would not. Rather than relying on the *p*-value alone, there has been a call for more consideration of **power** estimates and **effect sizes** in order to determine the importance of the statistical results (e.g., Norris, 2015; Plonsky, 2015). There has also been the recognition that statistical significance does not always equate to practical significance. Thus, practical significance has been used as a term to indicate the real-world meaning of a study's findings, which may or may not coincide with the statistical significance observed in the study. Studies with small samples, and those interested in small effects or relationships, will have less statistical power and therefore be unlikely to reach statistical significance. It is not appropriate to equate such findings, however, with a lack of importance for theory and/or practice.

Norris, J. M. (2015). Statistical significance testing in second language research: Basic problems and suggestions for reform. *Language Learning, 65*(Supp. 1) 97–126.
Plonsky, L. (2015). Quantitative considerations for improving replicability in CALL and applied linguistics. *CALICO Journal, 32,* 232–244.

Pretest

A test that is administered before a treatment, for two main reasons: the first is to assess learners' knowledge, often of a targeted linguistic form, before any intervention occurs from the researcher. The pretest can then be used as a baseline for measuring how much learners improve as a result of the treatment, based on their performance on a **posttest**. Another purpose of a pretest is to investigate the similarities or differences between groups at the beginning of a research study. In many cases, researchers include several experimental and control groups in their design. In ideal cases, the groups are randomly selected from the **population**, thereby helping to ensure comparability among groups. However, often in L2 research, researchers do not select participants randomly. Rather, researchers may rely on a convenience sample that may be drawn from or consist of **intact classes**. Particularly in these latter cases, it is important to ensure that all groups of learners are equivalent in their proficiency level or knowledge of the specific linguistic structures being targeted in the study. For example, learners in one class may have self-selected because they thought a particular teacher might be easier than another. Thus, their proficiency scores might be lower than another group's scores, even though the institution has labeled their proficiency levels as equal. A pretest is one way to ensure that any differences among the groups are statistically non-significant. If pretesting indicates that the groups' scores are statistically different, then certain steps should be taken before the groups can be validly compared. Using an **analysis of covariance (ANCOVA)** is one method of dealing with pretest score differences. Running inferential statistics on **gain score**s rather than on raw scores is another option. (See Plonsky, 2013 for more on pretesting, or the lack thereof, in SLA research.) It is also important to remember that pre-treatment differences may exist between groups even if their scores do not result in a statistically significant p-value. In other words, a p of greater than .05 should be not equated with an effect size of zero; the absence of evidence is not always evidence for the absence of a difference (see Godfroid & Spino, in press; Plonsky, 2015).

Godfroid, A., & Spino, L. (in press). Reconceptualizing reactivity research: Absence of evidence is not evidence of absence. *Language Learning*.

Plonsky, L. (2013). Study quality in SLA: An assessment of designs, analyses, and reporting practices in quantitative L2 research. *Studies in Second Language Acquisition, 35*, 655–687.

Plonsky, L. (2015). Quantitative considerations for improving replicability in CALL and applied linguistics. *CALICO Journal, 32*, 232–244.

Priming

A phenomenon by which the likelihood of an occurrence of a specific linguistic structure or phenomenon is increased by an earlier occurrence of the same. For example, if a person uses a specific word or phrase in a conversation, it is statistically more probable that the same word or phrase will be used again, either by the same speaker or by their interlocutor. Priming has been used in L2 research to determine if learners are sensitive to certain input: Learners may conduct a task in which a specific structure is produced by the researcher, or a confederate of the researcher, who unbeknown to the participant, is providing them with input designed by the researcher. After the task, the learner's output is analyzed to determine if the primed structures are used. In an example of a priming study, McDonough and Mackey (2008) had EFL learners participate in communicative tasks in which one individual, unbeknown to the other individuals, was asked to use scripted, developmentally advanced-stage questions, such as the following *Wh- question + auxilliary + inverted pronoun* example. After the scripted interlocutor asked a question with the pre-specified question form, the authors analyzed the participants' responses to determine whether the same question form was subsequently used. Results of the investigation indicated that priming did occur; that is, participants who were exposed to ESL question forms showed greater gains in ESL question formation development on **posttests** than participants who did not receive priming.

P

Example of priming (McDonough & Mackey, 2008, p. 39):

Scripted interlocutor: *Why did you decide to work in Bangkok?*
            Participant: *uh because I would like to study master degree in*
            Bangkok // what do you like to do in your free time?

McDonough, K., & Mackey, A. (2008). Syntactic priming and ESL question development. *Studies in Second Language Acquisition, 30*, 31–47.

McDonough, K., & Trofimovich, P. (2008). *Using priming methods in second language research*. New York: Taylor and Francis.

McDonough, K., & Fulga, A. (2015). The detection and primed production of novel constructions. *Language Learning, 65*, 326–357.

Trofimovich, P., & McDonough, K. (2011). *Applying priming methods to L2 learning, teaching and research: Insights from psycholinguistics*. Amsterdam: John Benjamins Publishing.

Principal components analysis

A type of **factor analysis** that is primarily distinguished from exploratory factor analysis (EFA) in its handling of **variance**. Specifically, whereas EFA is concerned only with common variance, that is, the variance resulting from **correlations** between variables, principal components analysis (PCA) is concerned with, and able to model, all variance in the data set: the variance in each variable (item), variance between variables (i.e., covariance; correlations), and error variance (Tabachnick & Fidell, 2013). Though the differences between PCA and EFA have been the object of much debate in the statistical literature (e.g., Conway & Huffcutt, 2003), in practice, the results from the two procedures are generally quite similar and the distinction is not commonly made in applied linguistics research (see Loewen & Gonulal, 2015). However, it is advisable to use EFA when interested in exploring the underlying relationships rather than reducing the number of variables in a data set.

Conway, J. M., & Huffcutt, A. I. (2003). A review and evaluation of exploratory factor analysis practices in organizational research. *Organizational Research Methods, 6*(2), 147–168.

Loewen, S., & Gonulal, T. (2015). Exploratory factor analysis and principal components analysis. In L. Plonsky (Ed.), *Advancing quantitative methods in second language research* (pp. 182–212). New York: Routledge.

Tabachnick B., & Fidell, L. (2013). *Using multivariate statistics* (6th ed.). Boston: Pearson Education Inc.

Publication bias

The tendency by authors and journals to publish studies that have statistically significant results. Publication bias is problematic because it can distort the importance of certain theoretical and empirical perspectives within a discipline. First, a lack of **statistical significance** does not necessarily imply a lack of **practical significance**, and conversely, not all statistically significant results are indicative of great theoretical or practical value. For example, statistically non-significant results can be important for evaluating theoretical and research hypotheses, and their exclusion from print can lead to the suppression of empirical evidence supporting (or opposing) certain theoretical positions. Publication bias is of particular concern when conducting synthetic research, such as **meta-analysis**, because such analyses are often based exclusively on published results. However, in an effort to counteract publication bias, some meta-analysts include unpublished studies, sometimes referred to as fugitive or grey literature. There are also several well-developed techniques established by meta-analysts for examining whether and to what extent publication bias may be present in a given domain: such techniques include the use of **funnel plots**, trim-and-fill, and the fail-safe N (see Rothstein, Sutton, & Borenstein, 2005).

Rothstein, H. R., Sutton, A. J., & Borenstein, M. (Eds.). (2005). *Publication bias in meta-analysis: Prevention, assessment and adjustments*. Chichester, England: Wiley.

P

Q–Q plot

A graphic representation of the distribution of scores in a data set in order to assess the **assumption** of **normal distribution**. A Q–Q plot charts the observed values from a data set against the values that would be expected if the data were normally distributed. The expected values are represented by a straight diagonal line, while the observed values are grouped into quantiles that split the data into equal segments. These quantiles are represented on the Q–Q plot by individual dots. The closer the dots are to the diagonal line, the more normally distributed the data set. In Figure 30, the trajectory of the dots varies considerably from the diagonal line, indicating a non-normal distribution. However, in Figure 31, the dots are much more closely aligned with the diagonal line, meaning that the data are more normally distributed.

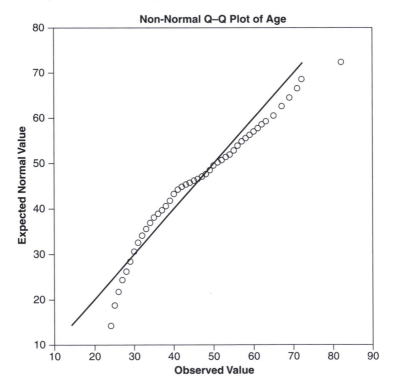

Figure 30   Q–Q plot of a non-normal distribution

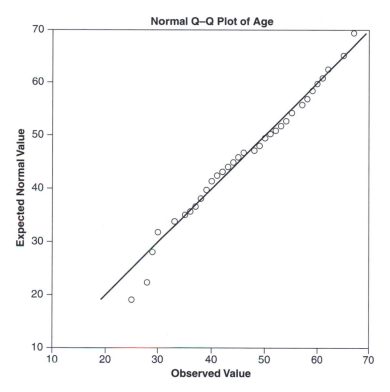

Figure 31 Q–Q plot of a normal distribution

Q–Q plots are similar to **P–P plots**; however, in P–P plots, the dots represent individual scores rather than quantiles. Because there are no specific criteria for deciding how similar the diagonal line (i.e., expected values) and the individual dots (i.e., observed values) must be in order for the data to be considered normally distributed, it is advisable to also conduct a **Kolmogorov–Smirnov** or **Shapiro–Wilk test** and examine a histogram of the data to investigate the assumption of normal distribution. However, a Q–Q plot can provide quick, visual information about the data.

Qualitative research

Empirical inquiry based on non-numeric data. In applied linguistics research, nearly all **constructs** of interest are qualitative in nature. Very often, though, researchers quantify qualitative phenomena. For example, L2 speaking fluency and discourse complexity are linguistic in nature; however, they have frequently been investigated by using the number of words per minute or the **frequency** of pre-noun modifiers, respectively. Similarly, language learning aptitude has often been determined by learners' scores on the Modern Language Aptitude Test. In another example, rater bias has been investigated by using the **percentage** of variance in ratings due to rater background. However, the **validity** of investigating qualitative phenomena quantitatively has been questioned: "Not everything that can be counted counts, and not everything that counts can be counted" (Cameron, 1963, p. 13). Often quantification of qualitative phenomena has been done for ease of measurement or analysis, but quantification of data separates researchers from the original or natural state of the data. Fortunately, even though applied linguistics has traditionally relied more on quantitative than qualitative analyses (Gass, 2009), there are a number of well-developed methodologies for conducting qualitative research. These methods include, for example, observations, **interviews**, **ethnography**, **discourse analysis**, and **conversation analysis**. As with quantitative analyses, these techniques have largely been imported from related disciplines such as sociology, anthropology, and education. Qualitative research is distinguished from quantitative efforts not only by the nature of the data analyzed but also by the techniques used to analyze the data. Whereas **quantitative research** generally works within a **positivist/postpositivist** paradigm, qualitative research is often situated within **constructivist** or critical theory paradigms, which, unlike positivism and postpositivism, accept and work with the multiple realities resulting from different perspectives (e.g., learner, teacher, and researcher).

For a thorough overview of qualitative methods in applied linguistics as well as numerous references for different types of qualitative techniques, see Friedman (2012).

Cameron, W. B. (1963). *Informal sociology: A casual introduction to sociological thinking.* New York: Random House.
Friedman, D. (2012). How to collect and analyze qualitative data. In A. Mackey, & S. M. Gass (Eds.), *Research methods in second language acquisition: A practical guide* (pp. 180–200). Malden, MA: Wiley Blackwell.
Gass, S. (2009). A survey of SLA research. In W. Ritchie, & T. Bhatia (Eds.), *Handbook of second language acquisition* (pp. 3–28). Bingley: Emerald.
Richards, K. (2003). *Qualitative inquiry in TESOL.* New York: Palgrave Macmillan.

Quantitative research

The analysis of numeric data. At its most basic, quantitative research involves analyzing numeric data. However, at its broadest, it encompasses an entire **ontological** and **epistemological** perspective. Put simplistically, quantitative research employs a positivistic perspective that assumes that truth is knowable, and that through accurate measurement and analysis, the truth about a given **construct** can be discovered. The predominant research paradigm in applied linguistics has been quantitative, with quantitative studies outnumbering qualitative ones (Gass, 2009).

In quantitative research, there are two primary methods of analyzing and interpreting data. The first is through the use of **descriptive statistics**, which provide information about the average datapoint, as well as the distribution of the data. Such descriptive statistics include the **mean** and **standard deviation**. Second, there are **inferential statistics**, which allow researchers to make generalizations based on the nature of the data. There are many different inferential statistical procedures, although *t*-**tests** and **analysis of variance** (ANOVA) are the most commonly used in applied linguistics research. **Correlation, regression**, and **chi-square** are also fairly common. More advanced statistics that are less common and less well-known in applied linguistics research include **structural equation modeling, factor analysis, cluster analysis**, and **discriminant functional analysis** (Loewen et al., 2014).

Gass, S. (2009). A survey of SLA research. In W. Ritchie, & T. Bhatia (Eds.), *Handbook of second language acquisition* (pp. 3–28). Bingley: Emerald.

Lazaraton, A. (2005). Quantitative research methods. In E. Hinkel (Ed.), *Handbook of research in second language teaching and learning* (pp. 109–224). Mahwah, NJ: Erlbaum.

Loewen, S., Lavolette, B., Spino, L., Papi, M., Schmidtke, J., Sterling, S., & Wolff, D. (2014). Statistical literacy among applied linguists and second language acquisition researchers. *TESOL Quarterly, 48*, 360–388.

Quasi-experimental design

A study in which a dependent measure is compared for two or more groups. Quasi-experimental design is a less rigorous version of **experimental design**. For example, quasi-experimental design does not require **random selection** or assignment of participants. Instead, participants may constitute a convenience sample. In addition, **intact classes** may be used for different groups. Another difference between experimental and quasi-experimental design is that the latter does not require a **control group**. In such cases, a quasi-experimental study might have two treatment groups, which receive different treatments, making it possible to consider how those two groups perform relative to each other; however, without a control group, it is not possible to determine if the groups would have performed significantly better than a control group that did not receive any treatment. Much of the quantitative research in applied linguistics is quasi-experimental, rather than experimental.

Questionnaire

A data elicitation method consisting of a series of questions. Often these questions are designed to elicit numerical responses, which can then be easily submitted to statistical analyses. Questionnaires are used frequently for large-scale data collection, because they are generally quick and easy for participants to complete. However, questionnaires are sometimes criticized because researchers impose their perspectives through the questions rather than letting respondents raise issues and topics that are important to them. Thus, a combination of questionnaires and **interviews** can provide

Q

both extensive and in-depth perspectives on a topic. In general, the terms questionnaire and **survey** are used interchangeably, although sometimes a survey is viewed as somewhat broader in scope. Questionnaires are a commonly used data collection instrument in applied linguistics research.

Sample questionnaire items from the Strategy Inventory for Language Learning (SILL), Part E (rated on a scale from 1, "Never or almost never true of me" to 5, "Always true of me")

- I try to relax whenever I feel afraid of using the L2.
- I encourage myself to speak the L2 even when I am afraid of making a mistake.
- I give myself a reward or treat when I do well in the L2.
- I notice if I am tense or nervous when I am studying or using the L2.
- I write down my feelings in a language learning diary.
- I talk to someone else about how I feel when I am learning the L2.

(Oxford, 1989, p. 3)

Writing good questionnaire items can be difficult and time-consuming. Table 18 shows the development of two questions from a questionnaire on isolated and integrated L2 instruction, as the researchers attempted to clarify the language and refine the construct under investigation.

Table 18 Development and revision of questionnaire items

First version	Second version	Third version
I find it helpful when the instructor teaches a grammar point found in that text.	I find it helpful when the instructor teaches a grammar point while we read the text.	I find it helpful when the instructor teaches grammar while we read a text.
I find it helpful if the instructor teaches a grammar point on its own before or after reading a text.	I find it helpful if the instructor teaches a grammar point before reading a text.	I find it helpful to learn a grammar point before I read it in a text.

Source: Spada, Barkaoui, Peters, So, & Valeo (2009, p. 73).

Dörnyei, Z., with Taguchi, I. (2010). *Questionnaires in second language research: Construction, administration, and processing* (2nd ed.). London: Routledge.

Oxford, R. (1989). *Language learning strategies: What every teacher should know.* New York: Newbury House/Harper & Row.

Spada, N., Barkaoui, K., Peters, C., So, M., & Valeo, A. (2009). Developing a questionnaire to investigate second language learners' preferences for two types of form-focused instruction. *System, 37,* 70–81.

r (see Correlation)

R-squared (*R²*)

An **effect size** that indicates the magnitude of the relationship between two variables. As the name implies, R^2 is closely related to the *r* **correlation** statistic. Statistically, R^2 is derived by squaring a correlation estimate (*r*), with the resulting value indicating the percentage of shared **variance** between the two variables in question. For example, a correlation value between two variables of *r* = .6 could be squared to determine that 36% of their variance was shared, that is, common to the two variables. R^2 is also found in the output from **multiple regression** analyses. In this case, R^2 expresses the percentage of variance in the criterion variable that can be accounted for by one or more predictors, thereby providing information about the adequacy of the regression model. The greater the R^2 value, the better the model, because the predictor variables account for more of the variance in the criterion variable. For example, Egbert and Plonsky (2015) found that a small set of linguistic and stylistic predictor variables (e.g., word length, presence of a results section) could explain 31% (R^2 = .31) of the variance in conference abstract ratings. It is important to note, however, that similar to correlation coefficients (*r*), R^2 does not imply causality. Instead, it provides information about the association between two or more variables.

R^2 is also closely related to the **eta²** effect size index, in that both are interested in explaining variance. Eta², however, is more commonly associated with ANOVA and is therefore used to explain variance as a function of group membership (i.e., based on a categorical **independent variable**), rather than the correlation between two **continuous variables**.

Egbert, J., & Plonsky, L. (2015). Success in the abstract: Exploring linguistic and stylistic predictors of conference abstract ratings. *Corpora*, 10, 291–313.

R statistical software

A free software program and programming language that can be used to compute statistics. One of the primary advantages of R is that it is free, unlike other software packages such as **SPSS** and SAS. However, one disadvantage for many users is that rather than using dialog boxes and drop-down menus to conduct statistical procedures, R is command-line-driven and users must write syntax in

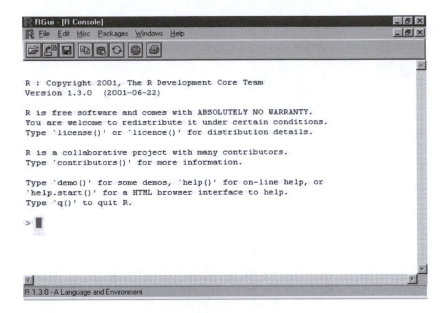

Figure 32 Screenshot of the R command-line interface

order to perform analyses (see Figure 32); consequently, learning to use R can be challenging for researchers who are unfamiliar with statistical syntax code. This approach can be challenging but, some would argue, requires researchers to possess a better understanding of the statistical procedures they employ (e.g., Mizumoto & Plonsky, in press). Although R is used by some researchers in applied linguistics, it is not as common as SPSS (Loewen et al., 2014). There does seem to be a move towards R in applied linguistics, mirroring a similar trend in other sciences (e.g., Muenchen, 2014). As of this writing, for example, there are at least three textbooks written for linguistics that cover different techniques using R in part or in whole (Gries, 2013; Larson-Hall, 2015; Plonsky, 2015). Applied linguists' use of R has also been bolstered by its utility as a tool for analyzing texts or **corpora** using R packages designed for this purpose (Gries, 2009; Michalke, 2014).

Baayen, R. H. (2008). *Analyzing linguistic data: A practical introduction to statistics using R.* Cambridge: Cambridge University Press.

Gries, S. Th. (2009). *Quantitative corpus linguistics with R: A practical introduction.* New York: Routledge.

Gries, S. Th. (2013). *Statistics for linguistics with R* (2nd rev. ed.). New York: De Gruyter.

Larson-Hall, J. (2015). *A guide to doing statistics in second language research using SPSS and R* (2nd ed.). New York: Routledge.

Loewen, S., Lavolette, E., Spino, L., Papi, M., Schmidtke, J., Sterling, S., & Wolff, D. (2014). Statistical literacy among applied linguists and second language acquisition researchers. *TESOL Quarterly, 48,* 360–388.

Michalke, M. (2014). *koRpus: An R Package for text analysis. Version 0.05-5.* [Computer program.] Available from http://reaktanz.de/?c=hacking&s=koRpus

Mizumoto, A., & Plonsky, L. (in press). R as a lingua franca: Advantages of using R for quantitative research in applied linguistics. *Applied Linguistics.*

Muenchen, R. A. (2014). *R passes SPSS in scholarly use, stata growing rapidly.* Available from http://r4stats.com/2014/08/20/r-passes-spss-in-scholarly-use-stata-growing-rapidly/

Plonsky, L. (Ed.) (2015). *Advancing quantitative methods in second language research.* New York: Routledge.

R Core Team. (2014). *R: A language and environment for statistical computing.* [Computer software.] Vienna, Austria. Available from http://www.r-project.org/

Random effects

The investigation of a variable in **quantitative research,** in which not all possible categories are investigated. For example, the variable of treatment duration can be considered a random effect in studies of the effectiveness of L2 instruction, if researchers divide participants into groups of zero, short, and long duration. This effect can be considered random because it would be possible to have additional groups with shorter or longer treatments. Random effects can be generalized beyond the treatment groups: for example, a "subject" variable consisting of the participants in the study is not exhaustive, and the researcher wants to generalize the findings beyond the specific participants who took part in the study. In contrast, **fixed effects** include all of the possible conditions that a researcher is interested in, and can be generalized only to conditions containing the same set of variable categories. In academic research, most variables are treated as fixed effects; however, some statistical programs, such as **SPSS** and **R**, allow researchers to designate a variable as a random or fixed effect.

Cunnings, I., & Finlayson, I. (2015). Mixed effects modeling and longitudinal data analysis. In L. Plonsky (Ed.), *Advancing quantitative methods in second language research* (pp. 159–181). New York: Routledge.

See **Mixed effects modeling**

Random selection

The manner in which participants are chosen for a research study. Random selection involves two related concepts: random sampling and random assignment. Random sampling is a characteristic of experimental research design, in which participants from a **population** are chosen with equal opportunity of being selected. For practical, and perhaps obvious, reasons, this practice is quite rare in applied linguistics and many other social and education fields; however, in a study of explicit L2 instruction, de Graaf (1997) randomly selected two groups of 28 participants each from a larger sample of 200 people.

A related procedure, random assignment, involves arbitrarily assigning different treatment conditions to participants. In so doing, each individual participant has an equal chance of being included in each condition, thus greatly decreasing the likelihood of pre-treatment differences between or within groups. Thus, in an experimental classroom study of Spanish university students, for example, random sampling would mean that any Spanish student had an equal probability of being selected, as well as an equal chance of being placed into one of the treatment groups. Random sampling and random assignment are important because they help ensure that the findings of a study are not influenced or biased by external variables. However, many SLA studies do not use random sampling due to the difficulties of randomly selecting participants. Furthermore, when investigating L2 classrooms, researchers may actually lower the **ecological validity** of the study by placing students in artificial, albeit randomly selected, classes. Instead, classroom researchers often choose a convenience sample, using **intact classes** which may be composed in non-random ways: for example, more motivated learners might take an early morning class, while less motivated learners might take one in the afternoon. Consequently, differences in L2 proficiency between the groups at the end of a research study might be due to motivation as well as the **treatment** provided in the study. Another type of sampling, which is used more frequently in **qualitative research**, is purposive sampling, in which researchers select participants based on specific criteria: for example, Carless (2007) selected 11 secondary school teachers to interview for his study based on recommendations from community contacts. In general, random sampling is uncommon in applied linguistics research; however, studies sometimes use **pretesting** to investigate the comparability of research groups before the treatment begins. Finally, if a study does not use random sampling, it is considered **quasi-experimental**, rather than experimental.

Carless, D. (2007). The suitability of task-based approaches for secondary schools: Perspectives from Hong Kong. *System, 35*, 595–608.

de Graaf, R. (1997). The eXperanto experiment: Effects of explicit instruction on second language acquisition. *Studies in Second Language Acquisition, 19*, 249–297.

Range

A measure of **dispersion** or variability in a data set. Another more commonly used measure of dispersion is the **standard deviation**. One or more of these measures should be reported along with a measure of **central tendency** when reporting **descriptive statistics** for a **quantitative research** study. The range is calculated by subtracting the lowest score from the highest one in the data set: thus, if the range of scores is from 10 to 25, the range would be 15. Sometimes instead of including the range in their reporting of descriptive statistics, researchers simply provide the minimum and maximum scores, as seen in Godfroid and Uggen's (2013) presentation of posttest scores in their study of German irregular verbs (mean = 3.13, SD = 3.21, range = 0–11). Finally, the range is strongly affected by **outliers** in the data.

Godfroid, A., & Uggen, M. S. (2013). Attention to irregular verbs by beginning learners of German: An eye-movement study. *Studies in Second Language Acquisition, 35*, 291–322.

Rasch analysis

A set of models, based on **item response theory**, designed to evaluate and analyze assessment and testing data. Rasch models estimate the relative roles of and relationship between item difficulty and other testing parameters, such as test-taker ability and rater leniency/severity. More concretely, Rasch Analyses provide test analysts with information about the likelihood (expressed in **logits**) of test-takers responding correctly to a given test item as a function of other test parameters. The analysis also allows for comparisons of parameters on a standardized interval scale (the logit scale), which is generally presented visually and can be interpreted quite intuitively. In addition to ease of interpretation, Rasch models can be applied to different types of items and data. These and other benefits over traditional or classical test theory have prompted major growth in the use of Rasch models among applied linguists in recent years (McNamara & Knoch, 2012). The analysis itself, however, can be challenging to newcomers, involving numerous decisions and procedures related to the nature of the data set in question (see Knoch & McNamara, 2015).

Révész (2009) conducted a Rasch Analysis in her study of the effects of task characteristics on L2 development during interaction. The analysis revealed that recasts and contextual support were both beneficial for development, which she presented in Figure 33.

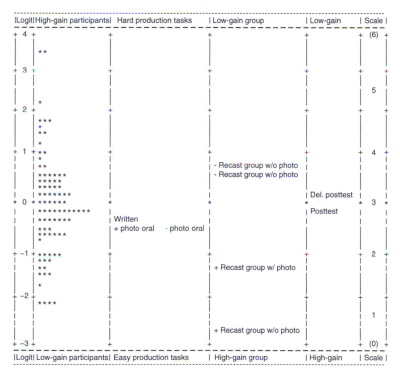

Source: Révész (2009, p. 459).

Figure 33   Facets map resulting from a Rasch analysis

Barkaoui, K. (2014). Multifaceted Rasch analysis for test evaluation. In A. J. Kunnan (Ed.), *The companion to language assessment*. Malden, MA: Wiley. DOI: 10.1002/9781118411360. wbcla070

Knoch, U., & McNamara, T. (2015). Rasch analysis. In L. Plonsky (Ed.). *Advancing quantitative methods in second language research* (pp. 279–308). New York: Routledge.

McNamara, T., & Knoch, U. (2012). The Rasch Wars: The emergence of Rasch measurement in language testing. *Language Testing, 29*(4), 553–574.

Révész, A. (2009). Task complexity, focus on form, and second language development. *Studies in Second Language Acquisition, 31*, 437–470.

Ratio

A number used to express one value in relation to another value. Often, a ratio is used to allow comparisons across conditions when counts are unequal. For example, a researcher may wish to compare the **frequency** of recasts during task-based interaction across multiple learner **dyads**. Unless the amount of time taken to complete the task is controlled, there may be differences in task length, making direct comparisons uninformative. By creating a ratio of the number of recasts per minute, the researcher can minimize the effects of different task durations. Another example of a ratio, used in vocabulary research, is the **Type-Token Ratio**, which compares the number of unique words (types) with the number of total words (tokens) in a text as a measure of lexical diversity.

Ratio-scale variable

A variable that is measured on a numeric scale that includes an absolute zero point. Similar to **continuous variables**, ratio variables are measured on a scale that has equal distances between each point on the scale. Age and **reaction times** are examples of ratio variables used in applied linguistics research. For reaction times, the difference between 400 and 500 milliseconds is the same as the difference between 1,400 and 1,500 milliseconds, namely 100 milliseconds. In addition, a score of 0 milliseconds indicates an absence of time. Ratio-scale variables are not commonly used in applied linguistics; furthermore, the primary difference between ratio and continuous scales, which is the presence or absence of an absolute zero point, rarely has practical implications in the field.

Reaction time

A measure of how quickly participants respond to the appearance of stimuli. Reaction times, usually measured in milliseconds, are frequently used in psycholinguistic studies to examine the processing load presented by the stimuli, with the assumption that longer reaction times correspond with heavier processing loads and/or greater difficulty. An example of reaction time research comes from Vainio, Pajunen, and Hyönä (2014), who used reaction times to investigate word recognition in Finnish by Chinese,

Russian, and Finnish L1 speakers. Among other results, the researchers found that, unsurprisingly, L1 Finnish speakers had significantly faster overall (average) reaction times (e.g., $M = 665$, $SD = 130$) compared to Chinese ($M = 927$, $SD = 192$) and Russian native speakers ($M = 880$, $SD = 175$). However, Chinese and Russian speakers did not differ significantly from each other.

Reaction times have also been used in self-paced reading and **eye-tracking** studies in which participants progress from word to word in sentences that may be grammatically or semantically anomalous. Participants may take different amounts of time to advance to subsequent words, and such differences might indicate participants' sensitivity to the anomaly. When used to measure participants' judgments (e.g., real word vs. non-word), reaction time data are often accompanied by a measure of the participants' accuracy. For instance, in the example from above, the Finnish participants' mean error rate was just 1.3 ($SD = 2.4$), compared to 10.5 (5.1) and 8.8 (15.6) for the Chinese and Russian speakers, respectively.

Jiang, N. (2011). *Conducting reaction time research in second language studies*. New York: Routledge.

Vainio, S., Pajunen, A., & Hyönä, J. (2014). L1 and L2 word recognition in Finnish: Examining L1 effects on L2 processing of morphological complexity and morphophonological transparency. *Studies in Second Language Acquisition, 36*, 133–162.

Reliability

The consistency with which an **instrument** measures something. Consequently, reliability refers to whether or not, upon an additional measurement, the results would be more or less the same. Reliability is a prerequisite for instrument **validity**, but it does not guarantee it: that is, an instrument may be very consistent and stable (reliable) without necessarily measuring what researchers claim it is measuring. Reliability is primarily a concern of **quantitative research**.

Reliability appears to be little understood (Brown & Bailey, 2008; Loewen et al., 2014), and it is often left out of reports of applied linguistics research (e.g., Derrick, in press; Larson-Hall & Plonsky, 2015). Perhaps contributing to these issues is the fact that there are multiple types of reliability, each of which can be estimated using a variety of indices. The first and most commonly measured type is instrument reliability (or internal consistency), which refers to the extent to which the items on a particular test or scale measure the same construct. For example, if a researcher is using a **questionnaire** to measure participant motivation, it is important for (a) items to be answered in a consistent manner, (b) items measuring the same construct to be highly correlated, and (c) participants to score similarly if the questionnaire was administered on more than one occasion (e.g., Brown 2014; Douglas, 2001).

R

Internal consistency can be estimated using a variety of indices such as **Cronbach's alpha**, KR20, and Spearman–Brown. Cronbach's alpha, for example, takes all of the items on a test and correlates them with each other to determine the extent to which respondents answered questions in a similar and consistent manner. For example, learners taking an L2 proficiency test should be relatively consistent, with higher proficiency learners getting similar questions correct, and lower proficiency learners patterning differently. Another statistical method for calculating reliability is to use the split-half method, in which a test or **survey** is divided into two parts and the similarity between the two parts is calculated. Both Cronbach's alpha and split-half produce **correlation** coefficients.

Another type of reliability refers to the consistency of data coding or rating. **Inter-rater reliability** provides an estimate of the consistency of data coding or rating across multiple raters. For example, if researchers have several coding categories that they are using, they need to ensure that those categories are applied consistently across raters. One way to assess coding reliability is by having another individual use the same coding criteria to determine if she or he arrives at the same categories for the same data. Alternatively, a researcher may code a set of data and then come back to it at a later time to recode it. Again, if a coding scheme is reliable, the two coding sessions should produce similar results. This is called **intra-rater reliability**. In the case of inter- and intra-rater reliability, researchers must decide how much data needs to be recoded in order to demonstrate that the coding has been (or at least can be) conducted reliably. Ideally, the entire data set should be double-coded, and in some cases, particularly with smaller data sets, this might be the case. However, in many cases only 10% or 20% of the data is double-coded. There is no predetermined percentage of data that needs to be double-coded. If coding 10% of the data results in a high reliability score, then it may be acceptable not to double-code more. However, in cases where reliability is lower, it might be desirable to code a larger percentage and/or to recalibrate raters before continuing.

There are also several indices designed to estimate inter-rater and intra-rater reliability. One is by simple **percentage** agreement, in which researchers simply calculate the number of items that were coded similarly by the two raters. Alternatively, **Cohen's kappa** can also be used to measure inter- and intra-rater agreement. The index differs, however, in that it accounts (i.e., adjusts) for the fact that some agreement might occur by chance. Consequently, Cohen's kappa is a more conservative measure of reliability than percentage agreement, and estimates of reliability based on Cohen's kappa tend to be lower than those based on percentage agreement (Plonsky & Derrick, under review).

There is no absolute agreement on what constitutes acceptable reliability scores. Obviously, higher is better. However, what might be deemed acceptable or appropriate might differ from one domain or context to the next (Brown, 2014). A much higher rate of reliability might be expected in high-stakes assessment situations, for example. In order to guide future interpretations of reliability, Plonsky and Derrick (under review) combined (i.e., meta-analyzed) 2,244 reliability estimates across 500 individual reports of L2 research. Their results point to a wide variety of observed estimates across the major types and indices, with typical estimates for internal consistency close to .80 (closer to .90 for inter- and intra-rater reliability). They also found reliability estimates to vary depending on the index employed, as well as according to several study and instrument features.

Bachman, L. F. (2004). *Statistical analyses for language assessment.* New York: Cambridge University Press.

Brown, J. D. (2014). Classical theory reliability. In A. J. Kunnan (Ed.), *The companion to language assessment.* Oxford: Wiley Blackwell.

Brown, J. D., & Bailey, K. M. (2008). Language testing courses: What are they in 2007? *Language Testing, 25,* 349–383.

Derrick, D. J. (in press). Instrument reporting practices in second language research. *TESOL Quarterly.*

Douglas, D. (2001). Performance consistency in second language acquisition and language testing: A conceptual gap. *Second Language Research, 17,* 442–456.

Feng, G. C. (2014). Intercoder reliability indices: disuse, misuse, and abuse. *Quality and Quantity, 48,* 1803–1815.

Larson-Hall, J., & Plonsky, L. (2015). Reporting and interpreting quantitative research findings: What gets reported and recommendations for the field. *Language Learning, 65*(Supp. 1), 125–157.

Loewen, S., Lavolette, B., Spino, L. A., Papi, M., Schmidtke, J., Sterling, S., & Wolff, D. (2014). Statistical literacy among applied linguists and second language acquisition researchers. *TESOL Quarterly, 48,* 360–388.

Plonsky, L., & Derrick, D. J. (under review). A meta-analysis of reliability coefficients in second language research. [Manuscript under review.]

Repeated measures analysis of variance (see Analysis of variance)

Repeated measures design

A study that involves collecting data from the same individuals on multiple occasions. Repeated measures design is also called **within-subjects** or **within-groups design.** A common repeated measures design involves a **pretest** and at least one **posttest** to measure participants' performance before and after a **treatment** of some kind. Some statistical tests assume that the data are independent, meaning that one datapoint is not influenced by another. Because participants in repeated measures pretest/posttest studies contribute two or more sets of scores, their responses are more likely to be correlated than if the tests were taken by different individuals. This lack of **independence** reduces the amount of variance in the data. Repeated measures designs, therefore, employ specific statistical tests that account for repeated measures data in order to compensate for this relationship between data points. Paired samples *t*-tests, repeated measures ANOVA, and **Friedman's ANOVA** are all tests that are appropriate for repeated measures data. For example, Riazantseva (2012) used repeated measures ANOVA to investigate the effects of written corrective feedback on the accuracy of L2 students' writing. She collected three types of written data (in-class essays, in-class summaries, and at-home summaries) at the beginning and end of the semester. Because all students participated in all data collection sessions, a repeated measures design was appropriate.

In addition to the previously mentioned tests which allow only repeated measures variables, there are some tests that allow both **between-groups** and within-groups variables. For example, mixed design ANOVA is often used in quasi-experimental research studies to investigate the pretest and posttest performances (within-subjects) of several different treatment groups (between-subjects).

See also **Between-groups design**.

Riazantseva, A. (2012). Outcome measure of L2 writing as a mediator of the effects of corrective feedback on students' ability to write accurately. *System, 40*, 421–430.

Replication

The process of investigating a previously researched topic, using the same or only a slightly altered methodology as an earlier study. Replication is an important component of advancing knowledge in an academic discipline because researchers can ascertain whether the results of the previous studies are durable and consistent when compared to the replication results. Replications are also useful in determining the extent to which findings of a given study can be generalized to other learners, target features, settings, and so forth (Plonsky, 2012). Exact replications are rare in applied linguistics research; however, partial replications or conceptual replications are somewhat more common. In partial replications, many aspects of the previous research design are kept the same; however, one or two key features are altered. For example, Winke (2013) replicated Lee's (2007) investigation into the effects of textual input enhancement. Similar to Lee, Winke used a **pretest/posttest** design to assess learners' knowledge of English passive verb forms. In addition, both studies used a free recall test to measure reading comprehension. However, in contrast to Lee, Winke used a different reading text and a different coding scheme for the free recall test. The most important difference between Winke's and Lee's studies was that Winke used eye-tracking technology to measure learners' eye movements while they read the passages. Thus, Winke replicated the same or similar **constructs** as those in the previous study while changing certain research design features. Finally, although there is not a strong tradition of replication research in applied linguistics, the field appears to be gradually accepting its value and conducting more replications. Evidence to this effect is found, for example, in: (a) a recently edited volume on this topic (Porte, 2012), (b) special replication issues in two prominent journals in the field—*Journal of Second Language Writing* (2012, volume 21, issue 3) and *CALICO* (2015)– and (c) an invited colloquium on replication at the 2015 Conference of the American Association for Applied Linguistics.

Gass, S., & Valmori, L. (2015). Replication in interaction and working memory research: Révész (2012) and Goo (2012). *Language Teaching, 48,* 545–555.

Lee, S.-K. (2007. Effects of textual enhancement and topic familiarity on Korean EFL students' reading comprehension and learning of passive form. *Language Learning, 57,* 87–118.

Plonsky, L. (2012). Replication, meta-analysis, and generalizability. In G. Porte (Ed.), *Replication research in applied linguistics* (pp. 116–132). New York: Cambridge University Press.

Plonsky, L. (2015). Quantitative considerations for improving replicability in CALL and applied linguistics. *CALICO Journal, 32,* 232–244.

Porte, G. (2012). *Replication research in applied linguistics.* New York: Cambridge University Press.

Porte, G. (2013). Who needs replication research? *CALICO Journal, 30,* 10–15.

Smith, B., & Schulze, M. (2013). Thirty years of the CALICO Journal—replicate, replicate, replicate. *CALICO Journal, 30,* i–iv.

Winke, P. M. (2013). The effects of input enhancement on grammar learning and comprehension: A modified replication of Lee (2007) with eye-movement data. *Studies in Second Language Acquisition, 35,* 323–352.

Research ethics

A concern with the morality of research practices. Most applied linguists associate research ethics with institutional and government regulations, prescribed by independent ethics committees and ethical review boards, commonly referred to as **institutional review boards** (IRBs) in the United States. These committees serve a protective function by approving only research that ensures the ethical treatment of research participants and limits any potential risks. In education and the social sciences more generally, research into ethical issues also constitutes an important area of empirical inquiry. Early concern with research ethics occurred in the mid twentieth century in response to human experimentation in World War II Germany, as well as the Tuskegee syphilis study and the Stanford prison experiment in the United States. In addition, the more recent high-profile retractions of research findings and a growing awareness of data fabrication across the sciences (see Fanelli, 2009) underscores the ongoing need for attention to research ethics. However, until quite recently, there has been little consideration of research ethics in applied linguistics, but this trend appears to be changing. Evidence of momentum in this area includes:

- Special issues on research ethics in *The Modern Language Journal* (see Ortega, 2005) and *TESL Canada Journal* (see Kouritzin, 2011).
- Thomas' (2009) guidance for applied linguists interested in devoting greater consideration to ethical issues in their research.
- De Costa's (2014) discussion of ethical issues involved in ethnographic research.
- Specialized symposia held at the 2014 conferences of the American Association of Applied Linguistics and the International Association of Applied Linguistics, resulting in an ensuing edited volume (De Costa, 2015).
- The *TESOL Research Agenda* (2014, p. 4).
- Plonsky, Egbert, and LaFlair's (in press) discussion of **data sharing** in the context of research ethics.
- Sterling's (2015) dissertation on research ethics and **informed consent** in SLA.

De Costa, P. I. (2014). Making ethical decisions in an ethnographic study. *TESOL Quarterly*, 48, 413–422.

De Costa, P. I. (Ed.) (2015). *Ethics in applied linguistics research: Language researcher narratives*. New York: Routledge.

Fanelli, D. (2009). How many scientists fabricate and falsify research? A systematic review and meta-analysis of survey data. *PLoS ONE 4*(5), e5738.

Kouritzin, S. (2011). Ethics in cross-cultural, cross-linguistic research. *TESL Canada Journal, 28*, i–iii.

Ortega, L. (2005). Methodology, epistemology, and ethics in instructed SLA research: An introduction. *Modern Language Journal, 89*, 317–327.

Plonsky, L., Egbert J., & LaFlair, G. (in press). Bootstrapping in applied linguistics: Assessing its potential using shared data. *Applied Linguistics*.

2014 Research Agenda Task Force. (2014) *TESOL research agenda*. Retrieved 15 December 2014 from: http://www.tesol.org/connect/tesol-resource-center/search-details/activities/2014/04/18/2014-tesol-international-association-research-agenda

Sterling, S. (2015). Informed consent forms in ESL research: Form difficulty and comprehension. Unpublished doctoral dissertation. Michigan State University.

Thomas, M. (2009). Ethical issues in the study of second language acquisition: Resources for researchers. *Second Language Research, 25*, 493–511.

Research hypothesis

A prediction made with respect to the outcome of a research study. In addition to posing one or more **research questions**, researchers are often also interested in making predictions about the results of their studies. Such predictions are usually motivated by theory and/or previous studies and, like research questions, can be one- or **two-tailed** (i.e., directional vs. non-directional). In an example of the former, Trofimovich and Baker (2006) hypothesized a positive relationship between learners' amount of L2 experience and their ability to produce segmentals accurately in the L2. A non-directional hypothesis would propose a relationship, but would not speculate on whether the relationship was positive or negative. Finally, a **null hypothesis**, stated either along with or in the absence of a directional or "alternative" hypothesis, states that no such effect or relationship will be observed. For example, a null hypothesis for Trofimovich and Baker's study would postulate that learners' amount of L2 experience has no effect on their L2 segmental production ability.

See also **One-tailed hypothesis/test, Two-tailed hypothesis/test**.

Trofimovich, P., & Baker, W. (2006). Learning second language suprasegmentals: Effect of L2 experience on prosody and fluency characteristics of L2 speech. *Studies in Second Language Acquisition, 28*, 1–30.

Research question

A question that establishes the main purpose of a research study, by specifying the issue(s) that the study seeks to address. Most studies are guided by one or more research questions, which are usually stated explicitly at the end of the literature review of a written research report (Plonsky, 2013). These questions can be broad or narrow in scope, with broader questions found more frequently in qualitatively oriented research, and narrower questions in more quantitatively oriented research. An example of a broader research question comes from Du's (2013) research on study abroad in China: *"Do students improve their fluency in Chinese after a semester of Mandarin Chinese language studies in China?"* (p. 133). A narrower question is found in Révész, Sachs, and Hama's (2014) investigation of task complexity: *"Do different intended levels of task complexity result in different levels of cognitive load during task performance, as measured by expert judgments, performance on a secondary task, and eye tracking?"* (p. 623).

Research questions also vary in their wording. It is common to find research questions posed as yes/no questions, such as the previous examples. This type of question necessarily yields a minimally informative yes/no answer, which is often provided by the significance or non-significance of a statistical test. For this reason, it is generally advisable to frame the research questions (and subsequent analyses, results, and interpretations of those results) in a more graded fashion, or to include additional, follow-up research questions. Examples of these types of questions were included in the previously mentioned studies:

What is the effect of time–on-task on students' fluency development? (Du, 2013, p. 133).

What is the effect of task complexity on the acquisition of the English past counterfactual construction under task conditions where recasts are provided? (Révész et al., 2014, p. 623).

Du, H. (2013). The development of Chinese fluency during study abroad in China. *The Modern Language Journal, 97,* 131–143.

Plonsky, L. (2013). Study quality in SLA: An assessment of designs, analyses, and reporting practices in quantitative L2 research. *Studies in Second Language Acquisition, 35,* 655–687.

Révész, A., Sachs, R., & Hama, M. (2014). The effects of task complexity and input frequency on the acquisition of the past counterfactual construction through recasts. *Language Learning, 64,* 615–650.

Research synthesis

A systematic, empirical approach to reviewing research studies on a specific topic. More specifically, research synthesis and **meta-analysis**, which is a type of research synthesis, comprise a set of well-established techniques for summarizing and drawing conclusions based on previous research. As such, this approach operationalizes the notion that no single research study can provide a conclusive answer to any theoretical **hypothesis** or **research question**. Research synthesis also provides an empirical approach to reviewing previous studies thus leading to more objective, valid, and replicable results. Toward these ends, synthetic research treats each study as a "participant," which is systematically "surveyed" using a coding scheme based on the substantive and methodological features particular to the area in question. Saito (2012), for example, synthesized the effects of pronunciation instruction. Based on a principled set of inclusion criteria, his study located and obtained a sample of 15 research studies, each of which was then coded for different features (e.g., segmentals vs. suprasegmentals) hypothesized to influence the effectiveness of pronunciation instruction. The results of each study, indicating the presence or absence of statistically significant gains in pronunciation, were then considered together in order to arrive at a consensus regarding the effectiveness of instruction. Overall, Saito found that pronunciation instruction is generally effective.

It is common for research syntheses to use **effect sizes** to measure and record the results from each research study in the sample. Effect sizes, which indicate the strength of the results, can then be aggregated via meta-analysis to understand the overall effects, as well as to investigate the variance present in such effects both generally and as the result of moderator variables. For example, Lee, Jang, and Plonsky (2015) were interested in the effects of pronunciation instruction as well. Their study differs from Saito's, however, in that their results were based on effect sizes, which enabled a more nuanced illustration of the effects of pronunciation instruction overall and as a function of **moderators** such as length of treatment and type of outcome measure employed. For instance, Lee et al. found that short-term instruction was less effective than longer-term instruction, with effect sizes of $d = 0.62$ and $d = 1.32$ respectively.

Despite the many advantages of taking stock of a particular domain via research synthesis (or meta-analysis), this process also carries with it several challenges (e.g., Ellis, 2015). For instance, because of their exhaustive nature, research syntheses can be prohibitively time-consuming. Another challenge stems from the often incomplete reports of primary research, which necessarily yield incomplete data sets at the secondary/synthetic level. For a more thorough discussion of these and other challenges found in research synthesis, see Oswald and Plonsky (2010).

Ellis, R. (2015). Introduction: Complementarity in research syntheses. *Applied Linguistics, 36,* 285–289.

Lee, J., Jang, Y., & Plonsky, L. (2015). The effectiveness of second language pronunciation instruction: A meta-analysis. *Applied Linguistics, 36,* 345–366.

Norris, J., & Ortega. L. (2006). The value and practice of research synthesis for language learning and teaching. In J. Norris, & L. Ortega (Eds.), *Synthesizing Research on Language Learning and Teaching* (pp. 3–50). Philadelphia: John Benjamins.

Oswald, F. L., & Plonsky, L. (2010). Meta-analysis in second language research: Choices and challenges. *Annual Review of Applied Linguistics, 30,* 85–110.

Saito, K. (2012). Effects of instruction on L2 pronunciation development: A synthesis of 15 quasi-experimental intervention studies. *TESOL Quarterly, 46,* 842–854.

Robust statistics

A set of statistical techniques that allow researchers to carry out parametric operations on their data without satisfying the statistical **assumptions** associated with **parametric statistics**. L2 data often do not meet such assumptions, because they are not normally distributed or the sample size is too small. Robust statistics can be used in such cases for more powerful analyses. One robust statistical technique is **bootstrapping**, a resampling procedure introduced to applied linguistics by Larson-Hall and Herrington (2010) that randomly resamples from an observed data set to produce an outcome that is more stable, and that could only otherwise be obtained from a much larger sample (e.g., Efron, 1979; Plonsky, Egbert, & LaFlair, in press).

Another robust statistic is means–trimming, which, as the name implies, involves running statistical analyses after trimming a specific **percentage** (e.g., 5%, 20%) off the tail ends of the distribution. By doing so, the mean scores being compared in a *t*-test, for example, are less sensitive to **outliers**, particularly when the analysis is based on the small samples typically found in applied linguistics research. Consider, for example, the following (raw) data, published in Donaldson's (2011) study comparing left-dislocation in French by ten non-native (NNSs: 19, 28, 35, 39, 41, 43, 47, 47, 55, 56) and ten native speakers (NSs: 17, 21, 23, 25, 35, 39, 42, 70, 94, 107). Using a traditional statistical approach, the two groups have **means** and **standard deviations** of 41 (11.5) and 47.3 (32.0), respectively. However, according to the **Shapiro–Wilk test** of normality, the distribution of the NS group is borderline non-normal ($p = .045$), and both groups have datapoints that

R

could be considered outliers, such as 19 in the NNS group and perhaps even all three of the final values in the NS group. In this situation, applying a robust technique such as means-trimming would be appropriate, with 5% trimming being a good option because trimming a greater percentage would result in an even smaller sample size with this data set. **SPSS** also provides trimmed scores in its "Explore" output (ANALYZE → DESCRIPTIVE STATISTICS → EXPLORE). The resulting trimmed means for the groups are 41.4 (NNSs) and 45.7 (NSs), and although the trimmed means are quite similar to the original means, the NS trimmed mean in particular appears less affected by the three high, outlying values. Consequently, conducting parametric statistical analyses based on these more conservative values rather than the original values would be more appropriate.

Donaldson, B. (2011). Left dislocation in near-native French. *Studies in Second Language Acquisition, 33*, 399–432.

Efron, B. (1979). Bootstrap methods: Another look at the jackknife. *Annals of Statistics, 7*, 1–26.

Larson-Hall, J., & Herrington, R. (2010). Improving data analysis in second language acquisition by utilizing modern developments in applied statistics. *Applied Linguistics, 31*, 368–390.

Plonsky, L., Egbert, J., & LaFlair, G. T. (in press). Bootstrapping in applied linguistics: Assessing its potential using shared data. *Applied Linguistics*.

Wilcox, R. (2005). *Introduction to robust estimation and hypothesis testing*. Burlington, MA: Elsevier Academic.

Rotation (see Factor analysis)

R

Sample

A subset of a **population**, which is represented in writing by *N* or *n*. A primary goal of inferential statistics is to make inferences and generalizations about a population based on the information provided by a sample. The size of a sample is determined by the researcher. In qualitative studies, the sample size may be only one or two individuals. Alternatively, a sample may consist of the entire population, especially if the population itself is relatively small and accessible; however, such instances are rare. A larger sample size is more representative of the population, resulting in less **sampling error** and therefore greater **validity** and **reliability** of the analysis. However, gathering a large sample may not always be feasible; nevertheless, researchers attempt to obtain a sample that is small enough to be practical, but large enough to still provide an accurate representation of the population. According to the central limit theorem, a randomly selected sample size of 30 is often considered to adequately reflect the features of the population and mitigate the influences of individual variation.

There are several methods for obtaining samples. A random sample selects individuals or data by chance, with no external manipulation. Alternatively, convenience samples rely on those individuals who are most readily available. A common convenience sample in applied linguistics research consists of students in an L2 classroom who are taken as a whole group. Finally, a purposive sample selects individuals based on specific selection criteria deemed important by the researcher.

Sampling error

The difference between a statistic based on a **sample**, such as a mean, and the **population** value for that statistic. When selecting a sample, it is assumed that the sample will not be an exact representation of the population. Even if a sample is randomly selected in an attempt to minimize differences between the sample and the population, there may be a disproportionate presence of specific characteristics in the sample, resulting in either an overestimation or underestimation of the variables or values in the population. Large sample sizes help reduce the sampling error because they provide a better representation of the population; however, very large samples are relatively uncommon in applied linguistics research.

Sampling error also comes into play when comparing group means in a quasi-experimental study, for example. In such analyses, a researcher is hypothesizing that any differences in scores between the two groups are due to the **treatment**. However, there may be differences that are not attributable to the treatment but are instead due to other variables that the researcher did not measure and/or is unaware of. This difference represents the sampling error, and can be represented statistically in the spread of the 95% **confidence intervals**. The greater the distance between the lower and upper confidence intervals, the greater the sampling error.

The effects of sampling error can have important consequences for the validity of a research study, with the greater the sampling error, the lower the validity. For example, Flege and Liu (2001), in their study of age and length of residence of L2 proficiency, claim that "the lack of an effect of length of residence in some previous studies may have been due to sampling error" (p. 527). They argue that taking into account confounding variables, such as age of first exposure and amount/type of exposure, is necessary.

Flege, J. E., & Liu, S. (2001). The effect of experience on adults' acquisition of a second language. *Studies in Second Language Acquisition, 23*, 527–552.

Scatterplot

A graph that represents individual datapoints of two different ordinal, interval, or scale variables on the x axis and y axis of a graph, respectively. A scatterplot is one way to visualize data, and it can be particularly useful for determining the existence and nature of a relationship between the two variables. For example, a scatterplot can reveal a positive linear relationship in which an increase in one variable is associated with an increase in the other. Such a relationship would be represented by a scatterplot in which data points were higher the farther right they were on the graph. Alternatively, a negative linear relationship occurs when, as the values of one variable increase, the values of the other variable decrease. This type of relationship would be portrayed in a scatterplot by a downward left-to-right slope. In addition, a scatterplot can be helpful in identifying **outliers**, those individual datapoints that are outside the main cluster of scores. The scatterplot adapted from Egbert and Plonsky (2015) in Figure 34 indicates that there is a generally positive relationship between the length (in words) of a conference abstract and the rating it receives. That is, longer abstracts tended to receive higher scores in their sample. In this case, a regression line was added to the scatterplot in order to help visualize the relationship between the two variables. It is important to remember that the relationship between two measured variables is not always best captured by their **correlation** (*r*). This statistic, though very useful, can obscure non-linear and/or **curvilinear relationships** that may be present and that are best observed by examining the data visually using a scatter plot.

See also **Loess line.**

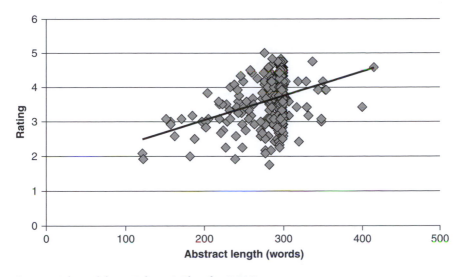

Source: Adapted from Egbert & Plonsky (2015)

Figure 34 Scatterplot

Egbert, J., & Plonsky, L. (2015). Success in the abstract: Exploring linguistic and stylistic predictors of conference abstract ratings. Corpora, 10, 291–313.

Scree plot

A **line graph** used in **factor analysis** to plot eigenvalues in order to help researchers interpret the number of factors to retain. Eigenvalues are represented on the y axis, while the variables or factors are represented on the x axis. The eigenvalues are plotted from highest to lowest, resulting in a descending slope. Researchers generally retain the number of factors that occur to the left of the point of inflexion, which is the place where the initial steep slope begins to level off. Factors to the right of the point of inflexion, with a shallow slope, are not retained for the analysis. There can be some subjectivity in deciding exactly where the slope levels off. In Figure 35, component number 3 might be designated as the inflexion point, in which case two factors would be retained. However, one could also consider component number 7 as the point of inflexion, in which case six factors would be retained. Because of this subjectivity, researchers often use scree plots as one of multiple means for choosing the number of factors to retain, including more objective measures such as Kaiser's criterion of retaining factors with eigenvalues over 1.0.

Loewen, S., & Gonulal, T. (2015). Exploratory factor analysis and principal components analysis. In L. Plonsky (Ed.), *Advancing quantitative methods in second language research* (pp. 182-212). New York: Routledge.

S

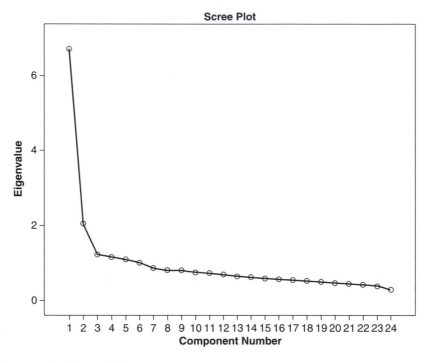

Figure 35   Scree plot

SE (see Standard error)

SEM (see Structural equation modeling)

Shapiro–Wilk test

A test that determines whether a data set meets the **assumption** of having a **normal distribution**. The Shapiro–Wilk test compares the distribution of the actual data against a hypothetical, and normally distributed, set of data using the same **mean** and **standard deviation** as the real data. If the results of the test are non-significant, it means that there is no difference between the two distributions, and the researcher can state that the assumption of normal distribution has been met. However, if the test result is statistically significant, then the data can be assumed to have a non-normal distribution. As an example, Kahng (2014), in a study of language fluency, used a Shapiro–Wilk test to investigate the distribution of speaker repetitions and corrections per minute. The test revealed that the data were not normally distributed (p = .001 and p = .002, respectively).

The Shapiro–Wilk test is similar to the **Kolmogorov–Smirnov test**, but the former has more power to detect non-normal distributions and is more appropriate with sample sizes under 50. However, both tests are sensitive to sample size and may be more likely to return a significant result for a large sample size, even though the violation of normal distribution may be slight. Consequently, it is important to use multiple methods, including **skewness** and **kurtosis** values, and visual inspection of graphs, to investigate the assumption of normal distribution of data.

Kahng, J. (2014). Exploring utterance and cognitive fluency of L1 and L2 English speakers: Temporal measures and stimulated recall. *Language Learning, 64*, 809–854.

Significance level (see Statistical significance)
Also known as **alpha level.**

Skewness
The degree to which a data distribution is non-normally distributed, with the majority of values occurring on one end of the scale. Skewness can be investigated by visual inspection of various graphs, such as **histograms**. If data are normally distributed, and not skewed, then they will produce a **bell curve**, with the mean in the center of the graph. In addition, all measures of central tendency—mean, median, and mode—will be relatively equal. However, if the data are skewed, the peak of the curve will be situated either to the left (positively skewed as in Figure 36) or right (negatively skewed as in Figure 37) side of the graph. In a positively skewed data set, the measures of central tendency will generally be ranked mean > median > mode, while with negatively skewed data, the ranking will be reversed, mode > median > mean. In addition to visual representations, some statistical programs will provide a skewness score. Because an **assumption** of **parametric statistics** is **normal distribution** of data, skewness presents a problem, which may be solved, in part, by conducting non-parametric or **robust statistics**.

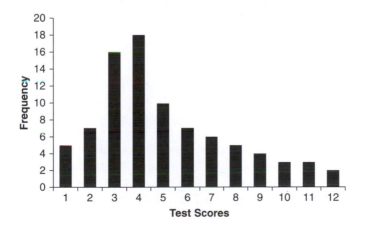

Figure 36   Positively skewed distribution

S

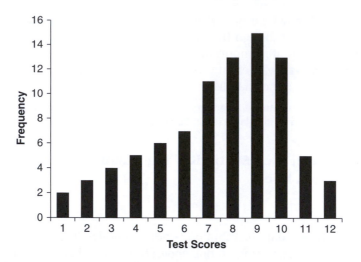

Figure 37   Negatively skewed distribution

Sphericity

An **assumption** of repeated measures analysis that, somewhat simplisti-cally, the variances from each participant are equal across data collection points. Bartlett's test of sphericity and Mauchly's test can be used in **SPSS** to determine if the assumption of sphericity has been violated. Violations of sphericity may be countered by applying the Huynd-Feldt correction or the Greenhouse-Geisser estimate, both of which are provided by SPSS output for repeated measures **ANOVA**. For example, Trenkic, Mirkovic, and Altmann (2014), in their study of processing constraints by L1 and L2 speakers, report using the Greenhouse-Geisser correction when the assumption of spheric-ity was violated for their within-subjects (i.e., repeated measures) ANOVA.

Trenkic, D., Mirkovic, J., & Altmann, G. (2014). Real-time grammar processing by native and non-native speakers: Constructions unique to the second language. *Bilingualism: Language and Cognition, 17*, 237–257.

SPSS

A software package that is frequently used to compute descriptive and inferential statistics. In large part, SPSS uses a set of user-friendly drop-down menus and dialog boxes to enable non-statisticians to do statistics. Unlike **R**, it is not open-source, and there is a licensing fee. However, its ease of use, and the fact that many people have been trained on it, no doubt contribute to its ongoing popularity. SPSS is currently the most commonly used statistical software package in applied linguistics (Loewen et al., 2014).

There are four view screens in SPSS. First, "data view," in which raw data are entered and stored, is formatted as a spreadsheet with each column representing a variable and each row representing a case (see Figure 38).

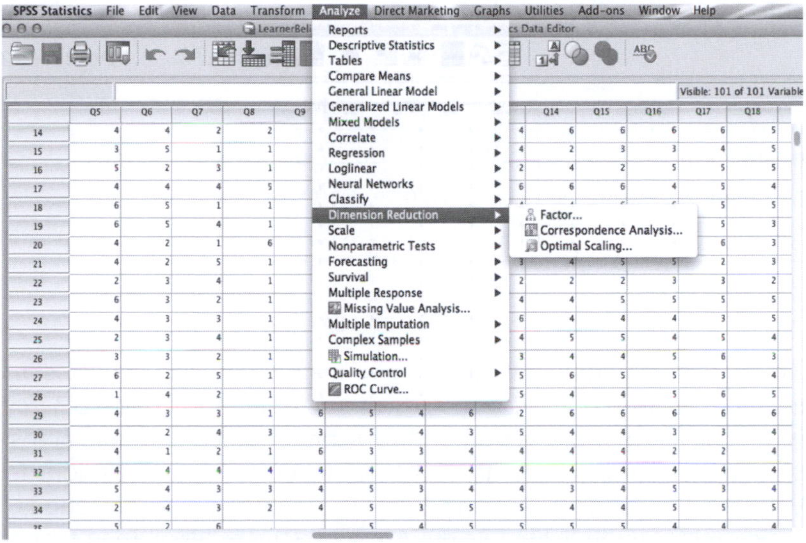

Source: Reprint Courtesy of International Business Machines Corporation, ©
International Business Machines Corporation.

Figure 38   Data view screen in SPSS

In addition, there is a drop-down menu at the top of the screen that enables
researchers to choose the types of statistics and operations they would like
to perform. The second type of screen is the "variable view," which is where
the analyst inputs information about each variable being analyzed, such as
whether it is numeric or "string" (i.e., text) and the level of measurement
(i.e., nominal, ordinal, continuous). Next is the output viewer, where the
results of statistical tests are displayed. The fourth and final type of screen
is the syntax editor, in which researchers can insert their own syntax scripts
to run statistical analyses as they see fit, rather than using the drop-down
menus that SPSS provides.

    http://www-01.ibm.com/software/analytics/spss/

Loewen, S., Lavolette, B., Spino, L. A., Papi, M., Schmidtke, J., Sterling, S., & Wolff, D.
    (2014). Statistical literacy among applied linguistics and second language acquisition
    researchers. *TESOL Quarterly, 48*(2), 360–388.

Standard deviation

A descriptive statistic that indicates the spread of scores within a data set.
It is the square root of the **variance**. The larger the standard deviation, the
more spread out the scores. The standard deviation is not a standardized
unit. It is expressed in the same unit as the mean, and as such, it must be
interpreted in relation to other standard deviations in the analysis. For
example, Table 19 reports the means and standard deviations for three tests

Table 19   Group means and standard deviations

Groups	Pretest		Posttest 1		Posttest 2	
	M	**SD**	**M**	**SD**	**M**	**SD**
Treatment 1	13.4	3.9	20.9	3.9	20.9	3.5
Treatment 2	13.2	4.9	19.2	5.2	19.9	5.3
Control	13.3	3.1	14.7	3.0	14.1	3.3

from a quasi-experimental study on L2 instruction. The similar standard deviations for the control group on the three tests (3.1, 3.0 and 3.3, respectively) indicate that the spread of their scores was comparable across the tests. Furthermore, in comparison to the higher standard deviations for the treatment 2 group (4.9, 5.2, and 5.3), the lower standard deviations from the control group indicate this group's scores were less varied than those of treatment 2 group.

Standard deviations should always be reported along with mean scores when reporting descriptive results: (a) so that readers can interpret the data for themselves, and (b) because they are necessary for synthetic analyses such as **meta-analysis** (see Norris, Plonsky, Ross, & Schoonen, 2015).

Norris, J. M., Plonsky, L., Ross, S. J., & Schoonen, R. (2015). Guidelines for reporting quantitative methods and results in primary research. *Language Learning, 65*, 470–476.

See also **z-score**

Standard error (SE)

The amount of random variance that is not explained by any of the variables in a research study. The standard error, also known as standard error of the mean, results from the fact that no measurement entirely captures the **construct** that is being investigated. According to Field (2009), the standard error is the **standard deviation** of the sampling distribution, and it gives an indication as to how much variation there is across samples within a single **population**. Small values indicate that the sample is a good representation of the population, while larger values suggest that the sample may not be an accurate reflection of the population.

Field, A. (2009). *Discovering statistics using SPSS* (3rd ed.). Thousand Oaks, CA: Sage.

Statistical literacy

An individual's knowledge about statistics. Statistical literacy may refer both to knowledge about how to interpret statistics in research studies, as well as how to conduct and report statistical analyses. At the moment there is some movement towards improving statistical literacy in applied linguistics through the appearance of journal articles, books, and conferences specifically addressing **quantitative research** methods. The focus and the trajectory of these efforts largely parallel those found in recent decades in related fields such as education and psychology (e.g., Sharpe, 2013). There is also a nascent attempt to investigate the current state of statistical literacy among students and researchers, as well as to investigate how statistical literacy is gained. Several questions related to statistical literacy include: Are doctoral students required to take statistical classes during their studies? If so, how many and what do the courses cover? Are discipline-specific statistical classes provided within doctoral programs, or do students take statistics courses in programs such as education, psychology, and statistics? How do professors maintain or improve their statistical literacy?

Loewen, S., Lavolette, B., Spino, L. A., Papi, M., Schmidtke, J., Sterling, S., & Wolff, D. (2014). Statistical literacy among applied linguistics and second language acquisition researchers. *TESOL Quarterly, 48*(2), 360–388.

Norris, J. M., Plonsky, L., Ross, S. J., & Schoonen, R. (2015). Guidelines for reporting quantitative methods and results in primary research. *Language Learning, 65*, 470–476.

Sharpe, D. (2013). Why the resistance to statistical innovations? Bridging the communication gap. *Psychological Methods, 18*, 572–582.

Statistical power

The likelihood of finding a statistically significant relationship or effect in a sample if the effect is present in the **population**. The more power a study has, the less likelihood of a false negative, **Type II error**, in which researchers claim no statistical effect, even though one exists. In general, a power level of .80 or higher is desirable, and indicates that the analysis has an 80% probability of detecting a significant effect. As with **statistical significance**, statistical power varies as a function of sample size and **effect size**. Therefore, when a larger effect is anticipated or observed (e.g., $d \approx 1$), a smaller sample ($N \approx 35$) is needed to detect that relationship at the conventionally desired level of power = .80. Likewise, smaller effects such as $d \approx .2$ require a larger sample ($N \approx 400$) to have an 80% chance of finding the effect at the .05 level. It is possible to calculate a priori power before conducting a study, in order to determine how many participants are needed to achieve a statistically significant result. In addition, it is possible to calculate post hoc power after a study has been completed, in order to determine the study's likelihood of detecting a statistical effect. Unfortunately, applied linguistics researchers have generally paid little attention to statistical power, which is particularly concerning given that the **quantitative research** in the field has historically relied heavily on statistical testing with small samples. In fact, observed (post hoc) power has been estimated at just above .5 or 50%, barely more reliable than a coin toss (Plonsky, 2013; Plonsky & Gass, 2011).

Several steps can be taken to limit the debilitating effects of low power. First, researchers can determine adequate sample sizes based on a priori power analyses, rather than relying on convenience or convention to determine sample sizes. Second, when a study lacks statistical power (e.g., when the anticipated effect is small, or when working with necessarily small samples), researchers can avoid or limit their use of statistical testing, focusing instead on **descriptive statistics**. Finally, because performing multiple statistical analyses on the same data can lower statistical power, researchers could conduct fewer analyses. Fewer, but more reliable, results are preferable to more, but potentially unreliable, ones.

Crookes, G. (1991). Power, effect size, and second language research. Another researcher comments. *TESOL Quarterly, 25*, 762–765.

Lazaraton, A. (1991). Power, effect size, and second language research. A researcher comments. *TESOL Quarterly, 25*, 759–762.

Plonsky, L. (2013). Study quality in SLA: An assessment of designs, analyses, and reporting practices in quantitative L2 research. *Studies in Second Language Acquisition, 35,* 655–687.

Plonsky, L. (2015). Statistical power, *p* values, descriptive statistics, and effect sizes: A "back-to-basics" approach to advancing quantitative methods in L2 research. In L. Plonsky (Ed.), *Advancing quantitative methods in second language research* (pp. 23–45). New York: Routledge.

Plonsky, L., & Gass, S. (2011). Quantitative research methods, study quality, and outcomes: The case of interaction research. *Language Learning, 61*, 325–366.

Statistical significance

A probability ratio, within the range $p = 0-1$, that indicates the likelihood of finding a specified relationship among variables in a data set, even when no such relationship exists in the larger **population**. Statistical significance is often viewed as a litmus test for the importance of the results of **quantitative research** studies. The statistical significance of a **t-test**, for example, indicates the probability that a researcher would find the difference between groups, even if there were no such difference in the population. If the **p-value** of a t-test is $p = .03$, there is only a 3% probability that the difference between the two sample groups was found in error, and a 97% probability that the difference actually exists in the larger population. Likewise, the statistical significance of a **correlation** indicates the probability of obtaining the observed relationship between two variables in a specific data set if the true population correlation was actually zero, $r = 0$, and there was no relationship between the two variables. For example, a p-value of .05 for a correlation indicates that there is only 5% probability that the correlational relationship found in a specific study does not exist in the population at large.

Traditionally, researchers in applied linguistics and in other social sciences have used an **alpha** level of .05, indicating a probability of 5% or less, to determine statistical significance. By doing so, researchers guard strongly against a **Type I error**, in which researchers claim that there is a statistically significant difference even though one does not exist. However, strict reliance on a single cutoff point can lead to the reduction of continuous data into a simple and rather uninformative yes/no dichotomy: the p-value is viewed as either above the desired threshold, in which case the results are not statistically significant, or the p-value is below the threshold and thus the results are statistically significant. In addition, because p-values are dependent on sample size, statistical significance has been criticized as providing an unreliable or unstable indication of the magnitude of an effect or relationship. **Practical significance**, often discussed in contrast to and as an alternative to statistical significance, is expressed by an **effect size** and, as such, generally provides a more informative and reliable answer to the **research questions** being addressed (see Plonsky, 2015).

See also **Publication bias**.

Kline, R. B. (2013). *Beyond significance testing: Statistics reform in the behavioral sciences* (2nd ed.). Washington DC: American Psychological Association.

Norris, J. M., Plonsky, L., Ross, S. J., & Schoonen, R. (2015). Guidelines for reporting quantitative methods and results in primary research. *Language Learning, 65*, 470–476.

Plonsky, L. (2015). Statistical power, p values, descriptive statistics, and effect sizes: A "back-to-basics" approach to advancing quantitative methods in L2 research. In L. Plonsky (Ed.), *Advancing quantitative methods in second language research* (pp. 23–45). New York: Routledge.

Stem and leaf plot

A type of data display in which all of the raw scores in a data set are arranged to indicate the distribution of the data rather than using lines or graphs. In one sense, a stem and leaf plot resembles a **histogram** turned on its side. The stem and leaf plot in Figure 39 represents the ages of the participants in Loewen et al.'s (2014) study of **statistical literacy** in applied linguistics. The first column, labeled frequency, represents the number of datapoints for each line. For instance, the first line has seven cases. The second column, labeled stem, represents the first value of the observation, while the leaf column represents the second value, and contains each case. For example, the stem and leaf for the first row indicate that there were seven participants aged 24. The second row indicates that there were 41 participants ranging in age between 25 and 29. Each individual in the **range** is represented in the leaf column by an individual numeric value. Thus, the study included four 25-year olds, nine 26-year olds, and so forth. A stem and leaf plot provides information about the distribution of the data, and in this case, the higher number of observations in the 20s and 30s indicates a positively skewed distribution.

```
Age Stem-and-Leaf Plot

Frequency  Stem   Leaf

7.00        2     4444444

41.00       2     55556666666667777777888888889999999999999

58.00       3     0000000000000111111111111122222222223333333333334444444444

43.00       3     5555555555666677777777788888889999999999999

27.00       4     000000000001111122222334444

21.00       4     555666777788899999999

17.00       5     00000012222233444

17.00       5     55555666667788899

7.00        6     0011223

8.00        6     55557799

2.00        7     12
```

Figure 39   Stem and leaf plot for participant age

Loewen, S., Lavolette, B., Spino, L. A., Papi, M., Schmidtke, J., Sterling, S., & Wolff, D. (2014). Statistical literacy among applied linguistics and second language acquisition researchers. *TESOL Quarterly, 48*(2), 360–388.

Stimulated recall

A type of research methodology in which participants engage in some task or event, after which they are asked to report what they were thinking when they were doing the task. Often, video or audio recordings of the task are provided for the participants in order to help them recall their thoughts. As such, stimulated recall is a retrospective research method. Stimulated recall has been used in classroom SLA studies in which participants engage in interaction, and then after the class, the students are shown video clips of their interaction and asked to state what they were thinking at the time. For example, Kahng (2014) used stimulated recall to tap into the cognitive process of L1 Korean learners of English when they paused or hesitated during a speaking task. She played a recording of their spontaneous speech immediately after they produced it and asked them to comment on difficulties they had recalling words.

One issue with stimulated recall is its veridicality. In other words, how well does it measure what it purports to measure? One concern is that participants may not report what they were actually thinking at the time that the stimulus event took place; rather they might state what they are thinking at the time of retrospective reporting. In addition, if participants are not able to remember what they were thinking during the event, they might invent something that they think will please the researcher, rather than admitting that they do not remember.

Another issue is the length of the delay between the stimulus event and the stimulated recall session, because memory decay increases over time, limiting the degree to which participants can accurately recall their thoughts. In some research studies, the recall takes place immediately after the event, the preferred approach (Gass & Mackey, 2000); in others, the recall session may occur some time later, from several hours to a day or more.

Stimulated recall has been used as one method to measure the **construct** of noticing. In particular, researchers may analyze participants' retrospective reports for statements pertaining to various linguistic features that occurred in the discourse. If participants claim that they were thinking about these forms, researchers may claim that the participants noticed those forms. However, the **reliability** of such reports is sometimes questioned; therefore, some studies use additional methods to measure noticing in an effort to **triangulate** the data, and to investigate the utility of each measure.

Finally, some researchers are very strict in using the term stimulated recall to refer only to the elicitation of participants' thoughts at the time of the event. However, there are other types of retrospective reports. For example, in addition to trying to recall their thoughts during the event, participants might be asked to provide their current thinking or interpretation of past events.

Gass, S. M., & Mackey, A. (2005). *Stimulated recall methodology in second language research* (2nd ed.). New York: Routledge.

Kahng, J. (2014). Exploring utterance and cognitive fluency of L1 and L2 English speakers: Temporal measures and stimulated recall. *Language Learning, 64*, 809–854.

Structural equation modeling (SEM)

A set of relatively advanced, multivariate statistical techniques designed to model and explain a complex set of relationships among variables. Studies of L2 learning, teaching, use, and assessment usually include several—often many—variables, which is indicative of the inherently multivariate nature of the field. Further complicating matters from both a conceptual and statistical point of view, the nature of the relationship between these variables can take different forms. For example, the presence or amount of one variable can cause another to increase (e.g., the effect of instruction on learning), or two variables can be correlated (e.g., reading comprehension and vocabulary size). And of course, applied linguists are also interested in understanding hierarchical relationships (e.g., between **latent variables** and sets of measured variables). Structural equation modeling (SEM for short) provides a robust and flexible analytic framework for helping researchers address these and other types of relationships in the data, thereby clarifying the **constructs** represented. In applied linguistics, SEM is perhaps most frequently found in the realm of language testing, where

S

it is often used to uncover relationships within and among different types of learner knowledge and/or performance (e.g., In'nami & Koizumi, 2011, 2012). But SEM can also be used in quasi-experimental SLA research. Li (2013), for example, was interested in understanding whether the effects of both working memory and language analytic ability could be subsumed in one underlying construct (i.e., a latent variable) in moderating the effects of corrective feedback. To address this question, Li constructed a confirmatory SEM model. The results showed that both working memory and language analytic ability were part of the same construct, which Li referred to as aptitude. Furthermore, the relationship between this latent variable and L2 proficiency was argued to be causal in nature.

SEM is similar to **factor analysis**. Indeed, factor analysis can be considered a more basic subtype of SEM. For example, both SEM and factor analysis can be used in exploratory or confirmatory ways, depending on whether researchers have relatively few preconceptions about the relationships in the data or are testing a specific theoretical hypothesis. In general, however, the use of SEM is more similar to confirmatory factor analysis. Although both procedures can be used to reduce a set of measurements into fewer, correlated variables (i.e., factors, latent variables), SEM is generally more flexible in its ability to identify the types of relationships present in the data.

Hancock, G. R., & Schoonen, R. (2015). Structural equation modeling: Possibilities for language learning researchers. *Language Learning, 65*(Supp. 1), 160–184.

In'nami, Y., & Koizumi, R. (2011). Structural equation modeling in language testing and learning research: A review. *Language Assessment Quarterly, 8*(3), 250–276.

In'nami, Y., & Koizumi, R. (2012). Factor structure of the revised TOEIC® test: A multiple-sample analysis. *Language Testing, 29*(1), 131–152.

Kline, R. B. (2010). *Principles and practice of structural equation modeling* (3rd ed.). New York: The Guilford Press.

Li, S. (2013). The interactions between the effects of implicit and explicit feedback and individual differences in language analytic ability and working memory. *Modern Language Journal, 97*, 634–654.

Schoonen, R. (2015). Structural equation modelling in L2 research. In L. Plonsky (Ed.), *Advancing quantitative methods in second language research* (pp. 213–242). New York: Routledge.

Winke, P. (2014). Testing hypotheses about language learning using structural equation modeling. *Annual Review of Applied Linguistics, 34*, 102–122.

S

Study quality

A broad and variously defined notion related to how well a research study is designed, conducted, and reported. Study quality has been considered and operationalized most explicitly in the context of **research synthesis** and **meta-analysis**, where researchers often code primary studies for features related to both general and domain-specific notions of quality. Examples of study quality include the testing of statistical **assumptions** and the reporting of appropriate and sufficient statistical details. Results for quality-related features can be used for a variety of purposes. Some meta-analyses, for example, weight study effects so that studies of higher quality contribute more to the meta-analytic mean than those of lower quality. Other syntheses collect study quality data for more descriptive and evaluative purposes, seeking to describe methodological practices in order to guide future studies. Plonsky and Gass (2011), for example, coded for a number of study quality features related to designs, analyses, and reporting practices in a sample of 174 studies of L2 interaction. Their results pointed to several improvements taking place over time, such as the increased reporting of **effect sizes**; nevertheless, Plonsky and Gass also found persistent weaknesses, such as a lack of **pretesting** in quasi-experimental studies and the omission of important statistical data such as **standard deviations**. In addition to examining methodological features related to quality in the aggregate and over time, study quality can also be examined in relation to study outcomes (e.g., effect sizes). The rationale here, as described by Vacha-Haase and Thompson (2004) is that "effect sizes are not magically independent of the designs that created them" (p. 478). In the L2 domain, a small but growing number of syntheses have addressed these kinds of relationship showing, for example, larger effects for (quasi-) experimental studies that: (a) include a **delayed posttest** in their design, and (b) report **reliability** estimates (e.g., Plonsky & Gass, 2011).

Journal Article Reporting Standards Working Group. (2008). Reporting standards for research in psychology: Why do we need them? What might they be? *American Psychologist, 63*, 839–851.

Norris, J. M., Plonsky, L., Ross, S. J., & Schoonen, R. (2015). Guidelines for reporting quantitative methods and results in primary research. *Language Learning, 65*, 470–476.

Plonsky, L. (2013). Study quality in SLA: An assessment of designs, analyses, and reporting practices in quantitative L2 research. *Studies in Second Language Acquisition, 35*, 655–687.

Plonsky, L., & Gass, S. (2011). Quantitative research methods, study quality, and outcomes: The case of interaction research. *Language Learning, 61*, 325–366.

Vacha-Haase, T., & Thompson, B. (2004). How to estimate and interpret various effect sizes. *Journal of Counseling Psychology, 51*, 473–481.

Valentine, J. C., & Cooper, H. (2008). A systematic and transparent approach for assessing the methodological quality of intervention effectiveness research: The study design and implementation assessment device (Study DIAD). *Psychological Methods, 13*, 130–149.

S

Survey

A type of data collection that involves gathering responses to preselected questions. Often surveys are administered to a large number of participants, and indeed one of the advantages of survey research is its ability to gather large amounts of data. Surveys may consist of closed option questions, in which participants must respond by selecting one of several possibilities. For example, dichotomous yes/no, multiple selection, or **Likert scale** questions all provide participants with a limited number of response options. Often these responses are in numeric format. In addition, surveys may include short or longer answer questions, in which participants can provide their own comments on the topic.

One benefit of survey research is that it involves numerous responses to standardized questions, allowing the researcher to see how people respond to the same stimuli. However, one disadvantage of surveys is that they present an **etic** perspective, in which the researcher, rather than the participants, determines the topics and details of the questions. Consequently, there is little opportunity for participants to respond in ways or with answers that may be more meaningful to themselves, which may provide the researcher with unexpected insights into the topic.

Survey data are often submitted to statistical analysis because of the large number of responses. For example, Loewen et al. (2009) collected survey data from over 750 L2 learners regarding their beliefs about grammar instruction and error correction. The results were expressed on a 6-point Likert scale, and the data was subjected to both a **factor analysis** and a **discriminant function analysis**.

Survey data may be collected manually, with researchers administering pencil-and-paper surveys to individuals face to face or via the mail. However, currently many surveys are administered electronically through a number of survey websites. Regardless of the method of delivery, one issue to consider is the survey return rate. Often return rates are quite low, which opens the results to criticisms of bias, because it may be that certain types of individuals are more likely to complete the survey. For example, in their online survey of **statistical literacy**, Loewen et al. (2014) reported a survey return rate of 30%, and they suggested that the positive results found regarding statistics may have been, in part, an artifact created by more returns from quantitatively oriented researchers than qualitative ones.

Some people may make a distinction between a survey and a **questionnaire**; however, in practice, both terms are generally used interchangeably in applied linguistics research.

Dörnyei, Z., & Taguchi, I. (2010). *Questionnaires in second language research: Construction, administration, and processing* (2nd ed.). London: Routledge.

Loewen, S., Li, S., Fei, F., Thompson, A., Nakatsukasa, K., Ahn, S., & Chen, X. (2009). Second language learners' beliefs about grammar instruction and error correction. *Modern Language Journal, 93*, 91–104.

Loewen, S., Lavolette, B., Spino, L. A., Papi, M., Schmidtke, J., Sterling, S., & Wolff, D. (2014). Statistical literacy among applied linguistics and second language acquisition researchers. *TESOL Quarterly, 48*(2), 360–388.

Tagging

A practice common in **corpus** linguistics in which various elements of a body of written or spoken language are identified. Generally the tagging process involves assigning various grammatical or part-of-speech (POS) labels to words in the corpus. For example, the English word *jumped* could be tagged as [Regular Verb + Past Tense Marker]. In this way, researchers can enter search parameters in a corpus to find and count the feature(s) they are interested in. So if a researcher wishes to compare the occurrence of regular and irregular verbs in an English corpus, they could use the tags in the above example. There are several computer programs, such as the Biber tagger (see Biber, 1988), that automatically assign labels to every word in the corpus, and generally the accuracy rate is high, often up to 98%, especially for L1 speaker **corpora**. However, L2 speaker corpora can present specific challenges for tagging due to learner errors and interlanguage forms.

Biber, D. (1988). *Variation across speech and writing*. Cambridge: Cambridge University Press.

Denis, P., & Benoît, S. (2012). Coupling an annotated corpus and a lexicon for state-of-the-art POS tagging. *Language Resources & Evaluation, 46*, 721–736.

Thick description

A practice employed in **qualitative research** methods, such as **ethnography** and **case studies**, in which rich and detailed information is provided about specific research contexts, such as L2 classrooms, in order to assist in the interpretation of human behavior. Thick description provides transparency in data analysis because it ideally consists of researchers detailing the evidence that supports their interpretations pertaining to the research context. As observers of any setting, it is easy to speculate on the causes of certain actions (or inactions); however, such assumptions can lead to mistaken interpretations of a given classroom or culture. Thick description enables researchers to gain perspectives and insights not likely to be detected by lighter observational and analytical approaches. For example, De Costa (2010) discusses collecting a variety of data sources, including field notes, videotaped classroom lectures, and interviews, in order to provide a thick description of the English language learning trajectory of a Hmong refugee.

Although it is impossible for researchers to be aware of all potentially relevant background information or meaningful actions (or inactions) in a given setting, thick description allows researchers to present more justifiable interpretations. In addition, thick description provides research consumers with the opportunity to make their own decisions about the **validity** and trustworthiness of researchers' interpretations.

De Costa, P. I. (2010). From refugee to transformer: A Bourdieusian take on a Hmong learner's trajectory. *TESOL Quarterly, 44,* 517–541.

Geertz, C. (1973). *The interpretation of cultures: Selected essays.* New York: Basic Books.

Holliday, A. (2004). Issues of validity in progressive paradigms of qualitative research. *TESOL Quarterly, 38,* 731–734.

Think-aloud protocols

A type of verbal report in which participants verbalize their thought processes while completing a task. Like **stimulated recalls**, think-alouds provide the researcher with a window into the learner's attention and internal cognitive processing. Unlike stimulated recalls, however, think-alouds are a concurrent methodology, meaning that the researcher asks participants to think out loud as they are engaged in a task. The main benefit of this method stems from its simultaneous nature, which enables the researcher to capture learner cognition in real time as a task is being performed. For example, Spanish L2 learners in Leow's (1997) study talked out loud to themselves while completing a crossword puzzle that included irregular preterit verb forms that the students had not yet learned. Consequently, the participants often questioned these forms out loud, providing data about their noticing of the forms.

Despite the potential of think-alouds to inform our understanding of L2 learners' internal cognitive processing, some researchers have argued that think-alouds are not particularly insightful because they are not something that people normally engage in. In addition, the act of speaking aloud while performing a task may alter the learners' attentional foci, either positively or negatively. Such interference is referred to as *reactivity*. Bowles (2010) provides a full discussion on this topic, including a **meta-analysis** of studies examining the presence of reactivity in think-aloud research. Her conclusion is that, although there is some evidence of reactivity, such effects are not strong; thus, think-alouds can be used with minimal concern regarding their influence on task performance. Another potential drawback of think-aloud procedures is that there is no certainty that participants report exactly what they are thinking. In addition, some participants may find it difficult to verbalize their thoughts while completing a task. Finally, think-alouds are appropriate only with written, rather than oral, tasks. In spite of these limitations, think-alouds have been used with some frequency in SLA research to provide additional information about learners' cognitive processes during task performance.

Bowles, M. A. (2010). *The think-aloud controversy in language acquisition research.* New York: Routledge.

Leow, R. P. (1997). Attention, awareness, and foreign language behavior. *Language Learning, 47,* 467–505.

Transcription

The process of writing down what is said in audio or video recordings. In many cases, transcribing is done manually by the researcher; however, in certain cases, it is also possible to use software programs such as *InqScribe* and *Dragon*. Transcripts, rather than the actual recordings, are often used for analysis because they are easier to work with. However, transcription is very time-consuming. One rule of thumb is that it takes seven hours to transcribe one hour of audio recordings. Of course, the amount of time and difficulty of transcribing depends on various characteristics of the recorded data. For example, **interview** data are generally easier to transcribe than classroom interaction, with the difficulty of transcribing increasing with more individuals recorded. It can also be difficult to identify multiple individuals by voice alone on audio recordings. Additionally, standard L1 speech is generally easier to transcribe than L2 speech, particularly if the learners are at low levels. Finally, researchers must decide whether to include translations, transliterations, or grammatical codes with the original discourse.

The act of transcribing is an interpretative process, because the researcher must make decisions about the amount of detail to include in the transcription. For interview data, a broad transcription style might be used, in which there is a minimal amount of paralinguistic information recorded, and instead, the transcriber might focus on just the words if the analysis is looking primarily at the semantic content of the discourse. For example, disfluencies or false starts might not be transcribed because they do not necessarily contribute to the ideas that the speaker is expressing. However, other types of research that involve closer linguistic analysis call for much more detailed types of transcription. For example, in investigations of linguistic complexity, accuracy, and fluency, it is important to transcribe errors and disfluencies in order to conduct an accurate analysis. Additionally, in **conversation analysis** research, detailed information, such as pausing, intonation, speech rate, and voice quality, is important for analysis and is consequently indicated in a transcription. Some transcripts might also include information about gestures, body movements, and eye gaze that accompany speech.

When transcribing, it is important to adhere to a transcription key. This key, which should be included in written reports of studies that use transcribed data, provides a definition of the symbols being used in the transcripts. Although there are some generally agreed upon transcription conventions, there is by no means a standard method of transcribing. Thus, researchers need to indicate which symbols are used to indicate which types of linguistic or paralinguistic features.

In addition to research purposes, transcription and transcripts are sometimes used as instructional tools in an effort to draw learners' attention to the language that is being used in a specific context. For example, Huth

T

(2006) provided L2 learners of German with authentic transcripts of L1 German compliment sequences in an effort to increase learners' abilities to produce target-like compliments during role plays. Huth transcribed the role-play discourse for analysis. The examples in Table 20 include actual L1 data as well as student role-play data. In both transcripts, the English translation is provided in italics below the original German. In addition, the learner interaction contains symbols to represent non-linguistic aspects of the data, such as pausing or overlapping speech; however, the German compliment example does not, presumably because the latter is concerned primarily with the linguistic forms used to express compliments. Excerpts of the transcription key are also provided in Table 21.

Table 20   Sample transcripts

German Compliment (Golato, 2002, p. 557, cited in Huth, 2006, p. 2030)	Excerpt from student role play (Huth, 2006, p. 2043)
A: aber heute abend hier war's schön bei euch *but it was nice this evening here at your place* B: schön *that's nice*	libby: du hast uh ein (.) schönes jacke *you have uh a (.) nice coat* lind: ach danke *well thank you* libby: [( )- [( )- lind: [i mean <u>ja ich wises</u> he [he he *i mean <u>yes i know</u> he [he he* libby: [he he he

Table 21   Transcription notation examples

.	A period indicates a fall in tone.
,	A comma indicates continuing intonation.
?	A question mark indicates rising intonation.
<u>mine</u>	Emphasis is indicated by underlining.
( )	Items in doubt are enclosed with single parenthesis.
[I used [I saw	Utterances starting simultaneously are linked together with left-hand brackets.

Source: Huth (2006, p. 2046).

Huth, T. (2006). Negotiating structure and culture: L2 learners' realization of L2 compliment-response sequences in talk-in-interaction. *Journal of Pragmatics, 38*, 2025–2050.

Jaffe, A. (2007). Variability in transcription and the complexities of representation, authority and voice. *Discourse Studies, 9*, 831–836.

Stillwell, C., Curabba, B., Alexander, K., Kidd, A., & Kim, E. (2010). Students transcribing tasks: Noticing, fluency, accuracy, and complexity. *ELT Journal, 64*, 445–455.

Transformation (see Data transformation)

Treatment
The procedure or process in a quasi-experimental study that is being provided to the participants. The treatment, which can also be referred to as an intervention, is the variable that is being manipulated in the study, and as such, it is the **independent variable** that is hypothesized to have an influence on the **dependent variable**. In instructed SLA studies, the treatment often consists of a type of instruction or teaching method that is being investigated for its influence on L2 learners' linguistic proficiency. For example, in Loewen and Nabei (2007) there were three treatment groups, each of which received a different type of corrective feedback (either recast, elicitation, or metalinguistic feedback) during task-based interaction. The study also included two non-treatment groups that did not receive any corrective feedback. One was a **comparison group**, which participated in the communicative activities but did not receive any corrective feedback. The other group was a **control group** which took the **pretest** and **posttest**, but did not receive any treatment and instead, simply continued with normal classroom activities.

Loewen, S., & Nabei, T. (2007). Measuring the effects of oral corrective feedback on L2 knowledge. In A. Mackey (Ed.), *Conversational interaction in second language acquisition* (pp. 361–378). Oxford: Oxford University Press.

Triangulation
The process of verifying research findings by investigating a topic from another angle or perspective. Often triangulation involves using different data collection methods. For example, in a recent project involving the **construct validity** of **grammaticality judgment tests**, Godfroid et al. (2015) used **eye-tracking** data to investigate previous claims that timed grammaticality judgment tests are good measures of implicit L2 knowledge. These claims were made on the basis of exploratory and confirmatory **factor analyses** of participants' accuracy scores on a battery of tests designed to encourage the use of either implicit or explicit L2 knowledge, respectively. By triangulating the eye-tracking data and the accuracy data, the expectation is that the two types of measures may confirm the same hypothesis, thereby strengthening the claims that researchers can make. It is also common for applied linguists employing **mixed methods designs** to do so for the sake of triangulation (Hashemi & Babaii, 2013).

Godfroid, A., Loewen, S., Jung, S., Park, J., Gass, S., & Ellis, R. (2015). Timed and untimed grammaticality judgments measure distinct types of knowledge: Evidence from eye-movement patterns. *Studies in Second Language Acquisition, 37*(2), 269–297.
Hashemi, M. R., & Babaii, E. (2013). Mixed methods research: toward new research designs in applied linguistics. *Modern Language Journal, 97*, 828–852.

t-test

A type of **parametric** test that involves the comparison of two groups. There are several types of *t*-tests that are appropriate under different research design conditions. An independent samples *t*-test compares scores from two different groups. Such a test is used to compare whether two groups that vary by a certain characteristic are the same or different on a specific **dependent variable**. For example, a *t*-test can be used to compare the proficiency scores of two groups of learners at the beginning of a quasi-experimental study in order to determine if their proficiency levels are equivalent. In a similar way, VanPatten, Keating, and Leeser (2012) used an independent samples *t*-test to compare responses to comprehension questions by L2 and native Spanish speakers and found no statistical differences [$t(41) = .573, p = .570$].

The **assumptions** of an independent samples *t*-test are that the two groups are comprised of different individuals, that the data are normally distributed, and that the **variance** between the two groups is equal. In addition, the data need to be measured on a continuous scale.

Another type of *t*-test is the paired samples *t*-test, which compares the scores of one group on two different occasions, in a **repeated measures design**. For example, in a study investigating the effects of a pronunciation training program, Derwing, Munro, Foote, Waugh, and Fleming (2014) used paired samples *t*-tests to evaluate speakers' fluency on pretest and post-test speaking tasks. They found no difference in the number of syllables per second, with means of 2.18 and 1.99 ($p > .05$); however, the number of phonemic errors [40.7 ($SD = 8.56$) versus 32 ($SD = 7.9$)], was significantly lower at the posttest [$t(6) = 7.091, p < .001, d = 1.058$]. By definition, the data in this test are not independent; however, a paired samples *t*-test assumes that the data are normally distributed.

Currently in applied linguistics research, *t*-tests are often used in initial and more exploratory analyses, and it is unusual to find research studies that employ only *t*-tests in their analyses because they are somewhat limited in their sophistication. Nevertheless, *t*-tests can indeed give insight into the nature of differences between groups.

One practice that has fortunately fallen out of favor in applied linguistics research is the use of numerous *t*-tests on the same data set, because the more tests that are run, the greater the chances of a **Type I error** in which a statistically significant result is found even when one does not actually exist (Brown, 1990).

Brown, J. D. (1990). The use of multiple *t*-tests in language research. *TESOL Quarterly, 24*, 770–773.

Derwing, T. M., Munro, M. J., Foote, J. A., Waugh, E., & Fleming, J. (2014). Opening the window on comprehensible pronunciation after 19 years: A workplace training study. *Language Learning, 64*, 526–548.

VanPatten, B., Keating, G. D., & Leeser, M. J. (2012). Missing verbal inflections as a representational problem: Evidence from self-paced reading. *Linguistic Approaches to Bilingualism, 2*, 109–140.

Two-tailed hypothesis/test

A hypothesis that looks for differences on both ends of a data distribution, meaning that the researcher is interested in determining if either group is better or worse than the other. The *tails* that are referred to are the ends of the distribution on a bell curve where the scores tail off, as shown in Figure 40. If a **one-tailed hypothesis** was being employed, the researchers would be testing only one end of the distribution, to investigate, for example, whether one group in particular is better than the other. A two-tailed test is considered more conservative than a one-tailed test because it takes the **alpha** level (for example, .05 or 5%) and splits it between the two ends of the scale, looking to see whether differences fall within 2.5% of either side of the scale. However, a one-tailed test looks for all of the difference on one side of the scale, so there is a 5% possibility of finding a difference even if one does not truly exist. In general, two-tailed tests are the most common in applied linguistics research.

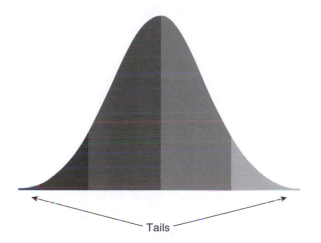

Figure 40   Bell curve showing 'tails' of distribution

Type I error

A false positive interpretation of statistical results. A Type I error occurs when a researcher mistakenly determines that a **statistically significant** relationship occurs in a data set when, in fact, no such relationship exists. In other words, there is no real-world effect in the **population**; however, the research claims that there is an effect, based on the results of the inferential statistics from a specific research study. As such, a Type I error contrasts with a **Type II error**, which concludes that there is no statistically significant effect or relationship, even though one does exist. The primary means by which quantitative researchers protect themselves from Type I errors is by setting an **alpha** level, which states what level of probability in making a Type I error is acceptable. The typical alpha level of .05 allows for a Type I error rate of just 5%, or 1 in 20 studies. However, given the **publication bias** among authors, researchers, and editors toward statistically significant results, as well as findings that confirm (rather than challenge) their hypotheses (see Plonsky, 2013), it is likely that more than 5% of published results contain Type I errors. Type I errors can also occur as the result of multiple comparisons based on the same data. In such cases, a **Bonferroni correction** can be applied to prevent such errors. A greater emphasis on **descriptive statistics,** including **confidence intervals** and **effect sizes**, can also help researchers move away from mistaken and/or dichotomous results (Plonsky, 2015).

Plonsky, L. (2013). Study quality in SLA: An assessment of designs, analyses, and report-ing practices in quantitative L2 research. *Studies in Second Language Acquisition, 35,* 655–687.

Plonsky, L. (2015). Statistical power, *p* values, descriptive statistics, and effect sizes: A "back-to-basics" approach to advancing quantitative methods in L2 research. In L. Plonsky (Ed.), *Advancing quantitative methods in second language research* (pp. 23–45). New York: Routledge.

Type II error

A false negative interpretation of statistical results. A Type II error occurs when a researcher fails to detect a significant relationship or difference in the data, even though the effect exists in the larger population. In other words, there is a statistically significant effect that is not discovered by the researcher. Type II errors contrast with **Type I errors,** which occur when a non-statistically significant relationship is interpreted as signifi-cant. The probability of committing a Type II error is expressed by β. If β is .1, there is a 10% chance that the researcher has failed to discover a significant effect. There is generally a trade-off between Type I and Type II errors. The more conservative researchers are in setting an **alpha** level, the more likely they are to commit a Type II error. However, if an alpha level is too high, researchers will commit a Type I error. The most com-mon cause of Type II errors is a lack of **statistical power**. Specifically, small samples and small **effect sizes**, both of which affect power, can lead to Type II errors. Unfortunately, researchers in applied linguistics have generally paid little attention to statistical power and Type II errors, a problem made more acute by the field's heavy reliance on **Null Hypoth-esis Significance Testing**.

Type-Token Ratio

A measure of lexical diversity or complexity. The Type-Token Ratio (some-times abbreviated TTR) is calculated by dividing the total number of unique words (types) in a sample of written or spoken language by the total number of running words (tokens). Therefore, the closer the Type-Token Ratio is to

1, the greater the lexical diversity. For example, sentence 1 has a Type-Token Ratio of 1 because every running word is unique, meaning that there is an equal number of tokens ($n = 8$) and types ($n = 8$). In contrast, sentence 2 has a Type-Token Ratio of .85 because the tokens *research* and *and* both occur twice in the sentence, resulting in a total of 13 tokens but only 11 types.

1. *Research methodology is an interesting topic of study.*
2. *Research design and research procedures are topics that require careful and deliberate thought.*

Underlying the use of Type-Token Ratio as a measure of lexical diversity is the assumption that individuals with larger vocabularies will use a larger portion of unique words in their writing or speaking. Godfrey, Treacy, and Tarone (2014), for example, examined L2 development in at-home and study-abroad contexts. Among other targeted skills, the authors were interested in the participants' lexical complexity and therefore compared the Type-Token Ratios of writing samples provided by both groups before and after their respective semesters of study.

Despite its intuitive appeal and mathematical simplicity, the use of Type-Token Ratio has been criticized because of the inflating effect of sample length on Type-Token Ratio scores. That is, "the more words (tokens) a text has, the less likely it is that new words (types) will occur" (McCarthy & Jarvis, 2007, p. 460). In addition, the Type-Token Ratio does not take into account the nature of lexical items, with the result that there is no differentiation between more sophisticated lexical items and more common vocabulary (Schmitt, 2010). A number of other measures have been proposed to overcome these weaknesses inherent in Type-Token Ratio, such as the Guiraud index, which accounts for frequency effects by placing the square root of word tokens in the denominator (Guiraud, 1954), and the D measure, which is based on a randomly chosen sample of 35–50 words from a given text (Malvern, Richards, Chipere, & Durán, 2004).

Godfrey, L., Treacy, C., & Tarone, E. (2014). Change in French second language writing in study abroad and domestic contexts. *Foreign Language Annals, 47*, 48–65.

Guiraud, P. (1954). *Les caractéristiques statistiques du vocabulaire.* Paris: Presses Universitaires de France.

Malvern, D. D., Richards, B. J., Chipere, N., & Durán, P. (2004). *Lexical diversity and language development: Quantification and assessment.* Basingstoke: Palgrave Macmillan.

McCarthy, P. M., & Jarvis, S. (2007). vocd: A theoretical and empirical evaluation. *Language Testing, 24*, 459–488.

Schmitt, N. (2010). *Researching vocabulary: A vocabulary research manual.* New York: Palgrave Macmillan.

T

Univariate statistics

Statistical techniques or operations that focus on a single variable, through the use of either descriptive or inferential statistics. The calculation of univariate statistics is often a first step in understanding a data set. For nominal or categorical data, such as gender or L1, for example, researchers might calculate descriptive statistics such as the **frequency** and/or **percentage** for each variable (e.g., 15 males, 19 females; L1 Spanish = 15, L1 Korean = 12, L1 Arabic = 9). For descriptive statistics for interval data, the most common univariate statistics are the measures of **central tendency**, such as the **mean** or **median**, and **dispersion**, such as **standard deviation** or **interquartile range**. As an example, DeKeyser (2009), in his investigation into the effects of study abroad, begins his presentation of quantitative results by providing participants' grammatical accuracy following their time abroad: "3 were rated as not having changed ..., 12 were rated up 0.5 point or more, and 1 declined by 0.5 point. Two students went up by more than 2 points" (p. 83). These results provide information about one variable.

In terms of inferential statistics, univariate statistics are those that examine a single outcome (or dependent) variable. For instance, a *t*-**test** investigates the difference between two groups on one dependent variable. Alternatively a one-way **analysis of variance** (ANOVA) examines differences among three or more groups; however, there is still only one dependent variable.

Univariate statistics are frequently discussed in contrast to bivariate statistics, such as correlation, that investigate the relationship between two variables, and **multivariate statistics**, such as **factor analysis** or **multiple regression**, that investigate the relationships among multiple variables. Procedurally speaking, univariate operations are generally conducted before more complex, multivariate statistics. For example, following his explanation of overall accuracy gains, DeKeyser (2009) then used **bivariate correlations** to examine the relationship between accuracy gains over time and a number of other variables such as aptitude and pre-study-abroad proficiency level.

DeKeyser, R. (2009). Monitoring processes in Spanish as a second language during a study abroad program. *Foreign Language Annals, 43*, 80–92.

Validity

A notion central to all research, although perhaps used more frequently in quantitative research, referring broadly to the substantive and methodological soundness of a study. In general, a study with higher validity is more trustworthy, meaningful, and accurate. Validity is also multifaceted, with several identified subtypes, including **construct validity**, **face validity**, **ecological validity**, internal validity, and external validity:

- Construct validity addresses whether a research study in general or a specific research **instrument** measures what it claims to measure. An extreme example of low construct validity occurs if L2 learners are given a writing assignment when a researcher is interested in their speaking abilities. A more realistic example of construct validity occurs in research on implicit and explicit L2 knowledge, in which considerable research has investigated which types of tests might be better measures of one or the other type of knowledge (e.g., Ellis et al. 2009).

- Face validity pertains to how participants view the activities in which they are taking part. For example, students taking an L2 proficiency test may not put in as much effort if they do not feel that the test is a good measure of their linguistic knowledge.

- Ecological validity refers to how well a research study aligns with the context it is investigating. Ecological validity is often an issue in classroom research in which it is difficult to control moderator variables. In contrast, laboratory studies can be more tightly controlled; however, they may be accused of having limited ecological validity because they do not necessarily reflect the realities of classroom learning.

- Internal validity relates to the degree of confidence that one can have that a research study has adequately controlled for as many extraneous variables as possible so that only the variables under consideration are influencing the results. There are numerous aspects to ensuring internal validity, such as choosing suitable participants, designing adequate instruments, following proper data collection procedures, and analyzing the data appropriately.

- External validity addresses the extent to which results of a specific research study are generalizable. Methods of increasing external validity include appropriate selection of participants and adequate description of the research methodology in order to allow **replication**.

In general, validity is best understood as a continuum from low to high, as opposed to dichotomously present or absent in a study. Researchers must make many decisions when designing and conducting a research study, and while it is usually not possible to eliminate all potential threats to validity, it is important to minimize as many threats as possible. Researchers should also explain and justify their methodological choices as much as possible in written manuscripts, in order to enable readers to appropriately evaluate the validity of the research. For example, random assignment of participants to experimental conditions constitutes a stronger research design, and enables more robust conclusions to be drawn regarding experimental effects. In applied linguistics, however, it is not always possible, ethical, or desirable to randomly assign treatment conditions; some researchers are more interested in preserving ecological validity and will therefore collect data from **intact classes**. In the end, the goal of research is to have high validity; however, it is important to realize that no study is perfect.

Cook, T. D., & Campbell, D. T. (1979). *Quasi-experimentation: Design and analysis issues for field settings.* Chicago: Rand McNally.

Ellis, R., Loewen, S., Elder, C., Erlam, R., Philp, J., & Reinders, H. (2009). *Implicit and explicit knowledge in second language learning, testing and teaching.* Bristol: Multilingual Matters.

VARBRUL

A statistical software package named for "variable rule analysis," designed specifically for running **logistic regression** analyses. VARBRUL was developed—and is most often used—by variationist sociolinguists interested in determining whether and to what extent a set of social, contextual, and linguistic **variables** predict the presence or absence of a given linguistic form (see Cedergren & Sankoff, 1974). For example, Carvalho and Child (2011) used VARBRUL to examine optional subject pronoun use in Uruguayan-border Spanish as a function of several social (e.g., gender, age) and linguistic (e.g., person, reflexivity of the verb, verb mood) factors. Carvalho and Child found that both age and gender were significant variables affecting the use of subject pronouns. Because VARBRUL's main function is essentially logistic regression, other types of programs can be used for the same analysis, including **SPSS**, GoldVarb X (a freeware version of VARBRUL), and the *Varb* and *Rbrul* packages for **R**.

Carvalho, A. M., & Child, M. (2011). Subject pronoun expression in a variety of Spanish in contact with Portuguese. In J. Michnowicz, & R. Dodsworth (Eds.), *Selected proceedings of the 5th workshop on Spanish sociolinguistics* (pp. 14–25). Somerville, MA: Cascadilla Proceedings Project.

Cedergren, H., & Sankoff, D. (1974). Variable rules: Performance as a statistical reflection of competence. *Language, 50*, 333–355.

Variable

An object of study in quantitative research that can have different values. Variables generally consist of characteristics of the people or contexts under investigation, and those characteristics can vary across individuals. For example, L1 background and L2 proficiency are two variables that might be of interest in a classroom-based study. Both of these variables are characteristics of the individuals in the classroom; however, first language and proficiency may vary from person to person.

There are different ways of classifying and conceptualizing variables, which affect the roles they can play in the study design. **Independent variables** are studied for their impact on **dependent variables**. For example, in much SLA research, researchers want to know what kind of effect a specific type of instruction (the independent variable) has on learners' proficiency (the dependent variable).

Variables can also be classified according to their level of measurement: (a) **categorical** or nominal variables, such as first language, consist of discrete groups, such as English, Spanish, or Chinese; (b) **ordinal** variables are rank-ordered and indicate the placement of scores in relation to the other scores in the data (e.g., first, second, third); (c) **continuous** variables, such as age, length of residence, or test scores, are measured on a numeric scale. The level of measurement of a variable can restrict the types of statistical operations that can be carried out on the data, with many statistical procedures applicable only to continuous variables. For example, L1 background or treatment condition might be assigned numeric values in a data file for ease of data entry (e.g., 1 = L1 Spanish, 2 = L1 Korean, 3 = L1 Chinese; 1 = Control group; 2 = Treatment Group 1; 3 = Treatment Group 2); however, these variables are still categorical and can only be used to calculate frequencies. An average score based on these assigned values, for example, would be meaningless.

Variance

A measure of **dispersion** of values for a given **variable**, indicating the extent of spread between the scores. Although the **mean** provides useful information about the **central tendency** and overall similarities in the data, the mean does not contribute any information about overall distribution of the values. Variance, then, indicates how close a set of scores is to the mean. If the variance is low, then the mean is a good representation of all the scores in the data; however, if the variance is high, then the scores are more spread out. In this sense, variance is conceptually similar to the **standard deviation**; in fact, variance can be calculated by simply squaring the standard deviation.

Indicators of data distribution, such as variance, are important because they specify the degree to which participants' scores vary. A large amount of variance in an experimental study may indicate, for example, that the effectiveness of the treatment varied substantially, which might indicate the presence of one or more **moderator variables** or **covariates**. Variance is also central to many statistical analyses of interest in applied linguistics. **ANOVA** (which is the acronym for analysis of *variance*), for example, compares the variance between all participants' scores to the variance of scores within each group, and the **eta-squared** value that results from an ANOVA indicates the **percentage** of variance in the sample that can be accounted for by group membership.

Variance is also used in several other ways to talk about the distribution of scores. For example, the amount of variance shared between two variables being correlated is calculated by squaring their correlation coefficient, also known as R-squared (R^2). Brantmeier, Vanderplank, and Strube (2012), for example, were interested in the relationship between self-assessed reading ability and reading ability measured by a more standardized instrument. The correlation between the two measured variables was $r = .229$. By squaring this value ($.229 * .229 = .05$), one can determine that 5% of the variance in each variable can be attributed to the other.

Brantmeier, C., Vanderplank, R., & Strube, R. (2012). What about me? Individual self-assessment by skill and level of language instruction. *System, 40*, 144–160.

V

Wilcoxon rank-sum test

A non-parametric statistical procedure comparing two independent groups by rank-ordering, from lowest to highest, participants' scores in each group and calculating a rank-sum score. If the rank-sum scores for the two groups are similar, then there is no difference between them; however, if the rank-sum scores differ considerably, then a statistically significant difference may be found. The lower the rank-sum score, the lower the rankings of the group, while a high rank-sum score reflects higher group rankings. The Wilcoxon rank-sum test is appropriate to use when the **assumption** of **normal distribution** has been violated, and when there are two groups comprised of different individuals. When reporting the results of a Wilcoxon rank-sum test, the test statistic, which is represented by W_s, should be reported, along with the **medians**, **range**, interquartile range, corresponding **z-score**, significance value, and **effect size**. The Wilcoxon rank-sum test is equivalent to the **Mann–Whitney U test**, which also compares the rankings of two independent groups that are not normally distributed.

Wilcoxon signed-rank test

A non-parametric statistical procedure comparing two sets of scores from the same participants when the data are not normally distributed. As such, the Wilcoxon signed-rank test is a **repeated measures** or **within-groups** test, and it is the non-parametric equivalent of a dependent or paired samples **t-test**, which may be used to investigate the differences between one group's **pretest** and **posttest** scores or the performance on two different data elicitation measures. The Wilcoxon signed-rank test ranks the differences between the two sets of scores, and assigns a positive or negative sign to the ranking. A positive sign indicates that the score on the second variable is higher than the first score, while a negative score designates a higher score on the first variable. Variables with equal scores are excluded. The sums of both the positive and negative ranks are calculated, and the difference between the two rankings is compared. When reporting the results of a Wilcoxon signed-rank test, the test statistic, which is represented by T and is the smaller of the two ranks, should be reported, along with the **medians**, **range**, interquartile range, significance value, and **effect size**; however, not all values always appear in published research articles. Using a Wilcoxon signed-rank test to compare perceptions of journal quality, Smith and Lafford (2009), found that Computer-Assisted Language Learning (CALL) researchers felt that they themselves viewed online journals as more rigorous than did their colleagues, ($z = -3.67, p = .0001, r = .67$) (p. 877).

Smith, B., & Lafford, B. A. (2009). The evaluation of scholarly activity in computer-assisted language learning. *Modern Language Journal, 93*, 868–883.

Within-groups design
Another name for **within-subjects** and **repeated measures** designs.

Within-subjects design
Another name for **within-groups** and **repeated measures** designs.

W

z-score

The distance that a datapoint falls from the mean, as expressed in **standard deviation** units. Conceptually, a z-score of 1 indicates that a given value lies 1 standard deviation from the mean of the group, assuming a **normal distribution**. Though most people calculate z-scores using statistical software packages such as **SPSS**, it is not a difficult operation to carry out by hand. First, each observed value is subtracted from the sample mean. Then, the result is divided by the standard deviation. Z-scores have several practical functions. Because they are standardized, z-scores can help in the comparison of data with means that are measured in different units. In addition, because of their correspondence to the mean, researchers often use a z-score of 2 or 3 as a cutoff point to identify **outliers** that are greater than the 97.7 or 99.9 **percentiles**, respectively. An understanding of z-scores can also aid in the understanding of the **Cohen's *d* effect size**, which can be interpreted in standard deviation units. However, whereas z-scores express an absolute distance from the mean, d values are used to express the difference in mean scores between two groups. Finally, in applied linguistics research, z-scores are not frequently used or reported.

Author Index

Printed and bound by CPI Group (UK) Ltd, Croydon, CR0 4YY